IS INDIA CIVILIZED?

ESSAYS ON INDIAN CULTURE

BY

SIR JOHN WOODROFFE

MADRAS

GANESH & CO., PUBLISHERS

1922

Printed by J. R. Aria at the Vasanță Press, Adyar, Madras.

CONTENTS

First printed : November, 1918
Second Edition: May, 1919
Third Edition : July, 1922
Revised and Enlarged

PREFACE TO THIRD EDITION

I TAKE the opportunity of this new Edition
to reply to some criticisms passed on the
last. Prominent among these is an Article
in the "Calcutta Review" in which the
opinion is expressed that I have not held
the balance fairly between Western and
Eastern Civilisation and, in particular, between Christianity and Brahmanism. As
regards this particular complaint I have
(with the consent of the "Calcutta Review")
reproduced the Article in the Appendix
so that the reader can judge for himself. I
wish however to say that the object of my
book ·is, in this criticism, misunderstood.
Of course this book is a defence of the
Indian case. It is a defence to a comprehensive attack on every aspect of Indian
culture. Naturally therefore I was concerned with what might be said in answer

vii

to the attack, that is in favour of Indian Civilisation. I am not the Prosecution. At the same time where the attack could rely on any facts which appeared to justify condemnation, I did not deny them. I said then, as I have said over and over again, that I was not blind to what can be urged against the India of to-day. Something may be said against every man and every people. Some of the Indian people have been unfaithful to their Dharma, in various ways. Some who claim to be orthodox are degenerate. Some who reject the Brahmanic Dharma have become "our foster-children" as an English Missionary called them, whilst others are mere "seat-arrangers" (to use an expressive Sanskrit term) socially, culturally, and politically of the Powers there be. These last two classes will suffer for their dissociation from their people. Round Dharma itself various kinds of Adharmik parasites have fastened during the course of the ages. But all this is not the concern of this book which is a short and summary answer to Mr. Archer's wholesale and uncritical charges. I observe in this connection that none of my adverse critics is willing to accept a brief for Mr. Archer, which is itself proof that his case is not a good one. What however they do not like are my criticisms on the Civilisation and the Religion "(for India only," since he calls himself a Rationalist) which he supports. If however what I have said is rightly understood I have nothing on this head to withdraw, but much (if I had the space) to add.

The writer of that review thinks that I have not sufficiently appreciated the merits of Christianity. Its merits were no part of the scheme of this little book. The existing literature on the subject is overwhelming. Millions of pounds have been spent in propaganda with results which show that in this, at least, money is not everything even in a Banya civilisation. Nor have I in claiming greatness for India's teaching intended to deny that Christianity has also its own greatness. All religions have certain fundamentals in common. I and those others who speak in any degree well of the Indian civilization are supposed, in the review cited, to claim an exclusive patent of merit for Vedantic religion. This position is characterised as " absurd "; doubtless. But I have never adopted it. I am well aware that all the religions have certain elements of worth in common, otherwise they would not be what they are. The Vedânta does not speak ill of any religion, but assigns to each its place, however much these religious sects may, amongst themselves, quarrel upon the question whether a place is to be given to any other religion than their own. I however was concerned with the religion of the "Idolatrous" "Heathen," at least the Indian part of it. The point was this, how could such a low grade people have principles so excellent that the Western Religions also laid claim to them? The answer of course is that the alleged ignorance of the " Heathen " and the lack of civilization is not justified, such an allegation being itself due to

x

ignorance and misunderstanding of the facts. It is clear that God has revealed Himself at all times and to all peoples according to their capacity to receive knowledge of Him. The Revealer is ever full and perfect, but revelation is conditioned by the mind to which it is made. No religion is absolutely false. No one religion is, according to Vedânta, free from some degree of falsity and imperfection.

Speaking of Indian doctrine I may here observe that the criticism which regards Shâkta teaching as distinct from " orthodox Vedanta " (whatever that may be) is founded on a misconception. The European man of a " religious " turn of mind is too often over-beset with sectarian notions. Nor is it the fact that the Shâkta system, which is just as much or as little " orthodox " as the Vaishnava, Shaiva or any other religious community has been " habitually misconstrued for centuries by all the leaders of Indian thought ". Where there has been misconception (for some criticism on this and other aspects of Hindu religion are well-founded), it is due to modern English educated Hindus and their English mentors.

My critic speaks of the true Vedantic doctrine of the " illusory nature of everything phenomenal ". This is a common but, in my opinion, an illusory criticism. I have dealt with the subject in my Book on " Reality ". Since its publication, I have read the observations of an Indian author in which he says that it is time that his people should turn their back on what he calls the " Theory of Unreality," since they have hard knots to disentangle in a region of Reality which requires all the attention and acumen which they can command. Perhaps it would be more accurate to say that the Vedantic doctrine should be studied and understood and that portion of it which gives rise to this conception may be put aside except by those who are really capable of understanding it. This and other doctrines require correct statement. My observations as regards ' Karma ' doctrine have been stated in the appended review " to be gravely misleading as an indication of the results it produces in Indian conduct, whatever may be said of (my) description for the meaning of the term on Philosophy ". But surely this or any other doctrine must be explained in its true form and not according to the corrupt misunderstanding of some of those who purport to follow it. A Guru of a friend of mine replied to a somewhat fatalistic observation of the latter that he who took a fatalistic view of life was no son of Kâli. The essence of the whole doctrine is that man is the master of his destiny. It is only the superstitious who believe that Vidhi writes the destiny of all children upon their foreheads. There is an astrological saying in the West that " fools are ruled by the stars and that wise men rule them ". In other words, man is born with certain tendencies; but whether or not those tendencies shall ripen into actuality in him depends upon his own action. One need not be the *Pashu* of anybody or anything.

In each religion we must distinguish its original principles and accretions. That "Christianity" is not necessarily Christ's teaching is shown both by the nature of what passes as such, and the history of the Churches, as also by the fact that all the Churches disagree amongst themselves what that teaching is. Each says that the "Christianity" of the other is not the true thing. It is Official Christianity which has been slow to recognise the merit of Indian teaching and to give credit for anything to the "Heathen". Vedanta kindly tolerates even the most ignorant of its detractors.

In passing I may say that I am not, as the criticism alleges, so ignorant of Christian doctrine, as not to know that it teaches both the Immanence as well as Transcendence of God; a fact which is supposed to have escaped my notice owing to my being too busy "in editing and translating the Tantras". What however I now say on, amongst other grounds, personal experience, is that the Christian emphasis is so commonly laid on transcendence, that the other aspect is often ignored and lost sight of. An example of this was told me recently. In an Indian school at which there were many Indian Christian children, the latter during a lesson on an English poem were asked " where was heaven ". The children's answer was that it was " up there in the sky," though, on being questioned, they were not sure if it could be reached by an aeroplane. Possibly they thought that it was too much " up there," and that the petrol supply would give out before they got to the heavenly destination. A little Hindu girl was then asked to give her answer when she replied " Heaven is in my heart". Here the beauty of the Hindu teaching shone forth. But what happened? All the other Christian children *laughed*. What was the value of the teaching which made them *laugh*. There is a Russian saying :— " God is a very long way up ; the Czar is a very long way off." The first part of the saying represents the ordinary western view.

I am not going to argue here the question whether the West or the East is the more "spiritual". It was enough for my Book to repute the ludicrous allegation that the Indians had no spirituality. As regards this again one must, as I have already said, distinguish between the typal civilization and its actual particulars. There is however one point on which I wish to observe. My critic affirms the religiousness of his countrymen on the strength of the patriotism shown by them in the Great War. But if they are in fact religious, what has the war to do with it? Some—many it should be said—had both affection for their country and the common sense to know that if they did not defend it, they themselves would be conquered. Some others were compelled to come in. If the first class of Englishman is a good Christian, then by their patriotism the Moslem Turks were good Christians. Under the circumstances, it is not Religion but a natural virtue, with which we are dealing. What is shown is the manliness of many, despite the degenerating influences of their civilisation. We may applaud the soldier without making him a Christian Hero? The point is worthy of remark as, it is one of those matters where self-interest is made to masquerade as self-sacrifice, causing laughter if not disgust in the rest of the world. In a book which I recently read, an American is reported as saying that his country came in to the war to save themselves. " I am glad," says the author that, " he did not put forward the case that they came in ' to save civilisation ' ", or as some say Religion, Morality or anything else. Regarding men in the mass these self-righteous statements are untrue. In another book ("Secrets of a Kuttite," by Capt. Mousley, p. 94) a frank author combines admiration for his country's great qualities with a knowledge of its weakness in this respect by his remark—" who would not mind being a Pharisee at the price of being an Englishman." In fact the less said about the Churches and the War, the

B

better for the former, with the exception of the Society of Friends which, has in all time consistently upheld Christ's teaching. The Pope also said a good word for peace but was called a Pro-German for his pains. The supposed charge of Materialism against the modern day Indian because he is engaged in secular affairs, industrial workings and so forth is based on a wrong view of what religion is. There is nothing either sinful or irreligious *per se* in such activities. All depends upon their nature and the intent and spirit with which they are undertaken. He may be a materialist after a visit to Europe; but there is no necessary connection between sin, piety, and a factory. All daily work is good which is dedicated to God and done in the spirit of such dedication.

It is too absurd to say that Western civilisation is beyond reproach and I have heard no one out of this country saying so. I have no desire, since I belong to that Civilisation myself, to do it an injustice.

What I have said is, indeed, very mild compared with what may be and has, in fact, been said by some English in their own country. The gist of the offence is that I have said it here, whilst others have said it there. The offence is against the false notions of " prestige " which prevail. But true prestige depends on real worth and not on the concealment of unworth and (since we are all imperfect) in routing out what is bad even if it be done " in the family ".

Again I did not say or suggest that all missionary enterprise was actuated solely by political ambitions. Take for instance Catholic Missionary enterprise in this country. It is mostly carried on by foreigners belonging to a super-national Church. In a colony of a country of one of those foreigners it may be different. There is no doubt however that Missionary enterprise has in fact often served political interests. I am here reminded of an amusing story which I recently read in Alan Lethbridge's " Elusive Africa " (p. 234) the author of which took it from the book on Nigeria by a missionary (C. H. Robinson) who had evidently a sense of humour. Some British schoolboys were told to write an essay on a British Colony and the following amusing answer came from one of them—" Africa is a British Colony. I will tell you how England makes her colonies. First she gets a missionary. When the missionary has found an especially beautiful and fertile tract of country he gets all his people round him and says 'Let us pray' and when all the eyes are shut up goes the British flag ". The same tale, said not in jest but earnest, is told by Mr. Villiers the war correspondent in his recent Book (Villiers, I. 180) regarding a conversation which he had with a Maori chief who, describing, what had happened to his country said : "First they sent missionaries who told us to look up to God. Then while we were looking up to heaven the English took our lands from us. Then we killed them, then you sent your red coats ; we fought and you crushed us and now here we are." Speaking again of Hawaii he says that in 1880 there was a native king " But as they always do the missionaries and other whites eventually stirred up trouble with the inevitable result—annexation by the United States. Hawaii was about to go through the mill, an ordeal all small and delightful primitive states have to pass through as grist to the millstone of modern civilisation; but though they come out flat and stale from a picturesque point of view they often become more profitable to outsiders as the result of their absorption by a bigger Power." (Chap. I. 182 and 183.) Talking of recommendations I saw in an Anglo-Indian paper a recommendation to the Indian people to give their attention to metaphysics, since, it was said, they were so suited to abstract thinking. Whilst so occupied their counsellors may take the opportunity of abstracting more material stuff. Many snares are spread to-day for the simple both in this country and elsewhere. But the people all over the world are ceasing to be simple and trusting. They are less willing to give credit and more desirous of cash even in heavenly dealings. The Indian people will I hope judge and act for themselves, whatever the result, whether in religion, metaphysics, industry and everything else. The first lesson in the present world is to rely on *oneself*; others may give advice and help us, but we are on the safe side in rendering ourselves independent of them. On the whole no one can look after our interests as we ourselves can do. Especially is this so in an age in which there is more hypocrisy and insincerity than in any other.

I leave this Review to pass to another point. I have been asked what I mean by being "true to oneself". That is —what is the self to which one should be true? This kind of darkness is not to be found in the most ignorant European. Those who ask such a question are honoured with a Self which however has evidently not made its presence known to them. A person who has not known his Self is no one. There are two good lines by the Dutch poet and epigrammatist De Genestet.

Wees uzelf zei ik tot iemand
Maar hy kon niet ; hij was niemand
Be thyself I said to *some one* but he
could not ; he was *no one*.

And so with a People and Race. If they are not *themselves* they are *no one*. But who is so blind as not to see that this ignorance is passing and that India, as a whole, is recovering Her (Indian) self-con-sciousness? What She will do with it is another question. There is a self-conscious-ness, class-consciousness, racial conscious-ness, national consciousness, human-consci-ousness, and cosmic consciousness. Indian Doctrine in the form of the Vedânta is famed for the last two. Under attack and during conflict, the second and third forms of con-sciousness are developing. The Authentic Voice of India has spoken. Having in part yielded to the attempts to mould Her, She now resists and *Resistance is the characteristic of a Self*. An atom of Matter is a self which holds itself together and resists. If it does not resist, it disrupts and ceases to be a self.

Another, as I have read, asks what the "somewhat grandiloquent term 'cultural conquest' means". I suppose he is one of those whose native sense has been conquered out of him. The late Governor of Bengal understood the point when he spoke of his sympathy (a word which has become too often an unhappy hack) with those who hold that "British Domination means also the imposition upon India of a civilisation that is not her own—one indeed which, if it is to prevail, must end by destroying her own." (See *Statesman*, June 20, 1922.) In my view however it is not a question of sympathy at all. If any people are unwilling, without first trying to do so, to hold their own, sympathy is wasted on them. Rather do they deserve contempt.

A statement by an English writer whom I have read suggested that the class of hostile criticism to which this book refers is a thing of the past. Not at all. It exists now and will continue as long as the cultural conflict lasts.

This cultural conflict is to be found in every historical process. It should be candidly recognised. It is only hypocrisy to pretend that it does not exist. Whatever may be said, the real facts, are clear enough. How often have we not recently heard the indignant complaint raised that this or that person or class was " opposed to Western civilisation ". What does this mean but that Western civilisation is *the* civilisation, that it is right for the West to impose it and that therefore it is wrong for the East to oppose it. That it has been and is being imposed is fully proved and the unsettlement of Indian Dharma is indeed one of the chief causes of the so-called " unrest," which alarms some and is as the refreshing Dew of Dawn to others.

It is a mistake then to suppose that Cultures do not conflict, or that these attacks from outside are (as one criticism I have read suggested) things of the past ; they are made to-day and will continue, for the whole world, as it is, is one vast system of attack and defence, of victory and defeat. I think it was Sir Fitz James Stephen who said both that "the British were the representatives of *intelligent* civilisation" and "that the only way to settle with the East is *to vanquish her intellectually*". Just so; and those who have not the intelligence to see this deserve to be vanquished by those who do.

Past criticisms are repeated to-day. Colonel Holditch ("India" 207) sometime ago described modern Hinduism as "the most contemptible religion in existence". The same thing is being said to-day. Thus recently the Rev. F. B. Meyer ("Evening Standard," March 16th, 1920), inveighing at Leicester against modern western immoralities, said: "The vast preponderance of our people have less religion in them than the Hindus or Kaffirs." This reference to Kaffirs reminds me of a note I recently read quoting the Argentine Rules relating to Immigration which exclude from landing the blind, deaf, dumb, paralytic, persons suffering from contagious diseases, gipsies *and Hindus.* These last are thus bracketed with incapacity and contagious disease. What the Indian people have to see is whether there is not something really wrong with themselves, and if so what it is that the world should rate them so disparagingly. In such cases they must set themselves to remedy it and compel the *respect* which is due to a self from its fellows. No people should know better than the Hindus with their doctrine of *Karma* that men get what they deserve. In my opinion one reason is to be found in the fact that there is both a lower and a higher people in India in a sense which does not apply to any of the more homogeneous European peoples. This fact is evidenced to-day by the caste system the meaning of which is not generally understood. But even the Higher India owing to its *poco curante, nichevo,* and *kuch parwa nahin* attitude does not secure the respect to which it is entitled.

There are of course other reasons which I do not go into here.

Thus again only some two and a half years ago, the Catholic Bishop of Plymouth wrote of the books "dignified" by the Sanskritists under the name "Sacred Books of the East" as being "gibberish," and so on. In so judging he spoke without the knowledge which some missionaries of his creed have shown. After all he and others may be excused to some extent (except for talking about what they do not understand,) seeing the often unintelligible translations of Eastern Books which are published. But the question is not one of Religion only. On November 7th, 1919, "The Daily Telegraph" (London), wrote: "There is *no* Civilization known to the world except that of Christianity." All then who are not Christians are uncivilized. Cardinal Bourne, speaking about this time at Watford, said: "When you come to nations where Christianity had not penetrated, there was no civilization in our sense of the word except *fragments* which they had *picked up* from the Christian Civilized Nations."

Last year, I received (I suppose for my edification) a number of the " Indo-Portuguese Review," which in the leading article weeps over the "baneful " and " pernicious " doctrines of Mâyâ and Karma which it says have " smothered patriotism," " undermined India's existence as a nation " making the people " seek absorption with Brahma to the detriment of all other lawful aspiration " ; and so on and so forth. It is some comfort to learn that the " absorption with Brahma," which is so much of a bugbear that one might suppose that the Race was in danger of extinction, is yet perhaps (to use a tedious phrase) to some extent a " legitimate aspiration ". These are, of course, familiar complaints ; but I learn from this Review for the first time that " the Mâyâ doctrine has distinctly taught them (the Indians) the modern-day cult of Non-co-operation "!! Poor Mâyâ has become a regular dhobi's donkey. Genuine sympathy from the

Indo-Portuguese and others will receive the thanks of the Indians who are a grateful people, but at the same time they will be sorry if these others and the Indo-Portuguese shed tears on their account without due reason.

Those who hold such views as those above mentioned must *necessarily* and logically seek to supplant Indian civilization by their own and no blame can be imputed to them. If others are in fact supplanted that is their affair.

But it is hypocrisy on the part of the conqueror to pretend that he had nothing to do with the conquest. The same people who! would like us to so believe protest against the supposed opposition of some Indians to " European civilization ". But why should there be this Indian opposition if Western Civilization were not invading this country and breaking up its old life? And why should the others protest against opposition to European Civilization if they were not in fact seeking to traduce it. Honesty is required here as elsewhere.

I should add to the words " no blame can be imputed " the qualification "provided they act sincerely and rationally ". Lord Stanmore, formerly Governor of Fiji, gives an instance of stupid and irrational cultural despotism inspired by " Christian " bigotry in a paper rightly called " Undue Introduction of Western Ways," read to the Anglican Missionary Conference in 1894, cited by Havelock Ellis (Psychology of Sex vi, 100). He says " they (the natives) have good ground for their dissatisfaction at the time when I visited the villages I have specially in my view. It was punishable by fine and imprisonment to wear native clothing, to wear long hair or a garland of flowers ; to wrestle or play at ball ; to build a native fashioned house ; not to wear shirt and trousers and in certain localities coats and shoes also ; and in addition to laws enforcing a strictly puritanical observation of the sabbath it was punishable by fine and imprisonment to bathe on Sundays. In some other places bathing on Sunday was punishable by flogging; and to my knowledge women have been flogged for no other offence". And yet my statement that missionaries may have changed their converts' names from (to give an imaginary example) Mukhyopâdhyâya to Muggins is questioned. The Catholic church on the other hand has often shown great sense in yielding to the habits and customs of Asiatic and African peoples and making Herself as presentable to them as possible. A recent instance of this I note from the Claver Almanach for African missions for 1922 (published in Rome via dell'Olmata 16) which recommends the Cult of the Black Virgin. There are, as it points out, in various countries statues and pictures representing the Blessed Virgin's features in black. I have myself seen and venerated one of the most celebrated Black Virgins at Puy de Dom. The Almanach I note says of the Holy Mother " If she inspires her true servants to portray her with the features of a negress does she not seem to invite the black races to approach her throne of Mercy in all confidence. Happy Blacks we may call them! Yes, fly to Mary! Throw yourself into her maternal arms : does she not bless your dark livery in order as it were to bear your resemblance?" This however is what Protestants call Mariolatry. Catholicism which hears in several features a resemblance to Hinduism has had to meet much the same sort of charges as the latter,—idolatry, mummery, immorality and so forth. It must be admitted however that more recently both outlook and action in these matters have improved. In a recent pastoral letter by the Anglican Bishops of the Indian Province it was said " We Christians ought to be attractive to the non-Christian world. The gentleness and reasonableness of Christ the Great Reconciler should shine out in us." This is all for the good. It would however have been more satisfactory if these good sentiments had been more widely felt or at least expressed before circumstance necessitated them. An

" attractive " attitude would have been appreciated and would have saved some sore backs in Fiji for instance. It must be noted however that the missionary has on occasions stood against the trader and the official to secure proper treatment of coloured races. They are now bound to do so if their religious propaganda is not to suffer. Therefore as one of them has recently said : —"it must be made plain that the Kingdom of God is not necessarily the same thing as the British connection". The crude truth of this statement makes one wonder at the previous states of mind of some which called it forth.

Of course, amongst the intelligent, there is some increasing appreciation such as, I may note, that of the Belgium author, Maeterlinck, who, thinking of " Nature's Horrors," says in his recent book, " Mountain Paths," that he " falls back upon the earliest and greatest of Revelations, those of the Sacred Books of India with a Cosmogony which no European conception has ever surpassed ". In the doctrine of

Karma he finds "the only satisfactory
solution of life's injustices". In the last
edition of my *Bhârata Shakti* I have cited
a recent pronouncement by Professor
Mackenzie on Indian religion and metaphysics. He writes ("Elements of Constructive Philosophy," 475) "The Religion
that is most nearly akin to a philosophical
reconstruction would seem to be that of
Brahmanism". I am glad to be able to
thus note an increasing appreciation of
Indian civilization. It will help to coun-
teract the bad feeling engendered by many
ignorant and unjust criticisms.

I cite all this however neither as good nor
bad *Chits*. We have had enough of *Chits*
in this country. I refer to it as a statement
of what is going on, and of views held
which show the necessity of stating India's
case. If Indian civilisation has any merit,
it is not because any foreigner to it has
approved it. If he has done so, it is because that Civilisation has merit, which
he has understanding enough to perceive.
As I have elsewhere said, India cannot

afford to allow the case made against Her
to go unanswered. Neither an attitude of
superior disdain nor slothful negligence
will do. Honesty first. To be sincere, that
is truthful, is the first thing. Open enemies
are the best and it is these we honour. The
worst are to be found amongst those who,
with a beguiling " sympathy," call themselves our " friends ". Sympathy is a noble
word and a still nobler thing—for what is
a sign of greater greatness than to feel
with and for others,—to feel with the heart
of the world. The word has, however, as
I have elsewhere said, become so greasy
nowadays both in East and West through
the handling of those who dishonour it by
their real thoughts and acts, that one has
to be on one's guard when reading or
hearing the soft word " sympathetic ".
Especially is this caution true for the
Hindus. Voltaire ("Fragments relating
to some revolutions in India ") spoke of
the Hindus as " a peaceful and innocent
people, equally incapable of hurting others
or of defending themselves ".

Some have to be stirred to see what is even before their eyes. Attacks on Indian Culture however have led and will lead to its defence and appreciation. Kâlîdâsa says:

Jvalati chalitendhanah agnir viprakritah pannagah phanam kurute
Prâyah svam mahimânam kshobhât pratipadyate hi janah.

" When the faggots are stirred the flame leaps. When the Snake is stirred it rears its hood. Through being stirred to action people mostly attain their proper greatness.'

Life has been and is still a struggle. It may be that those who speak of a general world-peace pleasantly dream. In any case during the immediately coming years India will pass an unhappy time. She also is to " go through the mill ". Therefore is it that we are under an obligation to all, who by their open words or conduct recall us to our duty of maintaining *ourselves*, without, so far as may be, injuring others. I repeat here from the last edition of my *Bhârata Shakti* a saying of the late George

Tyrrell : " I begin to think the only real sin is suicide or *not being oneself.*" In conflict the truth will not suffer as was proclaimed ages ago in this country. So also in the West it has been finely said : " Truth is like a torch : the more 'tis *shook* it *shines.*" So let them shake at the great tree of Indian Culture. It will be no harm should what is dead or parasitic fall off it, provided the Tree itself stands firm. In any case and for myself it is sufficient if the seed which produced it is still forceful to produce another.

The practical difficulty consists in making changes in the body of a civilisation without injuring the soul of which such body is the vehicle. But it is the nature of a vital people to solve these questions: or rather with such people Life itself supplies the answer. Signor Viglione, in his work on Algarotti (an eighteenth century Italian Interpreter of England) says " (L'Algarotti el Inghilterra) " with reference to his too flattering account of England :

"He belonged to a period of our history when imitation of the peoples beyond the Alps was not merely a fashion but a necessity, in order that we might learn from their habits of thought and life that which would enable us to *restore* the spirit and culture of our Nation."

There the end is well stated, whatever view we may take as to the means which should be employed.

It must not be supposed however that the influence as between East and West is exerted onesidedly only. As Oswald Spengler points out in his now celebrated work "Der Untergang des Abendlandes," there are to-day in Europe minds more Asiatic than many of the Asiatics themselves which means, so far as India is concerned, that whilst a large number of its people are being influenced by the West, some in the West, who are capable of understanding Asian civilisation, are being psychically modified by some of its ideas. Let India then continue to affirm *Herself*, standing fast, firm, and faithful until the time when She is able to impart and others are ready to receive what She has to say. She may then recall to the West Principles which both East and West held to before the latter's entry upon some paths of modern aberration. But who will listen to any message,—indeed who can give it—if it be not given by a free, thinking, and *respect*-earning Self.

Calcutta
1st July, 1922   J. W.

———

FOREWORD

THE question which forms the title of this book is of course absurd. Even the most antipathetic or ignorant would admit that India has a civilization (as he would say) " of sorts ". There is an acute difference as to the value of it. The question however is not mine but is raised by Mr. Wm. Archer, a literary and dramatic critic of note in his recent book " India and the Future ". He finds India as a whole to be in the state of " Barbarism ". " What does it matter if he does say so," said an Indian to me, adding " this is only the last of a long list of misunderstanding works abusive of our country and its culture ". That is so, though the number is increasing now-a-days of those who respect both. Yet this indifferent attitude is a mistake. India cannot at the present moment allow any charges against her to go unanswered. I have here given some reasons why, without

xli

waiting for the completion of a larger work I had in the first steps of preparation on the general principles of Indian Culture, Lordship over alien peoples at present ultimately rests on might, though particular circumstances may render its actual enforcement unnecessary. But (apart from such implied consent as may in any particular case be held to exist) the right which Power-holders to-day allege is *cultural superiority* and the duty to raise the ruled to the cultural level religious, moral, and intellectual of those who control. It is with reference to such a duty that Mr. Archer finds India to be barbarous.

Though his book is for want of sufficient knowledge, without intrinsic value as a criticism of Indian civilization, there are several matters which, apart from the general ground stated, make it a suitable object of reply. Unlike the general run of criticisms it is written not from a Christian but a " Rationalist " standpoint. It is next a typical instance of the cultural attack, (and vehement at that) for it assails the fundamental principles of Indian civilization and every form of its culture religious, intellectual, artistic and social. Its vehemence may offend some. For myself I greatly prefer a candid violence to insidious attacks made under cover of patronizing or beguiling " sympathy ". I do not refer to the feeling which rightly corresponds to that glorious, but to-day much-prostituted, word. As regards the matter of the book, " India and the Future " is largely a re-statement of commonly current criticisms. Therefore a reply to this onslaught is an answer to others. Lastly the book in question well evidences the political basis of the cultural attack. It makes an offer which may be nakedly stated in the following terms :—".Give up yourselves. Be like us. If you do, you have our support for (to use a tedious common place) your 'political aspirations.' You will not get it if you persist in your barbarism."

Mr. Archer thus treats of questions of practical politics now agitating this country. With these I am not here concerned and upon them I express no opinion. I deal only with the subject of Indian culture and I am here interested chiefly to show the three causes, racial, religious and political, which are at the back of the influences making for the cultural conquest of this country. It is obvious also that criticism of philosophic principles affected by any of these causes is not a detached and truly rational one. In judging of a civilization we must look to its fundamental principles. Indian thought, with its usual profundity and avoidance of arbitrary divisions, regards Philosophy as religious and Religion as philosophical. We must therefore go to first principles, however unfamiliar such a course may be to writers on Western civilization concerned with the external aspects of social and political life. It is right to say that the truth of such principles must be judged by their result—the test of Âyurveda. But we must compare results, and if one is more defective than another we must be satisfied that the principles are in fault. For other causes may be operating. Having lived in this country for a period of nearly thirty years I am well aware of the divergence between Ideals and Facts. The greater one's interest in India the more acutely is it observed. But this charge is one which, in varying ways, can be made in different degree against all peoples. We must also distinguish between what is essential and of value and what is mere *crust*. There are further some matters which evoke contempt in minds characterised by the organic shapeliness of Race. Well has it been said that any want of organic racial consistency means lack of moral and intellectual coherence; and that man, in the mass, fulfils to day his highest destiny not as an isolated individual but as a portion of an organic whole, as a member of a specific Race.

The question of the value of Indian culture is not merely an academic one. It has present practical bearing on the future of India and the World. I everyday ponder upon, and question myself as to, the future of this country. Will it preserve its essential character, that is culture ? I say " essential " because I am thinking of its enduring principles and of their general applications. Some things are still happening which might lead one to think that it will not. Thus after this Book had been sent to Press I read the report of a speech of one who has been called an Indian " leader " in which he said that " English institutions were the standards by which their (the Indians') aspirations were set ". We may all benefit by the example and influence of others. But it is the Racial Sun of those who speak in this way which is set. Is it possible to conceive of any ordinary, much less a leading, Englishman or Irishman, however friendly to and an admirer of, (let us say), France, saying that " French institutions were the standards by which his aspirations were set " ? He would think that *his own* perfected institutions and racial ideals were the standards according to which his aspirations should be set. Is it possible with such a frame of mind to have independence and nobility of spirit? But perhaps it and other like sayings are only evidence of the occasional lingering of the servient spirit of a disappearing generation into a newly opening age of nobility, courage, vigour and freedom. I greatly hope so. An Indian Reviewer of this book ("Ārya") thinks that I "make too much of that type of Indian who is capable of mouthing the portentous servile imagination that 'European institutions are the standard by which the aspirations of India are set' that, (he says) except for the rapidly dwindling class to which this spokesman belongs, has its truth only in one field, the political—a very important exception I admit, and one which opens the door to a peril of stupendous proportions; but even there a deep change of spirit is fore-shadowed". I am glad to hear this, for I have no desire to make of this evil more than is justified.

But is Indian civilization about to be renewed or to be broken up—another instance of that disintegration which has followed the introduction of Western civilization amongst Eastern peoples? Its poison does not harm the snake but is death to others. Who can be sure that the close of the War will not be followed by movements tending to the cultural conquest of the whole of the Asiatic continent. There are events and possibilities which point this way. Moreover there is a party amongst the Indian people themselves who favour, in varying degree, the introduction of Western civilization; a party which in the proposed new political order may be powerful enough to achieve its ends. In every way, the coming assault on Hindu civilization will be the greatest which it has ever had to endure in the whole course of its long history.

Hope as each of us may, we have yet to see what will issue from this time fateful for us all. Here however Mr. Archer, though he intended it not, gives consolation, to those who need it. For *his* complaint is against the attachment which the Indian people show for their culture and the stubborn resistance which India makes against Western innovations. And why should She not, seeing that, rightly or wrongly, the bulk of the ancient peoples of the East have never admitted the moral superiority of Western civilization. More-over Mr. Archer's book was written before, though published during the War, an event, which has, in so many ways, called that alleged superiority in question. Since I wrote the above, the last book of the late sociologist Mr. Benjamin Kidd came to my hands. After citing with approval Mr. George Peel's statement (" The Future of England " 169) that in Europe, History and Homicide are undistinguishable terms, and stating that the unfolding of the Christian Religion in the West has been an unparallelled record of fighting and slaughter, aiming at worldly triumph, he says that civilization has not yet arrived, for that of the West " is as yet scarcely more than glorified savagery " (120, 121). But bloodshed is not all. For it is unsoiling and honest compared with some things which have gone on in peace. Many to-day in this country would say to Mr. Archer and other would-be lecturers—" Physician heal thyself." Nevertheless European civilization, classic in its origins, has in the past displayed a greatness actively dominant in social and political life and in science and art. Whether it will continue to do so after present and coming revolutions is yet to be seen. In any case it is not to be imitated in neglect of the principles of Indian Culture except by such as are willing to confess their inferiority.

I have written from the standpoint of the Vedânta as interpreted by the Shâkta Âgama the principles of which effect a wonderful synthesis, through its " enjoyment-liberation " (Bhukti-mukti) doctrine, of the claims of the World and of the Spirit, the dual aspects of That which is in Itself One. As the Buddhist Demchog Tantra says "Let all avoid the extremes of worldly existence and selfish quiescence attaining success in the two ends. Let all become the Heruka Himsélf." I am not however concerned either to criticise or to establish the truth of any of the doctrines and practices here mentioned nor, (had I the desire) could I do so within the limits of this set of little Essays.

My object has been to state summarily and correctly the main principles of Indian civilization (incidentally removing certain common misconceptions) ; as also to explain the general cause of the attacks which have so constantly been made upon it. I would also urge now as ever the worship of beauty as true Form. How profoundly has it been said in Europe " Oh Middle Ages! when will your night leave us ? When will men understand that form is not an unimportant accident, a mere chance, but an expression of the innermost being, that in this very point the two worlds, the inner and the outer, the visible and invisible touch ? " To such as so understand, Dharma reveals itself in the beauty of all True Forms, racial and otherwise. To such again, all that is mishappen and botched is an offence.

li

In writing then of Indian Culture I have in mind not any soiled or hybrid developments of the time, but the principles of the civilization of old India, with its Dharma, Devatâ and Gomâtâ—a civilization in its depths profound, on its surface a pageant of antique beauty—the civilization of India of the Hindus. " This is to go back " I hear some one say. India might fare worse. But no man nor people *can*, in this sense, go back. If we be really vital however, we are able to, and will, maintain the present with the same splendid strength of the Racial Spirit which did the great deeds of the past.

Having referred in my last edition to the necessity of preserving Form or Type, and to the principles of the old Indian civilization at a time when it was flourishing (that is when its vitality expressed itself as Dharma, Devatâ and Gomâtâ) as also to the impossibility of " going back," I did not suppose that some readers would misconstrue my words as I learn they have done. These have apparently thought that I was making a case for Reaction. In one sense I am doing so, since I urge reaction against *subjection* to foreign cultural influences. This does not mean that what is foreign and useful and good may not be *assimilated*. Western civilization is a great, though a different, civilization from which much may be learnt. But to assimilate one must first be a strong free personality. I am not for reaction in the sense such readers suppose. Life is Life, that is something not fixed and inert, but a moving thing, a flow. What is past is gone beyond recall. The Universe is called Jagat or " the moving thing," for all is in movement which is not the serene and restful Ether of Consciousness in which that movement takes place. One movement is vibratory, the larger movement is admittedly cyclic. And it may be that the total cosmic movement is a spiraline one, in which the motion is both progressive and cyclic. In any case there is no possibility of staying at any particular point, of stereotyping for all time all the customs and beliefs of some past age. What I urge is growth with truth to Type. To use

Hindu terms, this means that the Indian inherited Sangskâra should be allowed free play. This can be done only by being oneself and by casting off the foreign cultural vestures which choke self-expression, and which, because they are foreign and borrowed, produce an unreal imitative life with all its automatisms, the reverse of that of a free personality. The Indian soul will then develop itself in what way it will. But as it will be rooted in its own racial inheritance, "what it wills" means the willing of an Indian will. The present in such case manifests the essence of the past life in its own forms. Action will spring from the Indian Sangskâra. A Sangskâra is not a particular thought, act or will, but the essence of individual and racial characteristics which, (as related to action) is a tendency. The Indian Sangskâra produced a particular result in the past. It will produce another to-day if left to itself. This is the Seed (Bîja) of Indian culture. Is it to be said that what has been done cannot be done again ? If that be true then India is played out. Her death approaches. Her last breath will help to vivify other living forms. But She Herself, as the material expression of the Indian Soul, will have gone. What of the men and women of this country? Some will of course be there, but only as the subordinate vehicles of another civilization, working out the aims and ends, industrial and otherwise, of the cultural victors. Possibly, with the diminution of racial vitality and the abolition of present caste rules, a new people may appear by miscegenation. Nature resorts to the latter when the blood grows thin. This however will not be, so long as the Racial Spirit is alive and maintains itself against the forces of disruption and decay, which, even when not in actual operation, ever threaten all peoples as the penalty for indifference, inaction, timidity and self-betrayal. From the Indian standpoint it is therefore the Type which must be preserved.

It is for the Indian people to say where they will go. What I urge is that the

Indian Spirit should *be itself* and thus have *cultural freedom*. When it has regained this, by study and appreciation of its own inherited ancient and grand culture, and by the casting away of all unassimilated foreign borrowings, it may go where it will. I have confidence that in such case, its way will be a right way—that is an Indian way. The inherited ideas and instincts (Sangskâra) of thousands of years will assert themselves. In any case I believe that Indian culture has value, and that its ideas, if spread, will have a beneficial effect on men at large.

I wish in conclusion to reply to some criticisms. I do not refer to such as are merely personal ; for these are of no interest to the reader who has the book before him. There are however some few general criticisms which misunderstand the scope and purpose of these essays, to which I reply in the hope of making the position here adopted clearer.

To begin with an English critic has taken objection to " my philosophical spectacles ". I have written from a Vedântic standpoint not merely because I think the Vedânta to be a great philosophy but because a defence of Indian culture must be based on Indian Principles of which it is an expression. The particular form of Vedânta here adopted is the Monistic (Advaita)—a standpoint which I have taken because it is widely held and is the best known to me. But though I have presented this Advaita in its Shâkta form, there are other versions against which I desire to say nothing. It is not my business here to persuade any one in this matter. Let each adopt that for which he has aptitude (Adhikâra). It is however one of the peculiarities of the Monistic philosophy that it so often attracts towards itself great hatred, though it is itself the most tolerant of all systems. There are Western thinkers to whom Monism (Advaitavâda) is like a red rag to a bull. Some get quite unphilosophically angry at it and denounce it as a pseudo-philosophy of the past. So this particular English critic tells us that he has " a contempt for the Absolute " by which inappropriate English term he means the Pûrna Brahman of the Advaita Vedânta. The strength of his contempt is greater than his understanding of this system, if we may judge from the statements he has made regarding it. For it has led him to say that any. one who, like myself, " presents a position such as this intellectual outlook as that of Indian culture, or at least a part of it, is not really and truly a friend of India ". I should be certainly sad if I was not in this matter on the side of the angels, but I really cannot help it if I do put forth Advaita Vedânta as part (and a very important part at that) of Indian culture. For the fact is that Vedânta is the essence of it. I am not here concerned to defend the correctness or otherwise of this philosophical position beyond the reply that it is absurd to regard it as so evil or culturally undeveloped a thing as to render anyone who presents it liable to the charge of being an enemy of the country of its origin. Such a statement argues so considerable ignorance and impudence as to make it worthy of inclusion amidst other ridiculous criticisms which I have collected in this book. The gist however of this criticism is a common one— a criticism against which this book is directed ; namely that Indian culture is not a true culture, and therefore no one who in any way gives countenance to it is a friend of the Indian people. What this critic means is that we should move away from these cultural untruths towards some universal and really truthful culture of the unborn future. He says that the fundamental character of humanity is wider than the ideals of the mere East or the mere West. This no doubt is as obvious as the proposition that the whole is greater than the part. The ideals of either he finds to be largely obtained from the past. With the defence of Indian ideals we are apparently not to concern ourselves, however much they may have been slandered. Such a defence is a " mere flutter a matter of insignificance " which has produced in him " a feeling of contempt touched by a sorry sense of amusement ". For he opines that mankind is pressing on to a new type of life, which however (I may observe) is as yet so unknown that the quiet thinker (to use his expression) is to endeavour to form a conception of what the best in it is likely to be. These are commonplaces of modern thought, though whether it is a correct notion that the future will entirely scrap the past and stand forth in that brand-newness, which is to many an evidence of truth, is another matter. Many, perhaps the majority, believe that the most fundamental truths are already known, though it is possible that the apprehension of them may be gradually deepened in the minds of those who were formerly ignorant. Other changes there are likely to be. To the Hindu as to the Christian the essential truths are already revealed, though there is continual need for their better comprehension and realization. There is therefore, for them, no necessity for the explorations of the quiet thinker in search of something he knows not what. In the Bible and in Jesus the truth is for the Christian revealed.

The Hindu finds it in the Vedas which are a projection of the Perfect Veda on to the finite planes. The full truth is, according to Advaitavâda, the experience of Îshvara Himself. In other Vedântic systems, truth is realised in the Beatitude which is association with Him. All this is not necessarily to adopt a static attitude, to deny the flow of life. It is merely an assertion that God, Soul, Morality and some other concepts are truths already attained, though in the course of time our understanding of them may become more and more conformable to the experience of the Revealer and therefore more perfect. However this be, and whatever be the ideas and hopes of the quiet though unsettled thinker, I am not here concerned with them but with meeting the charge that India is barbarous and all that is implied thereby. Present justice must be done before we speculate as to the future. My critic however considers that this small and imperfect attempt of mine to do justice to Indian civilization is as much a " nuisance," as the attack of

Mr. Archer and others upon it. For the result he thinks is bound to be an increase in the feeling of antagonism. I have no desire to promote this. On the contrary knowing that it already exists in an intense, but generally subterranean, form, I think that an attempt to do justice from the side from which unjustice has come may allay such feeling in those who entertain it, and tend to prevent others in future from doing anything which is likely to arouse it again. An effort to avoid ill-feeling is certainly praiseworthy. It is permissible however for those who are misrepresented, or for those interested in them, to enter defence. Those who make untrue charges cannot be permitted to say to others who reply to them " You must not do this, for if you answer and criticise me it will create ill-feeling ". The future may reveal some universal culture. But whether this be so or not, the first thing is to correctly understand and avoid unfounded abuse of that which exists. And amongst present cultures, India at least occupies a place in the first rank.

An Indian Reviewer, whilst approving the book as a " counterpleading" to that of Mr. Archer, calls me to account because I have not entered " an emphatic protest against the prevailing abuses of Hindu society," with the result that my book has proved " in the hands of the unscrupulously and obtusely orthodox a weapon of offence and defence against the attacks of reason and common sense ". I am certainly sorry if it has been used with this result. I cannot do everything at one and the same time. My object as I have stated was to meet a particular charge and not to administer a beating, however deserved, to Hindu society. Those who have a desire for chastisement will find many ready to satisfy it. They have only to look up the literature on India. At the same time in order to avoid being misunderstood I did state that I was well aware of the divergence between Ideals and Facts. I pointed out in several places what was bad, and exhorted the conscientious " Reformer " to fulfil his task. I said that a much stronger criticism than that of Mr. Archer

might be written against the present day
Hindus by avoiding misrepresentation and
stating the facts. I said that whilst the
character of Indian civilization was spiritual, this did not mean that the individual Indian of to-day was necessarily so.
Indeed many in this matter are below
individual members of the leading
European peoples. Some of these latter have
religion, which some Hindus of to-day
have not. Some of these latter again
believe in nothing but getting money and
advancing themselves, a notion which is
countenanced and perhaps derived from
those who belong to the inferior strata of
Western civilization. Some Europeans on
the contrary though without attachment to
"religion" as popularly understood,
are devoted to their country and race
and to Humanity at large. To answer the
question of an esteemed correspondent of
mine, the Bosphorus does not divide the
Kingdom of Heaven. The notion that the
West is entirely materialistic and that
every Indian is wholly devoted to unselfish

idealism is, like many another generality of its kind, incorrect. If any such exaggerated statements are to be found, it is due to the result of reaction to the undiscriminating, unintelligent, and prejudiced criticism of India which came from the West. It was the latter who first started this conflict. The character however of Indian civilization is distinctly and predominantly religious. But as to its present manifestation, the distinguished Bengali Scientist Sir P. C. Ray has recently written *a propos* of those writers who are ever holding up the Europeans as mere worshippers of mammon, that "they forget that the Hindu society *as it is* is thoroughly permeated with materialism". This is in part at least the result of Western influences. What I am in particular dealing with is the charge that the *character* of Hindu civilization is unspiritual and that the only genius which the Indian people have displayed is for "obfuscating reason and formalizing, materializing and degrading religion". Since the war which has shattered European society and riven it through

E

and through with hatred and economic and other jealousies, some Westerns have shown themselves particularly touchy on this question of the spirituality of the East. But their angry or plaintive claims to share in this coveted quality contrast oddly with former arrogant and offensive claims of theirs to sole possession of it and their denial of its existence amongst the Asiatic " Heathen ". This is the way of the world, in which those who are least considerate of the feelings of others are the most indignant at what they conceive to be a slight on their own. There are in short some irreligious Indians and some religious Europeans and the reverse. The general character of the present Western civilization and of ancient Indian culture is another matter.

Again my critic refers to my adjective " wonderful " as applied to the Varnâshrama Dharma and challenges any one to show an individual or family which to-day lives strictly by its ideal. That may well be so. I was referring to the ideal not to present facts, which as I have over and over again pointed out, are inconsistent with it. I wish to insist on this point, for I should indeed be sorry if anything that I had said was understood as countenancing any of the abuses into which, through a descending scale of degeneracy, Hindu society has fallen. All honour and encouragement on the contrary to those who are conscientiously working (particularly as regards the position of woman, deferred marriage, untouchability and other matters) for its betterment. But in this matter we must first know the facts accurately, and then understand what are the true principles of Indian civilization, and in what respect there is abuse. We must then consider whether the regeneration of India should proceed on Indian or on Western lines. If, in any particular, Indian civilization is deemed wanting, then recourse may be had to some other. It is however obvious to me that development must in any case be a truly Indian one. That is it must proceed from the Seed which has produced the Indian

Race. That Seed is not necessarily to be confounded with any of its past *products*. It should; if necessary, again *produce* for to-day. Nor must this question be confused with any form of religion. India has produced or adopted many forms—Brâhmanism in all its many divisions, Jainism, Buddhism, Mahomedanism and Christianity. An Indian soul can clothe itself with any form if retaining its own natural characteristics, it rightly interprets these beliefs and then, with freedom and knowledge, makes its own choice. Thus, as I have elsewhere said, the Indian Mahomedan has characteristics which are different from those of his co-religionists of other lands. And the same may become true of Christianity when the Indian soul receives its direct inspiration from the person of the Eastern Jesus, and not from the doctrinal and liturgical forms in which the West has (often ignorantly enough) presented His teaching. This is not again to say that all these forms are false or unsuitable, but that all these religions, according to their true

interpretation, must be first appropriated by
the Seed of Race and then develop from
such seed, and not be worn as something
which is without. In short let there be a
cleansing from all corruption, and then
freedom to follow the truth in that form in
which a man's aptitudes (Adhikâra) present
it to him. Those who think that I hold to
any particular past, or that I am in ignorance of, or indifferent to, present abuses
misunderstand me. I am for free-thinking.
One may nevertheless think freely and find
oneself at the end of it with beliefs which
are age-old.

Lastly an English critic complains of my
"unworthy attack on Western and, in
particular Christian civilization". This
charge is in its implication untrue. I have
certainly criticised some unworthy features
of Western civilization as many others have
done and are still doing. It will not be
pretended anywhere outside India, (where
for obvious reasons these criticisms are
distasteful) that Western civilization is
beyond criticism, and in every respect

superior to that of this country. If it were
so we should not have had the late war, nor
see Europe in the parlous state in which it
now is. Nor should we hear of " reconstruction ". The time has gone by, when owing
to the ignorance in this country of Western
conditions, it was possible to put forward an
artificially roseate picture of " Christian
Europe " (to whom for its goodness God had
given all forms of prosperity including the
mastery over Eastern peoples) in sharp
contrast with the darkness of the " Kingdom
of Satan " and the degradation of the
" Heathen ". All is far from being well
here. Indeed there is that which is rotten,
as there is in the West. But the Western
critic will not be heard, and cannot take
part in helping to put matters right, unless
he is fully truthful, free of all hypocrisy, and
unjustified pride. It is to be noted that
those critics, who show themselves so
sensitive to criticism against their own
civilization, have not a word to say on the
subject of the extravagant charges against
Indian civilization against which this book

protests. Such self-preoccupation is certainly not worthy. Nothing but ill is achieved by the commonly adopted position which, in the face of the facts, ignores on the one hand the grave faults in our Western civilization, and on the other the merits of the outlook on life which is that of the Indian tradition.

As regards " Christian civilization " my position was that, in so far as the West was not truly Christian, and had no other principles which were a worthy substitute, it was the proper subject of condemnation. This is not an attack on Christian civilization, but on a civilization which usurps that title. The doctrine of Jesus is essentially (that is in its highest form) Sannyâsa. I hope to compare it with the teaching of Hinduism on this point on another occasion. Meanwhile to Him all reverence. This may be said without approval of all theories, institutions, and civilizations which call themselves Christian. As an English writer (" The Nation ") has well said :—" the mission of Jesus was to restore spiritual mastery to man; to drive out the unclean spirits of violence and selfishness, hatred of enemies and neglect of neighbours. Jesus is essentially hard and simple; easy to understand, difficult to follow. And the trouble is that the world will not follow. It follows its own doctrine which has all but destroyed it. When society was called upon to put His plain meaning into effect, its leaders denied with oaths and curses that it was ever there." As Professor A. W. Rimington has recently pointed out (" The Conscience of Europe ") the influence of the Christian conscience in Europe has been for years past steadily undermined, and even the clergy who as representatives of their church should be a power above the nations have, with some exceptions in all countries, become violently nationalist partisans.

The ideal is the great Confraternity of Men, beyond all nationality, but reached through the training ground of a true nationalism. We must seek to look on the world as one organism of which all the separate peoples are parts. But this is just what no people, as a whole, will now do. To achieve this we must resolutely destroy all falsities. Whether it be realized or not the value of the effort remains. Let us then understand and value India's contribution to this wished-for result. This Confraternity may well exist with nevertheless differing national, or at least group, cultures.

The Reviewer whom I have first mentioned writes of " the need that some one should present to the educated Indian a statement of the ideals for which the West in its deepest and most earnest convictions stands ". " For in one way or another " (he says) " these ideals are as constantly misrepresented by persons in India for political motives as evident as those " which I find in Mr. Archer's Book. By all means let us hear what these are, seeing how modern Western theories are mutually destructive of one another. If there has been misrepresentation, as alleged, the purpose of this critic will not be attained

by contemptuous amusement at attempts
to secure a truer understanding of, and
therefore justice for, Indian civilization.
What is required is in the first place a
purging on both sides of any unjustified
feeling of superiority and of all falsities
wherever found ; then a condemnation of
such falsities and hypocrisies whether
English or Indian ; and lastly a true statement of the nature and value of either
civilization. The point of this book is not
that India is beyond adverse criticism,
either as to the principles of its civilization,
or their present day application, lack of
application, or misapplication. Nor is
Western civilization free from fault. My
point is that Indian civilization is continually misunderstood and misrepresented ;
that it has a value which is not appreciated
and that such faults as have been charged
to it may be matched with others (some
greatly worse) which can be shown to
exist in Europe. I see merits and demerits
in both—though as an snswer to Mr.
Archer's book, which deals with the latter,

I am naturally more concerned with the merits of Indian culture. If, as is finely said in India *Satyânnâsti paro dharmah* (there is no religion higher than truth) then the destruction of every falsity is a part of it. As the Veda of this " barbarous" people says " Truth will conquer." (*Satyam jayate*.)

Calcutta
May 31st, 1919   J. W.

IS INDIA CIVILIZED ?

*" Barbarian, barbarism, barbarous
—I am sorry to harp so much on
these words. But they express the
essence of the situation . . . There
are of course many thousands of
individuals who have risen and
are arising above it (barbarism),
but the plain truth concerning the
mass of the (Indian) population—
and not the poorer classes alone
—is that they are not civilized
people."*
"India and the Future" by
William Archer.

I

CIVILIZATION AND PROGRESS

FOR thousands of years man has seen
moving across the face of the world grand
migrations of peoples. From ages now

remote, waves upon waves of his tribes have clashed with one another, now conquering, now suffering defeat, exterminating, absorbing, now dispersed and again swarming to repeat the unending battle by which the Soul of Humanity has been tempered and brought to fresh expression. This conflict has continued until to-day and when I first wrote these words was terribly manifest. In later times there were added to the naked assault of the sword, economic invasions and struggles and more subtle cultural conflicts—for souls as well as bodies battle. During these immense periods and amidst inner and outer struggles man made his advance in social progress through various stages of savagery, barbarism, and civilization. Gradually culture developed in its various forms as Religion, Philosophy, Literature, Science, the Arts and Social Institutions. This evolutionary process has hitherto been effected by struggle in which one form of existence, whether as species or individuals, has made advance at the expense of others. The plant nourishes itself on the earth, the animal on the plant, man on the animal and plant and on his fellow men. Species conflict with species and individuals with individuals. For though man does not now (except amongst some savages) devour the flesh of his brother to build up his own; he yet still lives upon his fellow in other ways; warring upon and killing him to acquire his land and other wealth and to free himself of obstacles in the way of self-development; warring upon him economically, making himself richer at the other's expense; feeding or warring upon him culturally, either appropriating his psychical acquisitions where suitable, or destroying them where opposed to his own.

What is the meaning of this process called the "struggle for existence"? This phrase only denotes the superficial aspect of this conflict. Why this conflict at all and for what purpose and end?

Let us see what an Indian answer is. The one fundamental Substance or Consciousness (Chit) and its unmanifested Power

of activity (Chidrûpinî Shakti) appears
through this Power in dual aspect as Spirit-
Matter (Chitshakti and Mâyâ-Shakti) at
the same time mysteriously retaining Its
own nature (Svarûpa) as Changeless Spirit
or Consciousness (Chit). In the words of
the Veda the One said, " May I be many ".
The Spirit or supreme Self (Paramâtmâ)
whilst in one aspect retaining Its own
formless transcendency, in another aspect
becomes involved and immanent in Matter
which is the product of Its Power in order
that the individual selves (Jîvâtmâ) may,
in the world of form, enjoy and suffer the
fruits of their previous actions (Karma) in
successive births. This " Will-to-be-many "
is the start of the creative impulse. The
Will is not arbitrary. It evokes the fruit
of previous actions (Karma) and allows the
germs of past universes to fructify. At
the point at which the Cosmic Mind pro-
jects itself upon, and is conscious of, the
material plane, the universe of individual
selves is born in forms of varying development according to their previous cosmic

4

history. With the completed appearance of the Universe involution ceases and the evolving process commences, that is the evolution of matter so as to become a finer and purer vehicle of Spirit until Consciousness releases itself of mind and matter and enjoys pure unlimited and perfect transcendental experience. The Life-force (Prâna-shakti) which is a Power (Shakti) of the Eternal Being (Sat) moulds gross, and apparently inert, but in reality highly active, matter—with its constituent factors (Gunas) revealing (Sattva) and veiling (Tamas) through its activity (Rajas) Spirit or Consciousness—into the organized plant form, the consciousness of which is, as Chakrapâni says in the Bhânumatî, of a dormant or comatose kind. In the inorganic kingdom the active factor (Rajas) of Power (Shakti) as the material cause (Prakriti) makes the veiling factor (Tamas) suppress the ever concomitant revealing (Sattva) character of all material substance. Hence so-called " brute matter " appears as unconscious and inert though in truth it is

5

Consciousness deeply veiled in matter which is incessantly active. For the whole universe is in incessant motion and is hence called Jagat (moving). In plant life Tamas is lessened and Sattva more greatly reveals consciousness. The difference between plant and animal life has always been regarded by the Hindus as being one not of kind but degree. And this principle is applied throughout. This is not so according to Christian Theology according to which the body and soul of man is not like that of other living creatures; for their bodies and souls were made of earth whilst the body of man was alone made of earth and the. soul came from without, being breathed into it by God (St. Tho. i. p. q. xci. art. 1). According to that Theology, God of His own will made the universe " out of nothing ". It does not derive from pre-existing matter nor is God its material cause. There was an absolute first creation. The animals were created so that " man might recreate himself with the sight of so great variety and beauty of creatures; for

6

if it be so great a contentment to see an elephant what it will be to see so many together or some other beast which we had never seen ". When man was made, God afterwards, of a rib of his side, made woman to show, it has been said, that " he was not created principally to attend to generation as other living creatures are " for " work in matrimony is a work very base ". (Ven. Louis de Ponte. S. J. Meditations vi. 264, 272, 274.) Such notions are alien to both Indian and Modern Western thought.

Life and consciousness are not products of evolution. The latter merely manifests it. The individual self (Jîva) then manifests as an animal which is also full of darkness (Tamas), though in still lesser degree, owing to the greater prevalence of the revealing constituent (Sattva) of matter; for it shows a greater manifestation of consciousness which seems to display itself largely, if not entirely, in what we call animal wants. Animals are of higher and lower forms, the former showing a greater and greater manifestation of consciousness. At length the individual self (Jîva) clothes itself in the form of man, the birth which the Scripture calls so hard to get (Durlabha). If therefore man does not avail himself of the birth, so hardly won through innumerable ages, he is called a "Self-killer". In man Sattva more greatly predominates than in any purely animal form. Here consciousness recognizes its limited self or Ego and is fully awake to the objective world. Here it enters the world of ideas which are a superstructure on the fundamental substance or Consciousness and not its foundation or basis. Here also it enters the realm of conscious morality, one of the aspects of the eternal Dharma. This Dharma is the constituent principle of the universe ; that which makes anything what it is (Svalakshnadhâranât Dharma) and therefore governs and upholds (Dhâryate) all manifested being. But in man it exists in the form of what is generally called Morality or the principle of conduct, and in those concepts of his relation to all Beings, and to Being itself or God

8

which is the theological aspect of what we call Religion. Sattva which is the spiritual portion of man's vehicle of mind and matter because it reveals Spirit or True Consciousness manifests itself more and more in wise and saintly men, until in the accomplished (Siddha) Yogî the material vehicles which are a projection of consciousness disappear. He is then on release from the body (Videha mukti) identified with the Pure Spirit which is Consciousness-being-bliss (Sachchidânanda). There has always been this identity in fact but it is then realised. Thus as Matter more and more evolves, it becomes a more perfect manifestation of Spirit or pure Consciousness.

Just as the Gnostics (who in this borrowed from India) spoke of the Material, Psychical and Spiritual man; so the Indian Tantric scriptures divide humanity into three classes (according to the prevalence of the Gunas (into the Pashu or animal man in whom the veiling principle (Tamas) prevails; the Vîra or Heroic man in whom the active principle

(Rajas) is dominant; and the Divya or divine man in whom, owing to the abundant operation of the principle of matter which reflects and manifests Spirit (Sattva), the latter in increased degree of purity shines forth.

The meaning therefore of evolution is not merely the development of matter into more and more highly organised form ; but such organisation exists for the purpose of Spirit. Spirit which involves itself in that product of Its Power which is matter, organises that matter into finer and finer meshes until It is released from it.

The vital progressive impulse of which we are conscious is the impulse of Life to so organise itself that it may become a more and more perfect vehicle of Spirit. This impulse it is which organises matter into gradually ascending forms ; and which, when man is reached, works in him to effect his spiritual development. True Civilization is a process which has the same end. It may and does produce some material comfort but this is not an end in itself, but when rightly employed a means whereby man's mental and spiritual nature is given greater play on its increasing release from the animal cares of life. That then is true civilization which recognising God as its beginning and its end organises men in society through their material and mental vehicles with the view to the manifestation of Spirit in its forms as true morality and true religion. Thereby man first recognises his essential Divinity and then realises it in his conscious union with the Self as manifested in the whole Cosmic process and then as transcending it. For there is but one Shiva (" The Good ") who is thought of in dual aspect. From the transcendent aspect, Spirit (Paramâtmâ) changelessly and blissfully beyond all worlds (Vishvottirna) *is*. From the immanent aspect It by its power (Shakti) *exists*, that is appears in the form of the world (Vishvarûpa). As there is only one Shiva-Shakti or Consciousness and Its Power, it follows that, whilst in one aspect such Consciousness ever enjoys that Perfect Blissful Experience which the

Scripture calls the Supreme Love; in the other it both enjoys and suffers in the imperfect or world-experience. Whilst therefore neither in the Divine Ground or Godhead (Parabrahman) nor in the creative God or Lord (Îshvara) is there any duality of opposites; yet God in His form as creature, that is, *in* and *through* and *as* Man and all other beings, suffers and enjoys. Shiva appears both as the individual being (Vyashti) and as the collectivity (Samashti) of all finite beings inhering in the infinite and unlimited Lord. Religion, in its highest form, consists in union with "the Good" (Shiva) or God in both His and Her aspects; that is by identification in Vîrabhâva of the individual self with the totality of selves, with the cosmic process, and then with its Lord, which is known as the gross union of feeling (Sthûla Sâmarasya) in the world of a World-form with the World-Lord (Shivo'ham—I am Shiva); and the subtle union of feeling (Sûkshma Sâmarasya) beyond all world-forms in which the Self experiences the Self in all its perfections which is the completed Divyabhâva. We are each instruments in the eternal struggle of matter to free spirit. Know this and serve rightly. If man so understands the Cosmic process he will know why it is a struggle: and if he both thus knows and identifies himself in fact with it he will be freed of fear even in the presence of its most terrible forms. If beings fight with and devour one another in the early stages of evolution, it is to subserve the evolution of Spirit. Unconscious of it though most of them be, they are each a sacrifice on that altar on which the self is offered to the Self. In the nature of things past no other process was, in the first stages of development, possible. In the animal stage each being lives on others. Forms war with and devour forms. Races, nations and civilizations conflict and absorb one another. At the back of all is this Great Urge of Spirit clad in form to return to Itself, which we are apt to interpret in shallow ways as if such Urge were towards mere material existence lived in comfort as the end. Until the true end is reached there must be some suffering ; since imperfection persists until its achievement. Man moreover would rest upon the way and neglect the pursuit of his final ends. The clash of matter and mind-expression or cultures is the building up of better forms for the expression of Spirit. This clash of forms becomes less gross, and the necessity for it becomes less great, as the mass of men gain in moral value. At present one being lives on another ; one conflicts with another in the process of evolving and perfecting forms. In the same way souls in their cultural expressions are at war. What is inferior will be thrust out by what is better. Wherever and whenever also unrighteousness (Adharma) exists there must be a battle to overcome it for the establishment of Dharma. That this struggle on the whole subserves the development of forms and the greater manifestation of Spirit is clear. Otherwise it would be a meaningless and horrible conflict. But to justify each detail of this process may be more difficult for want of knowledge. Not only do men and animals war with one another, but nature in the form of storm and eruptive fire, in the earthquake and in disease war with both. We may believe, as Hindus do, that all being related, atmospheric and other natural disturbances only exist where man's Dharma is at fault; that the cause of happenings in this world may be only found in past universes; and we may remember that of the economy of the present world and of the functions of all its forms of life we have as yet but imperfect knowledge. Yet who, having faith in a Divine Order, can doubt that—whether every instance is capable of certain present explanation or not—the general nature and object of the process is revealed? Let each take up his position and fulfil his part therein without vulgar animal hatred. This, the doctrine of the Gîtâ, is one of the grandest doctrines which India has taught. As I write these lines, the morning paper reports the advice of an American clergyman preaching to the employees of a submarine boat company at Fort Newark. After consigning his enemies to Hell and advising the employees to " hammer the face off " his propagandist, the Reverend gentleman revealed the crudity of his " religious " beliefs in the following utterance : " when I stand before the judgment seat of the Almighty I want to be able to look my God in the face and tell him that I gave the Germans at least one good wallop before I shuffled off." This is not the spirit but the vulgar antithesis of that of which I speak ; and yet most probably, the preacher—a doctor of divinity—thought, as do betters of his cloth, that he was quite capable of teaching this country religion. Man should endeavour to do all acts, and should even righteously fight, not from personal animosity or with the desire for personal gain but selflessly as a soldier in the human hosts of the Lord to whom is dedicated the fruit of every action. Were all men of this spirit we should not see unjustified aggression. Or again according

16

to the sublime view of the Shâktas, man will know himself in all his actions to be Shiva and His Power the Universal Mother : saying " Shivo'ham " " I am Shiva ; " " Sa'ham " " I am She "; and will find that in his self-identification in and with theCosmic Process as the expression of a Power which is his own essential self, all vulgar hate, all merely personal desires and aversions are gone. He is Shiva in the form of the universe accomplishing its purpose. He who knows himself as such is the incarnate Spirit of World-Order. And when and in the degree that that World-Order is established, men will work *with* and not *against* one another and will even sacrifice themselves for one another ; knowing that if, in the past, evolution has advanced through discord, with spiritual knowledge the path is Harmlessness (Ahingsâ) and Harmony.

The same author in the work above cited complains that this country " in its inmost heart resents and despises progress ". We should know what he means by " Progress " and " Civilization " but he nowhere tells us. There are Indians who think in very nearly the same way as their teachers of the West do. One of such discussing the subject called himself a " Hindu progressivist". The bulk of the Indian people however do not believe in. " Progress " in the materialistic sense in which that term is commonly understood in the " liberty-loving and progressive " West ; to use a phrase which rolls off the tongues of some Indian politicians as if their country knew nothing of a liberty and progress of its own. But that is not to say that the people do not believe in progress at all. They have a different conception of it.

A young and very " modern " Moslem once said to me: " It was from the time that Europe became prosperous and fat that it became ' progressive '."

The remark is applicable to certain notions of " progress " ; such for instance as that which conceives progress as merely the increase of scientific knowledge, the development of industry, the conquest and harnessing of nature to serve man's material needs; and as a world getting healthier, richer, happier and generally more comfortable and refined and therefore more (in this sense) "civilized".

The notion of progressively increasing material comfort is on this view dominant. Moral improvement is also looked for, but as the necessary condition of an orderly, peaceful and industrious world. The lower expression of this ideal has been compared to a model farmyard with its healthy wellfed domesticity. Rude war has swept away these imaginings.

What was the impulse towards such and other "progress"? It has been rightly perceived that an impulse towards progress is inherent in man's nature. But the meaning and direction of the impulse was misunderstood. The message of the vital impulse made in the service of the unfolding of Spirit was read in material terms only. It is also a noteworthy peculiarity of Western notions of progress that they contemplate a future in which the whole world shall have arrived at an equality of high development.

And yet there has always been an impulse towards progress and a progress in fact. What is the meaning of the word " Progress " ? Most of those who use this and the term " Civilization " would be hard put to define with exactitude what they mean. From an Indian standpoint however this is clear : and it is from this standpoint that I write.

If by the term " Progress " we mean that at any particular time the sum-total of happiness is greater than it has been at any previous period, then it can be questioned whether progress is in this sense established. True happiness in this world consists in the natural harmony of Spirit, Mind and Body. Is there more of this to-day than formerly ? If there is one thing certain, it is the present lack of inner and outer harmony. Even from the material standpoint, the alleged progress is not proved. What is apparent is more happiness in some ways in one age and in other ways in another age. Thus medicine and surgery are more efficient to-day but the general healthiness of a primitive people had little need of them. Anæsthetics are urgently called for by our modern sensitivity. Earlier ages were able to bear suffering with both lesser pain and greater fortitude. If we are happier on account of our anæsthetic, they were so by their greater robustness. Is it better to have good dentists or good teeth and so forth?

If by "progress" is meant that the individual soul (Jîvâtmâ) evolves from lowly origins through higher forms to man, there is such progress. Ages before Lamarck and Darwin it was held in India that man has passed through 84 lakhs (8,400,000) of birth as plants, animals, as an "inferior species of man" and then as the ancestor of the developed type existing to-day. The theory was not, like the modern doctrine of evolution, based wholly on observation and a scientific enquiry into fact but was rather (as some other matters) an act of brilliant intuition in which observation may also have had some part.

True progress according to Indian notions is the increasing manifestation of Spirit through the gradual perfecting of its vehicles of Mind and Body. Each of these exhibits an increasing perfection of its own, psychical and physical, thus expressing more and more the true nature of the Spiritual Substance whence they both derive. This progress is displayed in the evolution of man from the animal, plant and mineral, and in his further development until, through an ever-growing knowledge and morality, he attains complete Humanity and therefore Divinity, since of this last, perfected man is the highest earthly form. True liberty is the freedom to develop oneself without hindrance along the path of true progress. As each individual varies in capacity and temperament, this involves the right to self-expression according to Svadharma, that is the morality geverning the particular self. If anarchy is to be avoided every society must place some restraint on its members. The nature of the freedom given differs. In one place there may be greater political liberty, in another greater intellectual or spiritual liberty. In some cases in Europe the latter has been wholly denied. So again it has been said that whilst there was under the late Russian Autocracy no political liberty, the restraints on social freedom were less than in England, the leader in what is called " political freedom ". In India there has been intellectual and spiritual freedom —the most valuable of all. This is evidenced by the great variety of religious and philosophical opinion in this country, Rationalism, Theism, Atheism and so forth, and the existence of a large number of varying religious communities. Provided that the social rules of the Hindu system are observed, one may think, believe and say what one will. The history of Europe on the contrary is marked by intolerance and abominable persecutions. Further it was, and is now open to any Indian to leave society and its rules and become a Sannyâsî

23

pursuing his way according to will. In Europe, and in particular amongst its Western peoples, state and social bonds are so many and close that it is not possible to escape them. Take for instance the case of a man whose religious ideas are those of harmlessness (Ahingsâ). It is only in England that a grudging recognition is given to such a conscience. Those too who are " conscientious objectors " . incur in general contempt and persecution. These people are in effect told that they may have an opinion and are then punished for having one. Outside England and on the Continent this liberty is denied. Even the Priest is made to fight. The Doukhobhors left Russia because liberty was not allowed them to give practical effect to their beliefs in this matter. Great credit is therefore due to England for her stand in this matter, spoilt though it be by the reluctance of the many to accept the principles which the true mind of their country has produced. But what is there in India against such spiritual liberty ? On the contrary even the

Kshattriya whose duty it was to fight might become a Sannyâsî and thereby give effect to his desire to injure no man. In the West there are restraints in all matters of daily life, the number of which is increasing yearly as evidenced by the number of laws enacted. An American writer says that it is an enlightening commentary upon the difficulties to be met in the evolution of the freedom of the individual, to read the Report of the Society of Comparative Legislation upon the Legislation of the British Empire. For the ten years ending in 1907, 25,000 new laws were made by men for the restriction of their own liberties in the British Empire. And how many more have been passed since then in a country which has claimed to uphold the liberty of the individual more than any other. " First " he says, " men strike off the chains of the church, of feudalism, which bind them, and then with a new system, with Self-government in a new era, they are finding that the new liberties must have new masters, and they turn to laws for their masters." There must be law but there can be too much of it. All the talk is now for " organization " which does not spell " liberty ". The mere right of a man to cast a vote every five years or so for the person who may " represent " him in Parliament is only but a portion, and not over big at that, of Liberty. The " liberty-loving nations of the West " have been in the past greatly, and still are to some extent, behind India in the matter of intellectual and religious freedom.

The term " Civilization " implies the living of men in community and therefore individual liberty is to some extent restrained by the duty which each has to others. But the State cannot constrain them from doing what is right or to do what is wrong. For right itself (Dharma) is independent of, and superior to, interests of State because the latter itself, like the individuals of which it is composed, is subject to the law of Right or Dharma which can be escaped by none.

II

EAST AND WEST

ONE of the oldest of problems is the conflict between East and West which is now becoming more acute owing to the growth of populations, increased communication, a closer contact of cultures, growth of knowledge, economic questions, the assertion of the Asiatic Consciousness, the intensity of the struggle for life and other causes. The whole world is now in ferment preparing for the next great advance in the evolution of the race. Once there was greater equality between East and West which was disturbed by the white man's conquest of the sea; leading in the case of the English to world dominion. Asia, however, once played her role. By a succession of vast onslaughts, She, as has been well said, " shook and hardened Europe to new life ". Before then, Greek and Roman had struggled for mastery with Oriental Empires. Thereafter the Huns carried fire and sword into the heart of Europe. Later the Arabs conquered Spain: and poured across the Pyrenees to be smitten by Charles the Hammer: and yet they retained parts of Spain for hundreds of years imbuing Europe with their great learning and culture. Then followed the Second Tartar invasion when the Mongols were defeated under the walls of Vienna largely by the aid of Hungarians, themselves nothing but Asiatics left behind from the flood of the first invasions of the fifth century. Finally, the Ottoman Turks, rivalling the military success of the Arabs, captured the whole Byzantine Empire and were only arrested after immense struggles along the line of the Danube, thus terminating in the fifteenth century the vast series of forays undertaken by Asia against Europe with which in the course of a thousand years there was an unending conflict. Through this hardening process the white man's position in the world was established. As

an American writer, whose conclusions I
here, in his own language, summarise ('The
Conflict of Colour' by B. L. Putnam
Weale) points out, another factor in·the
Evolution of the white races was Christianity, not because, according to his view,
Christianity as a religious system (that is
institutional Christianity) had special value,
but because it supplied just that inspiration
and organization which were needed by
rude and unimaginative peoples to give
them discipline and to intensify the conflict
with Asia and Africa. " The political mark
which the· Christian Church has conse-
quently made in Europe, can never be
wholly effaced ; though it is a mark entirely
different from anything which could be
anticipated from a reading of the Gospels "
with their essentially spiritual and other-
worldly and therefore Eastern message.
Thus by the time of the last Turkish forays
a new Europe was born and the position of
East and West was reversed. The latter
conquered the sea. To the European the
whole world was unmasked, and, landing

29

on the most distant shores, he made rapid conquests with the modern magic-explosive matter. If India be once again mighty, those who now ignorantly speak of Her as " uncivilized " will at least not dare to assert it. Whilst it is a demoniac notion that the power to harm alone gives civilized title, that power, it must be admitted, at least ensures a kind of human respect.

The Christian middle-ages (whatever was their practice, and it was often bad enough) possessed a beautiful ideal ; an ideal of human unity and of the blending of the spiritual and temporal. With the discovery of America and of the East and a declining Christianity, Europe cast its eyes abroad and became predatory. The sense of unity was lost and the period of base exploitation began. Money became more important than land (for Feudalism had rested on an agricultural basis) and " Vulgar Nationalism " (as a friend of mine calls it) arose, and being reinforced by the coarse Industrialism of the " Age of the Machine " became more and more aggressive, until in our day it has met with its natural retribution. The Portuguese, the Dutch, the French and the English imposed, by force and with desire for trade and loot, their will upon the Asiatic. The Spanish Conquistadores in the Americas were called by that humane Catholic apostle Las Casas " destroyers of the Indians ". The same or similar processes have gone on everywhere and amongst all colonising peoples —until times which are recent. So (to take one instance) at the other end of the world in Tasmania, Captain Stoney writes, " the aborigines were doing much mischief. Measures were taken in 1830 to drive them by a grand ' battue ' through Forrestiers' Peninsula. The expedition however failed; other plans were adopted, and they were at last all got together in Flinders Island where they gradually became extinct ". ("A Residence in Tasmania," p. 43.) "Thus," to use the words of the authors (T. A. Coghlan and T. T. Ewing) of the " Progress of Australia in the Nineteenth Century,"

" perished the sole survivor (Torganini) of a gentle race of savages whose horrible treatment by the early settlers of Van Diemans Land is a blot in the records of the British race " (p. 231). In India the work of conquest went on from the sixteenth century until the age in which we live. Throughout and in every instance there was the worship of brute force. The Portuguese, the Spaniard and the Dutch gradually lost their pre-eminence. Then followed England's struggle with the French when She at the close of the Napoleonic Wars was found the victor. Macaulay says that, until Clive went to India, the English " were despised as mere pedlars, whilst the French were revered as a people formed for victory and command ". But from the moment that England displaced France, her history became world-history and her land became covered with worldly renown. By the middle of the eighteenth century, just prior to the birth of the present European civilization, the force of the European attack had been spent and matters moved more leisurely ; but, as the independent author, I cite, says, the old tradition remained and was acted upon, wherever possible, strengthened by the inventions of a scientific age. Suzerainty was displaced by the notion of actual ownership. Later still, Power covered itself and its actions with what he calls some " pleasant fictions". To the honest these are hypocrisies which time will sweep into the sink of all other falsities.

Again, Asia reacts and as the author cited says : " In the far East the return swing of the pendulum is clear ; in the middle East it has commenced ; and elsewhere smaller oscillations have to be noted in Egypt, in Morocco, in Algeria and in the French Soudan."

This was written four years before the great European War. Of the great European Powers in Asia before that event, France and Holland occupied a subordinate positon to the Russians and the English. The predominance, as I write after the internal strife in Russia, rests with the last mentioned alone who, now that the war has ended, seems to hold the key to Asia. As Dr. Yujiro Miyake in his article on " The Future of Asia " written in January 1918 has said, " hitherto Asiatic countries have changed, so far as they have changed at all, diversely and independently according to their racial traits and history.- But at present great changes are going on in all countries of Asia simultaneously. It is a change more colossal, far-reaching and profound than any that has taken place in the past." Not the least of the influences operating is the late European War., This War, if read rightly, marks the close of an epoch of civilization, and, through it and its aftermaths, both the feudalism which yet lingers in Europe and particularly in England, as well as the modern purely materialist industrialism (at any rate in its present forms) is likely to disappear. Even now what was before 1914 is seen as an old world. The close of this epoch also definitely affects both the relations of, and balance between, East and West. The same writer

says that, " if the 850,000,000 people of Asia
become self-conscious and begin to display
the latent forces of democracy, the whirl-
winds for which Asia has been famous for
ages, will grow in magnitude and sweep
round the world. The whirlwind of Asia
has already circumscribed the globe and is
now just starting on its second circuit with
greater vehemence than on the first journey.
Already it is beginning to effect mighty
changes in Asia itself ". The movement is
of profound interest to a world seeking to
know where it will end. No wonder that
another writer of the same race (which
some think may assume the hegemony of
this movement) states that the Christian
missions are labouring harder than ever
since the War to extend their religion in
the East ; no wonder is it that missionaries
of race and culture are by attack or persua-
sion endeavouring to get the East to
adopt, in place of its present inherited
civilization, their own. The " coloured
peril " and the world-peace will, it is
thought, be more vastly diminished if the

East is westernised than if it retains its secular ideals and practices alien to the life of Europe. The cultural attack by Europe on the East is, in short, an effort to save its own psychic possessions by the assimilation of that which opposes them, and (let me at once say it) this is for Europe, in this era of conflict, right, if done in sincerity and with truth ; for each must defend his own. Similarly India's Dharma is to stand by Her cultural inheritance and to repel all assaults upon it. Were the English to absorb the Indian civilization which the spread of the English language, ideas and customs threaten, its people would not be monsters on that account. The act would only show that those of this country were fit to be eaten. It is for them to say whether they shall be so or not. Hitherto military might has been with Europe. By the exhaustion of the present War it will be shorn of much of this strength and will need all its powers to reconstitute itself internally ; possibly after social revolutions. Moreover there are signs that allegiance to

the reign of brute force in the west is
weakening and commencing (though the
way may be yet long) to disappear. But
apart from this, the Japanese writer in the
" Japan Magazine " has truly said, " the
lands where Confucious, Buddha, Christ and
Mahomed were born and taught (and wherein, we may add, the immortal Upanishads
appeared) are possessed of a power greater
than military force and may yet be able to
change the face of the whole world. They
have not much money or anything that
visibly impresses worshippers of the things
of this world, but they have vast numbers
of people, many of whom have brains and
souls more significant of real manhood and
real living than all the wealth of occidental
materialism ; " which, however, I may add,
is only a passing stage in what has been
(despite its modern vulgarians) a vital
civilization with elements of greatness.

The quotation above made refers to
spiritual power which is the true source of
all others. It has however been well
observed by an Indian writer in an acute

analysis of the present book ("Ârya" : December, 1918) that Spirituality is not the monopoly of India, but that the strength of, and the place assigned to, it vary in different civilizations. Thus a civilization may be predominantly material like the modern European culture, or predominantly mental and intellectual like the old Greek and (in a less degree) the old Greco-Roman culture, or predominantly spiritual like the still persistent culture of India. Though Mr. Archer does not admit that Indian civilization is at all spiritual, he concedes at any rate the predominance of what India believes to be spiritual when he says that " to study religion on its native heath you must go to India ". India's central conception is, as the reviewer cited truly says, that of the Eternal, the Spirit here incased in evolving matter, involved and immanent in it. Her religion is the aspiration to spiritual consciousness. Her whole Dharma or Law is founded upon it. Her philosophy, art and literature have the same *upward* look. Her progress is spiritual progress.

Her founding of life upon this exalted conception, her urge towards the spiritual and the eternal constitutes the distinct value of Her civilization, and Her fidelity, with whatever human shortcomings, to Her ideal, make Her people a nation apart in Humanity. But there are other cultures in the world led by a different conception. None is devoid of spirituality which is a necessary part of human being. " But the difference lies between spirituality made the *leading motive* and determining power of the inner and outer life, and spirituality existing only as a secondary power, its supreme reign denied, or put off in favour of intellectualism or a dominant materialistic vitalism. The former way was the type of many ancient cultures. But all nations with one exception have now fallen, or are falling away from it, and have in varying degress adopted, or commenced to adopt the economic, commercial, industrial, and intellectually utilitarian modern type." (This statement requires qualification, so far as the Catholic Church is concerned.

39

For that Church still represents in the west the older order of ideas. For this reason I think that the Syllabus of Pope Piux IX was an essentially honest document, shy of it as may be the modern Catholic seeking to explain it away). Indian alone, he says, has remained faithful to the heart of the spiritual motive. She is still obstinately recalcitrant as Mr. Archer angrily complains. She alone up to now has refused to surrender the worshipped Godhead, and to bow the knee to the reigning idols of rationalism and commercialism. To this situation there can be only one out of two issues. Either India will be rationalised and industrialised, or by her example and cultural infiltration, aiding powerfully the new tendencies of the West, She will spiritualise humanity. It is then profoundly said that the real question at issue is whether the *spiritual motive* which India represents is to prevail in Europe, taking there no doubt, new and other forms congenial to the West, or whether European rationalism and commercialism will put an end to the Indian

type of culture. Not whether India is civilised (a point no fair and competent man
disputes) but whether the motive which has
shaped Her civilisation, or the older European intellectual, or the more recent
European materialistic motive is to lead
human culture ; " whether the harmony of
the Spirit, Mind and Body is to found itself
on the gross law of our physical life, rationalised only, or touched at the most, by an
ineffective spiritual glimmer, or whether
rather the dominant power of Spirit is to
take the lead and force the intellect and
physical life to the highest harmony is the
real question. Whatever appearance of
conflict may be assumed for a time, it will,
since it will be in effect an assistance to all
the best that is emerging from the advanced
thought of the West, prove in reality the
beginning of concert on a higher plane and
a preparation for unity ". This is well said.
I would add only a word as to the importance of the reasonable conservation of
forms. Ideas only exist in men ; that is, in
bodies. They are only given objective

existence through other forms; that is, social and religious institutions and customs. If these untimely disappear, then whilst the ideas may to some extent pass over into other and foreign bodies they cease to have that strength and impulsion which comes from their persisting embodiment in the people who produced them. Hence whilst the substantial matter is that above described, it is necessary that the Indian social organism be conserved with what adaptation to circumstances as may be necessary. Indian culture can at present only exercise that full influence in the world, which is beneficial to the latter, if it continues to exist as the spiritual, intellectual and artistic expression of the Indian Peoples who evolved it, who therefore can best understand it, and who can, if they will but throw off all indifference and sloth, best propagate it.

III

WHAT IS CULTURE?

CULTURE is an expression of the soul or subtle body (Sûkshma Sharîra), a mode of the manifested Self in which it is related either as religion and philosophy to the one Spiritual Principle of all—that aspect of culture in which it seeks to give expression to the Inner Reality; or in which it is related to the outer Phenomenon, a manifestation of the Life Principle as Knowledge, as Will displayed in action, and as the Beauty of all perfect natural forms. The "Rationalist" author whom I have cited at the head of this work does not tell us what "Civilization" is, and many who, like him, have drifted from the sure anchorage of the world-wisdom enshrined in all the great religions, will also be at pains to say in what it consists or what is its end. Whilst culture is concerned with every aspect of life—material, intellectual and spiritual—it should not be one-sided since the Spiritual works and can only work through mind and body, its aim being spiritual development. India has always so taught; and in this consists its true civilization, however imperfectly it may have realised in fact its highest doctrine. A merely material or intellectual civilization bears within it a disease which leads to Death. The end of Culture is the realization of the Kingdom of Heaven *on earth*—" On Earth as it is in Heaven ". The " Kingdom " in an Indian sense is that of the Lord or Divine Self with which on Earth the purified human self is united. For these reasons the Shâstra says that those who have reached man's estate so hard to get (Durlabha) and yet neglect its true privileges are verily " self-killers ".

As each individual is Spirit (Âtmâ), Soul (Sûkshma Sharîra), and body or matter (Sthûla Sharîra), so is each race. Spirit throughout is one. Individual souls and bodies are particular expressions of the

44

common racial Psyche with the physical vehicle appropriate for its manifestation. The Racial Soul is itself ultimately a physical stress or stresses in the Universal Consciousness in the form of the Sangskâras or impressions left on the soul by its past incarnations, racial and individual, manifesting as mind and body. Each race both as the original typal imagination (Kalpanâ) and its materialisation is a particular form of the general Power (Shakti) who is the Mother of all. To the Hindu, India is thus in a literal and not merely figurative sense the Mother and (as a form of Her) the object of worship, that is God appearing as India. Therefore true service of Her is worship of Him. The author whom I have just cited has given the pinion that in patriotism as expressed by the Salutation to the Mother " Bande Mâtaram " may be sought " that reinforcement of character which is falsely declared to be the peculiar property of religion ". This is to misunderstand both the phrase and what religion is. By India is not meant a particular stretch

45

of the earth's surface peopled by men of varying worth and lack of it. Why should anyone worship these except in the belief, that it and they are a grand display of the Power of God to whom alone all worship is due and Who alone can be the inspiring principle of any effort towards national or racial regeneration and advancement?

What is called racial culture is, again, an expression of the Racial Soul enshrining Spirit, as such Soul displays itself in all those forms of thought (Jnâna Shakti), will (Ichchhâ Shakti) and action (Kriyâ Shakti) which are called Religion, Philosophy, Art, Literature and the Institutions of social life. As race and nationalities are in physical conflict, so are their souls and their cultures each trying to impose itself upon, to influence, or absorb the other. It must not be supposed that such cultural conflict is meaningless. No cosmic process is without meaning. It is in truth a fight for the Soul of the World for the purpose of its evolution; not that the persons engaged in such conflict are necessarily aware of, or impelled

by, any such motive. More often this is
not so. Individuals may act selflessly.
But past history shows us that the actions
of masses of men as races and nationalities,
are determined, in the main, by self-regarding motives, whatever may be the veil of
hypocrisy with which in modern times they
are covered. Just as man has developed a
sense of physical shame which makes him
cover his bodily nakedness, for he is no
longer natural and not yet divine : so he has
recently developed a sense of moral shame
which urges him to clothe his naked political
selfishness with apparent altruisms. Nothing
is more hateful than such hypocrisy to any
lover of the truth, nor a more fruitful source
of distrust among men, nor a greater enemy
of co-operation, if it be believed to be
possible, between naturally opposing
interests. Yet two things should be remembered. The first is that such hopocrisies
may be the presage of a better time when
honesty will be more generally regarded as
a state and a communal as well as an individual duty. And the second is this : even if

man is at present, in general led to become, an instument of the Divine Order through the belief that what It plans is profitable to himself, yet even his selfishness may promote what (though he intended it not) is good. The Divine Alchemy transmutes for its ends even the most rebellious elements. Those who have faith in God know that, notwithstanding all obstacles, He prevails. Dharma infinitely endures beyond the death of those who, spurning it, will yet be crushed by it.

The struggle between the peoples takes on a more massive shape when it assumes the age-long form of the contest between Asia and Europe. For there is what may be called an Asiatic as well as an European Consciousness. It may be hard to define each of these with clearness and precision ; the more particularly that there are races in Europe which are in fact Asiatic in blood and temperament just as some Eastern peoples are modifying themselves under western influences. As regards these last it has been said that some

Westerns now realize that though their inventions and their forms may be readily accepted, the spirit of the Eastern remains; and that, no matter how much externals may be altered, men retain certain unalterable qualities and ideas which are rooted in climate and environment; and more deeply (I may add) in their inherited Sangskâras. However all this may be, the Eastern and the Western now and for ages past have possessed distinctive qualities; though it is to be noted that the difference between the Hemispheres, which prior to the industrial epoch presented many points in common, has become accentuated since such date. Even to-day there is less difference between a Catholic adherent of the old Christian tradition and a Hindu than between the so-called " modernism " of the west and the culture of the latter.

Whilst India exercised an influence upon the culture of the Mediterranean peoples, it was, however, in accordance with its genius, no party to the armed attacks on Europe, only one of which (that of the Arab) directly contributed to the intellectual advancement of that Continent. On the other hand, notwithstanding some unimportant exceptions (such as the persecuting bigotry of the Portuguese), the European invaders were neither in a position, nor cared, to influence the life and thoughts of this country. They were satisfied with its money and other treasures. The Mahomedan rulers of India were, on the whole, (with some fanatical exceptions such as Aurangzeb) content to administer, without seeking to affect the beliefs and practices of the races which they ruled. Moreover, then both the rulers and the ruled were Asiatics. So also the early English settlers, first engaged in trade and then in conquest, did not concern themselves with what the Indian believed or did in matters not directly and materially affecting themselves. Their energies were devoted to the security of their position and trade. With, however, the gradual settlement of the country after the Battle of Plassey, English Culture was brought to bear on it. Even however in 1830, Sir Thomas Strange complained in his "Hindu Law" of "the almost universal indifference as to. what regards India further than as our own direct interests are involved". Both the trend of evolution and recent events have since led to a gradually widening outlook. The most important happening in the first half of the 19th century was the defeat of the Orientalist party amongst the English in India and the determination to forward the teaching of the English language. The importance of this decision cannot be over-rated, for thereby English ideas and ideals came in time to be spread throughout the land and were even accepted by some of its people in place of their own. The result of the famous Minute of 1835 was the resolution of the Government of Lord William Bentinck . " that the great object of the British Government ought to be the promotion of European literature and science amongst the natives of India and that all the funds appropriated for the purpose of education would be best employed in

English education alone ". Whatever might have been the views and aims of individual members of the English as opposed to the Vernacular party, a determining factor of the decision arrived at was the self-interest which has, hitherto at least, been the ultimate basis of all political action. In this particular instance, there was the utility to Government of Indians trained in the English language and other reasons which have operated till to-day when the English-educated Indians vastly exceed in number those to whom official employment can be given. Sir Charles Wood's Despatch of 1854 furthered English education and resulted in the formation of a Department of Public Instruction together with the outline of an University system. From this time forward English education was more and more organised in Government hands. Even private schools were subject to a system of inspection so as to approximate those institutions to the ideals and efficiency of Government schools. In 1882 Government control was somewhat relaxed.

In 1902 increased direction was insisted upon. Without going into details it may be said that practically the entire control of education and therefore of culture (so far as school and university training is concerned) is in the hands of the Government.

To this must be added other causes in conflict with the maintenance of the traditional culture—economic and social. Were it not that there has been no general primary education, and that such education as is now given is necessarily confined to comparatively few, and to the fact that there has been a rise of national consciousness, the whole of India was likely to have been Anglicised. All this is part of the process whereby a dominant race at first works by force of arms, and then, when free to do so, by cultural assimilation. Wherever there is resistance to such assimilation, there is a conflict of culture and ideals. There is in the present competitive stage of evolution no question (apart from the means employed) of right or wrong in such conflict for those with sincerity engaged in it. Indeed Dharma works through such conflicts for the establishment of what is right. Subject to the condition stated, any one nation, such as the English are entitled, if they can, to impose their culture (in the worth of which they believe) on others; the more particularly where, as in the case of India, so many showed themselves to be clamant for it and indifferent to their own. What other could they give? Perhaps in a future co-operative stage of evolution each people will be left to work out its own appropriate evolution according to what in India is called Svadharma. On the other hand, it was from their standpoint a sure and true instinct which led (what I may call) the fully Indian wing of the National Party to attempt the revival of Indian Culture and, notably, of Indian Religion. The same reasons naturally led to an opposition to that culture. This opposition has been accentuated in recent times by reason of what Mr. William Archer has called " aggressive

Hinduism ;" a phrase which reminds me of the complaint of the wolf against the lamb, and of the French sarcasm "This is a wicked animal. It defends itself when it is attacked". (C'est un méchant animal. It se défend quand on l'attaque.) It is noteworthy that the little work called "Aggressive Hinduism" is from the pen not of an Indian but of that ardent Irish-woman Sister Nivedita. There is no harm in attack if rightly made, and many hold it to be the best defence. Thus a distinguished Indian writer (in the " Arya .") says " where-ever the Indian spirit has been able to react energetically, attack, create, the European glamour has begun immediately to lose its hypnotic power. No one now feels the weight of the religious assault from Europe, which was very powerful at the outset, because the creative activities of the Hindu Revival have made Indian religion a living, evolving, secure, triumphant and self-assertive power, the seal being put to this work by the two events the coming of the Theosophical movement and the appearance

of Svâmî Vivekânanda at Chicago ".
There is (I may add) the less danger that
evil may result if positive action is taken
for the propagation of Indian culture than
in any other case. For its principles include
that of toleration, and the paramount
importance of the spiritual element in life.
It is on the contrary a distinct advantage
to the world that a wide and tolerant and
spiritual doctrine should be promulgated
abroad and thus made known to it. It is
otherwise when an intolerant doctrine
seeks to propagate itself by the subdual
of the liberty of others. By continual
assaults, often of a contemptuous and
abusive character, this country is being
gradually goaded into an active defence of
its culture. And it is well that it should be
so. When a blister is applied, the patient
may call out. But we do not lament at·
the cry. We say that the medicine works.
If India is aroused from its lethargy
thereby, such attacks, however unjust they
may be in themselves, will serve a useful
purpose so far as this country's culture is

concerned. There are many who misapply Yoga doctrines to cases for which they are not intended. Non-resistance is both in Christianity and Hinduism the mark of a Sannyâsî. But there are others who have renounced nothing but dignity and courage. He who is truly selfless needs no other weapon. But he who is in and of the world will protect himself by action. It is necessary for all to defend with sincerity what is of worth in the inheritance got from their forefathers if they would escape the death which shadows degenerate descendants. And such defence is now to some, but insufficient, extent being made. It is true that some, in their newborn enthusiasm and in a western spirit, speak of Indian religion and philosophy conquering the world, and a few, notably that man of upstanding courage, Svâmî Vivekânanda, have preached their faith abroad. The charge of aggressiveness on this account ill lies in the mouth of those who are continually (and may be naturally) vaunting the excellence of their own civilization, its faiths and practices.

India, however, true to its principles (in this matter different from those which have prevailed in the west) will never force itself by violence on any. It asks only a fair hearing, having trust that the truths, of which it believes itself to be the guardian, will of their own strength establish themselves. Truth, in whatever form, needs nothing but itself to win the minds and hearts of men. And so we see once more Indian ideas (without material aid such as that possessed by Christian Missions) commencing to influence the world thus rousing to strengthened combat all those who from racial, political and religious motives are opposed to them. A missionary who has lived in this country for a quarter of a century in a work published last year ('Christian Thought and Hindu Philosophy' by the Rev. A. H. Bowman) writes as follows :

"On returning to England after long absence, and trying to gather together the threads of theological study in the west, the author is amazed to find the extent to

58

which Hindu Pantheism has already begun to permeate the religious conceptions of Germany, of America and even England. Again and again in the following pages reference is made to the subject. It needs a far more subtle brain and cunning hand than the author possesses to describe in detail the extent of the danger with which this trend of thought must threaten, if not the present generation, certainly the generation following : but this ought to be done and to be done without delay." As regards "dangers," I say nothing, for I am not here concerned to establish the superiority of any doctrine, or practices, or to contend for the superiority of any civilization. Each man has his preferences and will seek the spiritual food he wants. Hinduism never thrusts on any one what he does not want. To me, though one may make greater personal appeal than another, all serve the ends of God who as Truth will alone prevail. Worshippers of the Vedânta will think that this passage reveals the reason why Indian civilization has been almost alone preserved throughout the ages ; and that this is because through its Vedântic teaching India was destined to be Jagad-guru—the Spiritual Teacher of the world. Each must meanwhile promote and defend what he sincerely believes to be true. I say " sincerely," for, as regards religion (the most important of all forms of culture), the man who defends a belief which he does not think to be true for merely racial or political reasons, sins by his untruth against the law of that 'Light' (Jyotih) which in Hinduism as in Christianity is the 'Illumination' (Prakâsha) which lights all in this world. I am only concerned here to show that India has, notwithstanding recent denials, a civilization of high value, and to explain the reasons which prompt the statement that it has not yet emerged from 'barbarism '.

Mr. Archer, in his book ("Future of India,") says that if a rational world-order be possible, the future of India becomes a matter of absorbing interest, because it offers, so to speak, a test case. " For one of the great obstacles to a stable equilibrium among the peoples of the earth lies in the immense differences in the development of the different races. If, in a case so conspicuous as that of India, the obstacle can be overcome, and one-fifth of the human race can in the course of a couple of centuries be emancipated from mediævalism and fitted to take a place among the peoples who are shaping the future, then the solution of the whole problem will at last be definitely in sight." This passage as usual assumes the entire superiority of the writer's civilization. Are we sure that there will ever be such " equilibrium upon the principles hitherto governing the Western peoples ? " Conflict will never cease until the reflection of the Great Peace is shrined in the hearts of men. Assuming equilibrium to be in this or a future stage of evolution possible, it may be that elimination of differences will lead to it. The question is, on whose side differences are to be eliminated and what is the nature of that equilibrium to be? The Western will ordinarily and naturally consider that, if there is to be an assimilation, it must be of East to West. Whether that will prove to be the fact will depend on the relative values of these general cultures and the strength of the adherence which they respectively receive. I will say with certainty that, whatever happens, the influence will not be wholly one-sided. Even the victors in racial conflicts bear the marks of the peoples they have subdued. Nothing is ever lost, all is transformed ; and that for the ultimate good.

In conclusion, I wish to point out a fact imperfectly realised by many but which has become very obvious since the close of the war. And it is this :—There is now no Asiatic country or people which is not either subject to, or under the protection or influence of Europe and (since the war) America. I do not exclude either China or Japan. Both have been and are subject to Western cultural influences and the first at any rate may, owing to its present state of disruption, come under more direct Western control. The powers have already quite recently served China with an admonition to put its house in order, which in the past, at any rate, has been a prelude to more direct intervention. Japan is now less powerful than before the war. She has no longer the protection given by the mutual jealousies of the European Powers such as they existed before the great war. She will be faced by a more solid block of Powers in the West acting both in Europe and in the parts of Asia they rule or control, and, in the West by the newly arisen military and naval power of America. All this tends to the predominance of Western influences. But physical force is not everything. In fact, it has no real value unless it works in the service of true ideas. Of these the East and particularly India has many. To save its civilization, it must make them acceptable to those nations which are mighty. Rome conquered Greece in a soldier's sense. But culturally Greece was the victor of Rome. India's good future depends, not on any power to exclude or to repel others by

63

force, for She cannot at any time within human foresight have such might, but on Her spiritual power to turn any who are inimical to, or even merely different from, Her, into Her friends and into adherents of Her essential cultural ideas. Success in this would mean that She would both preserve the essentials of Her civilization and would gain everything to which upon the application of Her own principles She was entitled. If She denies these principles She loses her own peculiar civilization, and will only gain what She can wrest by Her power, or what others may concede her, either upon the application of these latter's principles, or from concessions of expediency made for the protection of their self-interests.

This is so clear that it has always seemed strange to me that it has not been perceived. Those who are ready to desert their cultural inheritance for some supposed political advantage would do well to carefully consider the matter from this point of view.

IV

CONFLICT OF CULTURES

JUST as the bodies of races physically conflict, so do their cultures. Victory over the soul is greater than that over the body. Military and administrative control affects chiefly the latter. A cultural conquest means the subjection and, may be, destruction of the psychic possessions of the Racial Soul which is then transformed into the nature of that of the victor. Language affords a notable example of such cultural dominance. A people who abandon or who are compelled to abandon their language for that of another lose themselves. Language is the means by which cultural ideas are expressed and handed on. There are certain ideas and feelings which can be expressed by particular languages alone. Thus it is not easy to write metaphysics in Latin; whereas Greek and Sanskrit are

5

highly efficient for this purpose. There
are many terms in Sanskrit for which it is
impossible to find an adequate English
translation. In short, only a race's own
language can express its soul. Those who
speak a foreign tongue will tend to think
foreign thoughts: those who think in
foreign thoughts will have foreign aims
and tend to adopt foreign ways and so
forth. For these reasons dominant peoples
have sought to impose their language on
subject races as the completion of their
conquest. Spenser in his " View of the State
of Ireland" written in 1597, when complain-
ing that the English settlers spoke Irish,
says of this " abuse of language " that " as
it is unnatural that any people should love
another language more than their own,
so it is very inconvenient, and the cause of
many other evils," adding, " for it hath
ever been the use of the conqueror to
despise the language of the conquered and
to force him by all means to learn his."
" The words are the image of the mind, so as
they proceeding from the mind, must needs

66

be affected with the words, so that the speech being Irish, the heart must needs be Irish, for out of the abundance of the heart the tongue speaketh." He who to-day is both attached to his country and a man of sense will know both his own language and that of another. We may here call to mind the attempted enforcement of the German language on the Polish people; and in the British Empire the opposition to the Dutch language in South Africa and to the French language in Canada. Lately it has been made (so I read) an offence to teach any subject in French in the English provinces in Canada. It is hoped doubtless thereby to supplant in time French culture by that of the Anglo-Saxon. In this country there is no law which compels anyone to learn English; but compulsion exists all the same for those who would pass through School to University, who would qualify for Government service or for any professions. Mr. Hegarty in his work on the " Indestructible Nation " (that is Ireland) points out how the English first proceeded by force of arms, intrigue, plantations of settlers, rules as to language and customs and so forth and then by means of some of these and other methods sought to conquer the Irish *mind*. But as a whole in vain; for England had here to meet a people small in numbers yet great of spirit, proud of their inherited traditions and culture. Such direct or indirect imposition of culture is in the nature of things. Dominating races must necessarily affect others. Those who complain of it waste their time in what is futile. Instead of complaint they should maintain themselves and their own. Failure to do so is biological sin. What fails to find defenders is not worth preservation. Nothing is ever wholly and lastingly lost which is worth such preservation. What is absorbed is without the value which attaches to that which has the power to independently exist.

In the earliest times, food and desire for loot, and sometimes woman, were probably the chief impelling cause of battle. Now, conflict of races and their cultures is due to various causes—racial, religious and political. The first is at present rather of a negative, and the two others are of a positive character. The racial cause manifests, largely as a force passively resisting assimilation. Its most powerful manifestation is that in which it is combined with religion and politics or either.

The world is composed of beings which as classes and as individuals differ from one another. Man differs from man according to different colours and each coloured division is subdivided into various races. We call such differences of classes Types. These Types are varying aspects of the One Cosmic Mind. Being projected from Its Unity, it is reasonable to suppose that this projection was not without cause and that though types do, at one time or another, as all else, disappear, yet Nature intends and devises means for their perpetuation until the purpose for which they have been created, shall have been served. How are these racial types preserved ? The answer is—By what is called Racial Antagonism.

There is nothing "wicked" in pure Racial Antagonism for those who know no better. The antagonism is natural. Nature preserves her types by estrangement, distrust and even hatred, and not by love. For this reason, Western races of strong vitality will not cross with Africans or Asiatics. The stronger the vitality, the greater is likely to be the antagonism. The stronger the antagonism of a type, the less is the likelihood of its being influenced or absorbed by another. Until he receives a spiritual initiation, man is thus the enemy of man. This is the natural or animal law. There is then learnt a higher spiritual law which at first tempers, and ultimately abrogates, the other through the knowledge that all men are kindred expressions of the One Self.

Racial antagonism, however, is not today (at any rate upon the Eastern side) acute except where it is augmented by religious or political conflict. It undoubtedly exists; but I myself (with the author of "Conflict of Colour") doubt whether an

Asiatic positively hates or fears a white man simply because he is white. When he so hates or fears him, it is because of the latter's assumption of superiority ; and because of his past political aggressiveness which puts the former's country, wealth and culture in danger. Thus, the early European visitors to Asia were well received. So, again, the first travellers to Tibet were freely admitted into that land. When it was, however, discovered that a country into which a Western entered was in danger of being taken by his people, a natural racial antagonism was re-inforced to such extent by political considerations that a state of positive enmity was aroused and thus Tibet was closed to the Western world. The white man's dislike for the man of colour is, I think, natural and his contempt is largely due to the former's assumption of superiority and the latter's subservience and acknowledgment of it : a superiority which, so far as material force is concerned, has been justified for about the last two hundred years. When, however, an Eastern coloured people showed themselves the fighting equal of the Western, then racial antagonism did not stand in the way of exterior respect and political alliance. Even racial antagonism yields to political interest. Racial antagonism is thus, from the cultural aspect, rather something which resists attempts at assimilation than a force which seeks to impose itself on others. A meaner form of Racial Antagonism is racial jealousy which manifests itself, amongst others, in the Orientalists of lower mind and which is the cause of their constant belittling of things Indian. A Russian friend of mine and a great traveller told me some years ago that all the orientalists he had come across in this country and many elsewhere disliked, notwithstanding and perhaps because of their study, India and all its ways. As the religious and political factor did not come into play I asked him to what he attributed it, when he answered ' racial jealousy.'

In earlier times the religious factor was of great importance. Thus we read of

Crusades, Jehads and persecutions. These animosities still exist as between Christian and non-Christian religions, as also between Christians themselves; notable instances of which are the quarrels of Catholics and Protestants in Ireland and of Hindus and Mahomedans in this country.

The vital question of Religion which is the most important element of culture may be considered either from its own standpoint, or from that of racial and political interests. In more sincere ages the Christian religion was sought to be propagated on its own account, that is because of its supposed truth, and this is still the fact in the case of sincere believers. In the first case the meaning and nature of the conflict is clear. The Christian missionary still carries on warfare against Hinduism; which one of them has recently stated to be " a great philosophy which lives on unchanged whilst other systems are dead; which as yet unsupplanted has as its stronghold the Vedânta, the last and most subtle and powerful foe of Christianity."

("Christian Thought and Hindu Philosophy" by the Rev. A. H. Bowman).
After many centuries of occasional missionary effort and a century of constant labour
there are in this country not quite 4,000,000
Christians, and some 311,000,000 Indians
who are still what they were ; though
it is the fact that a considerable number of
the latter have been influenced both by the
sacred personality of Jesus and by certain
modern Western ideas which (it has been
pointed out) have come to the East in such
close association with Christianity that
it is not always possible to distinguish
between one influence and the other.

Jesus, however, did not bid His disciples
preach His word abroad to serve any
political or racial interests. It is true that
good may follow in the train of right and
religious living. But the vulgarity of
turning religion into a means of money-
making and Empire-building has been
reserved for our political and commercial
time. It is a greater abuse of what is
sacred when these manœuvres are worked

by persons who have no religious faith in the doctrines which, for other motives, they seek to propagate.

Institutional Christianity is not necessarily the same as the teaching of Jesus. It contains elements drawn from Western civilizations anterior and subsequent to His earthly manifestation, and is now associated with secular aims and ideals which are rather the product of modern social and intellectual developments than of His essentially unworldly Yoga doctrines; even though in some cases they may perhaps be harmonised. His teachings are what He in fact taught. " Christianity ". is what others thought He had taught; and it is worth just as much as their thought is worth and not more unless it be held (as Catholics do) that to the Church has been given a power of infallible interpretation; a claim which of course other Christian sects repudiate. Such universal truths as were taught by Jesus will, when rightly interpreted, find ready acceptance in India which also proclaims them. The

75

essentials of Jesus' teaching were said
before Him and have been taught by
others. The strength of Christianity consists
in the personality of its Founder. Acceptance of the Christian Religion will (if
at all) the more speedily come when
Christianity is no longer associated with
the notion that it is the religion of a ruling
western people and when its doctrines
receive an independent interpretation by
the Indian mind. That interpretation will
lead to something far different from what a
witty Irish writer calls a " Jolly Theology "
with its Christ in the character of " a good
sportsman," the " Padre " a " good fellow,"
the Ministry "the Parson's job " and so
forth. Meanwhile it does not accept
western interpretations of Jesus' teachings
from the hands of those who have a very
imperfect understanding of what they
mean. This country will honour only the
Christian Sannyâsî, whether living in or
withdrawn from the world. In ancient
times men were not hired to preach
Hinduism. Those who did were actuated

by love and duty only. Nor did nor does it try to thrust itself upon unwilling people or make their miseries or worldly ambitions its opportunity. At present the religious conflict is largely due to the fact that Christ's doctrine comes to this country in a Western guise, which is no essential part of it ; a guise which often misinterprets it. Thus an Indian might find in the Bible (as many Westerns now do) support for his theory of Re-incarnation and knowing what a Yuga is, he would not understand " Aeonian " loss to be the equivalent of " eternal damnation." It has been well pointed out (" Modern Review ") that even the late Pratap Chunder Mozoomdar who was western in culture and Christian in piety wrote of " the Oriental Christ " and not of the Anglicised or Western Christ. In addition to this, conflict is provoked by the fact that some missionaries have sought to de-nationalise their converts. Mukhyopâdhyâya (if they succeed by a rare chance in attracting a Brâhmana) becomes Muggins or the like. Dhoti and Chudder yields to shirt and trousers ; and the eating of beef erects a barrier against relapse into Hinduism. A different treatment is to be found amongst some Catholic missionaries who have gone great lengths to accommodate themselves to Eastern principles and practices, including caste in this country and ancestor worship in China. As regards the first I may refer to some of the South Indian Christian communities and, as regards the second, to the theological question known as the Dispute concerning the Chinese Rites. The Jesuit De Nobili, lived and dressed, wearing the sacred thread, like a Brâhmana and surrounded by Brâhmanas ; even administering the sacraments to Shûdras in such a way as to preserve against pollution. The Yezur Veda (Jesus-Veda) which Voltaire took to be genuine and attempted to use as a weapon against the pretensions of Christianity to all wisdom, was only an invention of one of its missionaries. Protestant methods have gone to the other extreme, though they have in recent times been softened. Possibly some may have

78

thought it advisable in these "nationalist" days to make some concession to Indian sentiment and culture, whilst others may have somewhat tardily discovered the wisdom which does not press for the acceptance of what is unessential.

Many instances might be given of the exploitation of Christianity in support of political interests. It was in this sense that it was said by a French minister, "Anti-clericalism is not an article of export :" for religion attacked at home was found to serve French Colonial aims and the maintenance abroad of French interests. And in other countries the Cross has been made synonymous with the Flag, and the Flag with Trade, whether, to use President Wilson's recent words, "the persons to whom it was taken welcomed it or not." What Asiatic or African has been consulted? In Europe Christianity has been for many centuries a strengthening (though for some time past a diminishing) force politically ; consolidating and giving strength to European civilization. There are, it has been said, ("Conflict of Colour," 119) those "who still believe that, as it will be in our day impossible to bar out the hordes of Asia and Africa, the only safeguard for Europe and the white man still lies to-day as in the past in Christianity ; and that the impossibility of allying themselves with other creeds is perhaps the reason why instinctively the great movement towards Christianising the coloured world is growing stronger and stronger in Anglo-Saxon countries as a sort of forlorn hope launched to capture an almost impregnable position." And so also it has been alleged that the Christianising of the Negro, weaning him from the militant bent of mind he assumes under Islam will, as diminishing racial and political danger, have in the future much greater political importance than it has to-day. The author cited is not ashamed to supply an example of Political Christianity of his own and to confess that " the part which the white man is politically called upon to play in Africa is the part " of " Delilah and no other " " for" if, he says " the black man is Christianised, his destructive strength is stripped from him, as was Samson's when his locks were cut." Elsewhere, that is in countries which have a real civilization and religion of their own, as in India, he thinks the hope of a general Christianisation is illusory, for " it is there looked upon as a disintegrating force, a purely European thing, aiming at destroying the most essential parts of social fabrics which have been slowly and painfully built up through the ages." He adds that " it is a strange fact which has often attracted the attention of unbiassed observers that Asiatic converts to Christianity are not only denationalised but (save in rare cases) are not morally benefitted ; the very effect of breaking away from the support of their natural environment being an unnatural one and therefore visited with bad effects." This is an observation many others have also made.

Mr. William Archer, who is not a Christian, writes in a somewhat similar strain : (" India and the Future ")—For him Christianity is only a " half way house " to civilization ; for nothing is apparently quite civilized unless it bears his " rationalist " approval. He says, however, that whilst he would himself " disown " the religion in his own land, it is good for India which he regards as an essentially unspiritual country. Its acceptance by the Indian people will bring them " half way " to true " civilization." Until they are according to a liberal interpretation leavened with Christianity (in which he himself personally disbelieves) they will be " unfit for freedom." That is, after the " half way house " stage is reached, the notions then acquired must be further " liberalized " when there will be competency for freedom. Freedom is, of course, political freedom for the political motive and standpoint is that of his book. The true religious missionary propagates his religion because he sincerely believes it to be the truth and that the truth will benefit India. Mr. Archer would, for political motives, foist upon it a " half way house " in which he himself disbelieves, in order that the Indian people may be thereby "civilized" enough for political freedom. Until that point of time, which seems from what he says to be remote, they are apparently not to have it. Because of the political service which missionaries thus render by the assimilation of West and East Mr. Archer says " that it did not long take him to throw off a vague prejudice against the missionary which he brought with him to this country."

A Japanese author Dr. Enryo Inouye in a recent article in the " Japan Magazine" shows that the Western has his imitators in this also in the far East. He writes :—
" Religion has always paved the way for extension of Western Nations overseas, and why should it not do the same for Japan ? In Africa, India, China and the islands of the South Pacific, Christianity always preceded the flag and opened a way for the development of the nations preaching the new religion. We have imitated the occidentals in other ways; why not in this way ? While Christianity is losing force in the home lands of its propagandists, it is

gaining force and influence in the countries overseas. It looks as if it were the policy of Western countries to take away from the forces of Christianity at home and apply the extra force to lands abroad to make way for the greater influence of the countries represented ; and this is especially true in the Orient." He, accordingly, advocates that the Japanese people should give every attention to the propagation of Buddhism in foreign lands " to prepare the way for our national influence and as the first step for the empire's future *enrichment*." The Buddha is thus made into a kind of political bagman.

All do not think this way. According to another view it would be better that " the whole band of missionaries were sent home ; for their interest in the native sometimes gets to the point of mawkishness, leading him to over-estimate his own importance and weakening his respect for authority" ("The East in the West" by Price Collier, 228-229). Another, an African traveller, (" Via Rhodesia " by Charlotte

Mansfield, 257) whilst observing strongly, against the Protestant missions, says, "Of all the missionaries, the Roman Catholics do the least harm, for they never preach equality, nor allow the natives to approach the level of familiarity in any way. They teach them to work, and to be clean, and above all to respect the white man. Therefore, politically as well as socially, they are to be congratulated." It is always Politics with a particular type of mind. It is not in such case a question whether Christianity is a true religion, and therefore good for the Indian or other people, but whether its promulgation subserves imperial or racial interests.

The Commercial note so characteristic of some forms of modern Western Christianity is seen in the "Church Advertising and Publicity Department" of "The Associated Advertising Clubs of the world;" the report of the twelfth convention which has just been published (Lippincott). The Executive Secretary's paper on the "First successful Church Advertiser" asserts that "the

Church was born with advertising plastered all over it" and closes with the assertion that "Christ did not do His own advertising. He created the talking points on the interests of the new Church." Great was the Company which published them. And the first successful advertiser was the one of this Company to get out and plaster the country side with posters reading " Repent, come and see one who claims to be the Christ. Hear Rabbi Jesus the teacher who has all the other Rabis guessing." Another clergyman writes " Why the world needs our goods " (that is Christianity); and others continue with papers on " Delivering the goods advertised " " Preparing the copy " for " Church advertising is the display window of the biggest business on Earth " and so forth. There is one thing in the West which is happily missed in the East (unless where the European has introduced it) and that is vulgarity in these and other matters. This " playing the role of Delilah," " half way houses," the whole vulgar policy of " Church Advertisement " and of " Bibles, Bottles and Battalions" will like other falsities fail of any good effect.

The religious factor in the conflict of East and West is becoming however of less importance in comparison with the conjoined racial and political factors. In the first place, Hinduism in the persons of its higher adherents has never been disposed to intolerance. Indeed in its higher form it has been so tolerant that it has been charged with being " indifferent to the truth." " Fanatical " or " indifferent" the blow is delivered both ways. The lower mind in India as elsewhere is not always free from narrowness but it has been in considerable degree influenced by the wide outlook of Vedantic teaching. Indian tolerance is not merely a matter of temperament. It is based on the doctrine of the relativity of ordinary human knowledge and, in part, of morals (though this does not exclude absolute principles in either case) and on the doctrine of Adhikâra, that is the teaching that all people are not fit for the same beliefs and practices, and that what is suited to the capacity, intellectual, moral, and spiritual, of each person is that which he may and should accept, follow, and practise. On the other hand, whilst there is still some talk of " heathen darkness," tolerance has became more widespread in the West. Large numbers have ceased to be " Christians " in anything but name; and believing Christians either from disposition or necessity have largely drawn in their horns of aggression. What are called " liberal " ideas are spreading. It is thought that religion is a private affair, that liberty of conscience is sacred, that the religion which any civilized country has evolved is presumably the best for it ; that if there be a revelation at all it has not been confined to one people, nor to the adherents of one faith and that religion, the essence of which is the upholding of our common humanity, should not be made a ground of conflict and of enmity between men. It is noteworthy that just as racial antagonism displays itself most strongly when combined with causes of political conflict, it is the same with religious antagonism. Thus in Ireland, the feeling between Catholic and Protestant would not be so acute as it is, were not the question of Home rule involved; and in India the differences between Hindu and Mahomedan are commonly said (with what truth I cannot say) to have increased since the recognition of separate Electorates and the struggle for Government patronage. So dominant are politics now-a-days that even religion is made to serve their purpose.

I do not here desire to discuss practical politics but certain general principles of universal application only with a view to ascertain their bearing on the cultural question now under discussion. The very fact of political dominance of one race over another involves either an unconscious or conscious influence on the latter's culture. Just as a commanding personality (whether he wills it or not) affects the men who surround him; so does a dominant race affect the people subject to it. In some cases the influence is automatic; in other cases it is predetermined. In either instance the result is the cultural assimilation of the subject race to that of its governors. If that subject race is savage, it is both for its good and for the profit of the ruler that it should be rightly civilized. As Macaulay, speaking for a commercial people, said "to trade with civilized man is more profitable than to govern savages." As regards India he expressed the opinion that it was a doting policy which would keep "millions of men from being our customers." Mr. W. Archer is of opinion that the lesson which this country has to learn is "to want more wants." There is nothing "spiritual" about this doctrine nor is it, as so crudely stated, a sound and satisfying one, at any rate from the point of view of those addressed. The Vishnu Purâna more truly says that by feeding your desires you cannot satisfy them. The former doctrine will not be found of benefit from any but the trader's standpoint. It is however the fact that the adoption of the counsel to "want more wants" may lead to the increased purchase of English motor cars, Scotch whiskey and so forth. The pockets of such a "civilizer" are filled when he gets the uncivilized to learn this part of his lesson. So on the banks of African rivers naked savages are taught to "want more wants" in the form of Brummagem beads and the like; they on their side parting with ivory to the white trader. It is on the other hand absurd to suppose that the Indian hugs his miserable poverty.

Conquered savages without culture, properly so called, take over that of their masters. But in the case of a country like India, which (pace Mr. Archer) is already civilized, the problem is not so simple. Two courses are open: either to leave the governed race to itself, subject only to the natural influences which flow from contact ; or to deliberately undertake a policy of "education" in accordance with the ideals of the Rulers. In this country we see both courses in operation. Politically there are advantages and disadvantages attending

91

either of the policies. If the people be left to themselves, as I understand is more or less the case in the Dutch Indies, there is always a certain danger from the continuance of interests, aims, and ideals alien to those of the rulers. On the other hand if the ruling race educates its subjects in its own culture, it must follow that in the degree such culture is acquired a claim to equality and governance will be made by the latter which the former may not, at any particular moment, be disposed to concede. On and before such cession of power certain advantages from the point of view of administration are gained by the cultural assimilation of the ruling and ruled races. This policy necessarily involves a time when all " inferiority " ceases to exist; and the two races either then enter into a partnership of administration, or the foreign ruling race altogether gives place to that which it formerly governed. These two possibilities are kept in view and present policy is framed with reference to them. Mountstuart Elphinstone said of India " A time of separation must come and it is for our interest to have separation from civilized people rather than a violent rupture with a barbarous nation." Sir T. E. Colebroke enjoined that meanwhile " we must apply ourselves to bring the natives into a state that will admit of their governing themselves in a manner that may be beneficial to our interests." He also added " as well as their own and that of the rest of the world ; " a qualification which means little, if anything, should the first aim be kept in view and acted upon. For if the subject interest be different from the ruling one the latter must be served according to the first part of this passage. If the former interest be the same as the latter there is no distinction at all. Cultural assimilation is thus a perfect form of conquest initiated by force of arms. Whilst it, in some degree, helps administration during the continuance of foreign rule; when that rule ends it considerably compensates for the loss of it by the amalgamation of material interests, aims and ideals which it effects. The cultural assimilation acts as a compensation for lost political control. Much the same results are attained by both. Whilst a foreign administration exists the subject people may be directed by external control in a direction which subserves the former's interests. But when that administration ceases, such people may serve the same class of interests of its own accord, if it has been first culturally assimilated with its former masters. The cultural conquest is so complete as to render political control (which in fact can be no longer kept) unnecessary for the furtherance of the former ruler's interests. Thus if the English were in a body to leave India to-morrow they would leave an uneffaceable, and in several respects good, cultural influence upon it. But in order that that influence should be both lasting and complete, assimilation (according to the policy discussed) must be brought to that stage in which political control may safely be surrendered without danger to the interests of those who formerly had possession of it, as also of the general civilization of which theirs was a particular form.

The cultural and political aspects are different sides of the same question. Again looking at the matter from the Indian standpoint ; whilst political Home-rule might be attained through adoption of the civilization of the foreign ruler, there would in such case no longer be a Home (in the Indian sense) to rule. Those who then ruled themselves would be an *alias* of their departed rulers; a people who in the language of Macaulay would be Englishmen in everything. but colour. His well-known observation is a classic-statement of cultural assimilation. There are already a certain number of this type whom their more racially-minded countrymen call " Black Englishmen." If Indian culture has value and is worthy of preservation) a matter which those who inherited it must determine) it is obviously their duty to resist any such cultural assimilation as threatens it. As I have said before and here repeat; the question of political loyalty must not be confounded with the right to the possession of one's soul even if the complete possession of it may (as I think it will) have in the future a political effect.

The British Government has given some support to Indian culture in its encouragement of Sanskrit and otherwise. Yet such is the air of suspicion in certain quarters in this country that some well-meant endeavours to promote Indian culture have been charged with being a machiavellian plan to keep the country enslaved and in ignorance. Such is the value which these persons attach to their culture. Thus an English educated Bengali who read the first edition of this book thought that it advocated a policy which, if pursued, would keep the Indian people " hewers of wood and drawers of water." Of some other work done several years back in furtherance of Indian culture it was said that its Author deserved a decoration from Government for " helping them in their work of keeping the people in the dark." When again in the interest of Indian|Art students, some mediocre Western paintings were sold and removed from the School of Art, Calcutta, and from the proceeds of their sale a fine collection of copper, brass, and other Indian objects of Art were purchased, a Bengali Paper charged the Principal of the School with purposely impeding the work of Indian artists with the object of reducing the people to the state " in which they were before the arrival of the English." The implication of all these statements is that those who have nothing but Indian culture are benighted. English culture is the light. But dark reactionaries wish to keep it from the people so that they may be plunged in ignorance, which is the natural state of the Indian people. Before the arrival of the English there may have been some philosophy or art but it was of a primitive character—and " We are long past all that " and so on. All this is due to the suggestion and Hypnosis to which I allude later.

To the Western Orientalists (imperfect in understanding though they may sometimes be) this country is indebted. The State

7

has adopted what it thought to be a policy of "neutrality" as regards Indian religion and has not consciously interfered with Indian law or custom except when the latter was deemed to be not consonant with humanity. The fact that English is the language of the ruling race has made its acquisition a practical necessity. For though there is no law compelling its acquirement, all by force of circumstances must learn it if they would not rest employed in humble services. The teaching of English and its literature has immensely forwarded English ideas to which there has been hitherto no sufficient counterpoise in the shape of the study of Indian literature. This can not however be subject of complaint against the State until a demand is made for it which is refused. In fact the Indian people (I mean the English educated section) have only in recent years commenced to value what is their own. Were this not so, it would not have been necessary in the case of some to place Indian culture under their nose and to say

" Look, see ; this is your own. It has value. Respect it." In one case (of which I am informed) there was Indian opposition in an Indian university to the appointment as lecturer on Indian philosophy of a mere "native Pandit." It was apparently thought that even Indian philosophy requires an English education before it can be taught and understood. Even now there are Indian professors of philosophy who have knowledge of European and American philosophical systems and know little or nothing of the Sângkhya and Nyâya or Vedânta. There are also persons who I believe take it more to heart if they are told that they do not speak good English, than if surprise is expressed at their not knowing their own language or knowing it properly. As regards Art it is only recently that the same section of the Indian people have taken any interest in its Indian form ; and that largely through the initiative and aid of Europeans.

Education again is almost entirely in State hands and has hitherto been substantially of an English character. If attention has not been paid to Indian culture it is due primarily to the fact that the English educated sections of the community have not, as a rule, made any demand for it. Some of them are quite content with "Indian Etons" and the like. How can the State be expected to understand or to teach Indian culture? Why should it give that for which there is no demand? It gives that which it considers best, namely its own ; and which, if accepted, will also it thinks, best serve its particular interests and the general interests of its own form of civilisation. The English moreover naturally suppose that that for which the Indian shows no appreciation is not worthy of it. It is for the latter if he values his culture to insist that it shall receive at least equal, if not preferential, treatment.

Again the presence of a powerful but alien civilization, naturally and without any State interference whatever, affects every department of Indian life. The joint-family and caste system seem to be weakening. Whether and how long they will exist only the future will show. The village life as it was is ceasing to exist. With the crowding into towns, English habits are acquired as also English modes of living. The old collectivist spirit has to some extent given way to individualism and so forth. Some of these changes were perhaps " inevitable " though 1 do not like the word. In the flood of change care must yet be taken that one is not swept off one's feet. Similar changes are of course at work in the West. M. Le Play in his books on the working men of Europe found in 1864—1878 the agricultural and family system to be almost everywhere undermined. And this is of course still more so in the present. Christian writers note with complacency the influence of the Christian Spirit in disintegrating Hinduism. But forces, in the form of the Modern Spirit, are at work in the west disintegrating Christianity.

Lastly the so-called " neutrality " of the State as regards Indian religion has in fact worked against it. As the French Catholics long ago pointed out to their anti-clerical Government there can be no such thing as neutrality where religion is ignored. True neutrality is to recognise and support all religions impartially. Indian religion has in the past been mainly learnt, where it has been learnt at all, from the mother ; herself as a rule lacking the education which is her right. As the schools and universities have hitherto ignored it, the youthful mind has followed its teacher's example. For the sake in part of cheapness,. and also in part of efficiency, Indian boys are sent to missionary schools or schools conducted by Christians, from which some students have returned to their homes in the belief that their parents (if they themselves had any belief) were dark " heathens." In this way the Indian Dharma is being lost and often no other definite conception of life and its duties has been acquired in its stead. For formal Christianity (it is admitted) has not made headway amongst what are called the educated classes. Many of these have shown themselves ignorant of, and indifferent to, the principles and practices of their country's religion. If it be replied that these are not taught in the State schools, those who have any regard for their religion should either insist upon a change in this respect or start schools of their own. I am' fully aware that there has come, in recent times, a change in Indian opinion as regards some of these matters but it has yet in general to be materialised; and I am now speaking of the past which has produced the present of which this book is a short review. Valuable work for instance is now being done by Sâdhus in spreading a knowledge of one of the crest-gems of Indian literature the Gîtâ; and the next generation may see (if the spirit which prompts this movement prevails) a wider appreciation of, and adherence to, the principles of the Vedânta and of its practical application in the various schools of Âgama—the Tantra Shâstras. There may also be an Indian form of Christianity.

Thus on the whole the influences at work have not been, and under the circumstances probably could not have been, such as to encourage the propagation of Indian civilization. To some extent these Western influences have worked for good ; in some cases they have had ill effects. One of the worst effects is the vulgarization of the refined Indian life as it existed in ancient times. I cannot think it good for India that it should altogether surrender its distinctive self. Others have co-operated in this work besides the State, namely missionaries by spreading Christian and Western ideas ; and lay writers and others who believe that the acceptance of Western principles of civilization will be for the good of this country as of their own. All these forces, whether official or private, will work, if not opposed, for the cultural assimilation of Indian to English civilization. It is obvious that, whilst in this the English are carrying out their Dharma, India has a Dharma of Her own to follow. For unless She admits that Her civilization is without value, and is ready to throw it on the scrap heap of things past and gone, She must uphold it. It is nothing to Her whether it be more politically advantageous to Her Western. Rulers that She should liken Herself to them or not. This is not Her's but their concern. As the Gîtâ says, each to his own Dharma : " Better one's own Dharma than that of another, however exalted."

What form the future may take we can not with certainty say. But of this I am convinced that if we each do our duty by our country and our forefathers and maintain what is best, and has not suffered corruption, in our respective cultural inheritances, the result of such rivalry cannot be other than good. Healthy rivalry is better than a cultural Olla Podrida. Nature Herself will effect the elimination of unnecessary differences. A good result is not likely to be attained if India wholly surrenders Her soul to foreign influences unless we assume (as I do not) that those influences are entirely good ; and that

Indian culture is so worthless that there is
nothing to be done but to get rid of it as
speedily as possible. It is because these
principles have not been hitherto generally
understood that predominance has been
given to the political aspect of India's future
to the neglect of Her cultural interests.
Political freedom is nothing for those who
have lost their souls and that Spiritual
Autonomy (Svârâjyasiddhi the Shâstra calls
it) which is the greatest of possessions. It
has been rightly said that the saying " For
what is a man advantaged if he gain the
whole world and lose himself or be cast
away ? " applies not only to the individual
but the Racial soul. This self-maintenance
of Indian civilization is also for the world's
good. Its further advance depends on the
guarding of all its spiritual and cultural
wealth, not by the neglect or abandonment
of any of it. The Universe is the Body of
the Lord and every fraction of it is as such
sacred. In the light of this idea when once
fully grasped it will be seen that whilst it
is the duty of each man and each people to

uphold sincerely and with right motive their selves and interests, it is not their own good but that of the world which they thus, under the guidance of Îshvara, ultimately serve.

In the cultural attack a considerable part has been taken by English critics of this country's civilization. The most recent and comprehensive of these attacks is the book by Mr. William Archer which has suggested the title of my own. Others have expressed themselves adversely touching either Hindu religion, or philosophy, or art or so forth. But Mr. Archer includes them all in one widely sweeping review, leading to the conclusion that this country is not yet " civilized " but in the earlier state of " Barbarism." His reviewer in the " Times " expresses himself well pleased at these conclusions. He like Mr. Archer is indignant that a few Europeans " have achieved · a cheap and very mischievous popularity amongst Indians " by assuring them that their " gods " (it is always thus with these people) and their culture " are far greater than ours " and " that there resides in the inner shrine of the Indian soul a transcendental spiritualism denied to the Western soul." He commends therefore the manner in which Mr. Archer " in very luminous chapters supported by unimpeachable authorities tears to pieces " these " myths ; " passing " under review the teachings of Hindu Philosophy, the masterpieces of Hindu literature, and the various manifestations of Hindu art *without finding anywhere any great moral or spiritual concept capable of uplifting a nation.*" Thus neither the Vedânta or Gîtâ contains any such concept, not to count the rest of Indian Shâstra. Then referring to self-government, the National Congress, and social reform (without which this class of English criticism is nowadays incomplete) and describing Mr. Archer as a genuine and candid " Friend of India," it concludes with the enunciation of the now prevailing policy of cultural assimilation by saying " It is in the slow process of *educating up India to our own ideals* that the only path lies which can lead India to salvation."

His book though not based on any real knowledge of the subject he discusses, being largely a restatement of criticisms passed by others before him, has yet peculiar interest for it reveals the motive which (though not in general expressed) underlies this and some other present-day writing of its kind. It is an example of the political aspect of the cultural attack to which I have referred in previous pages. What in effect Mr. Archer says is this:—A time must come when India will govern itself. Whether the country will govern itself independently or as a part of the British Empire he leaves to the future. The present condition however of India is barbarous, and therefore not in conformity with Western, and in particular English, civilization. It will be harmful to the interests of the latter and the world-peace if India is given political autonomy at the present time. For as his first cited Reviewer says:—" Hindu society as it has been moulded by many centuries of religious tradition, philosophic thought, and unchanging custom is almost inconceivably far removed from those out of which the democratic institutions of our own country have sprung." Before therefore such autonomy can be safely conceded, India must assimilate Herself to Western civilization, that is to (as he calls it) " the nations shaping the future ; " upon which movement it seems India is a drag. The position then is this :— India must either surrender her distinctive culture or renounce, until She does so, any hope of the political autonomy She seeks. If She will not change Herself, then She must remain in a political subjection which will ensure that She does no harm to anyone but Herself. Ruling and world interests will not then be endangered. If She elects to change and bring herself into line with the rest of the world, this cultural assimilation will remove all dangers which would otherwise attend the political autonomy She seeks. It is because of these political aspects of his book that his reviewer in the " Times " gives it a warm welcome and calls it " timely."

. As I have said before I am not here concerned with any question of practical politics and express no opinion whether such political autonomy should be given or refused, now or at any other time. I state simply the motives which prompt this attack (as also others which are made to-day) so that we may judge the value of this class of criticism which is neither disinterested nor endowed with knowledge. Criticism has true value only when given in detached service of the truth. Religion, philosophy, literature and art are subject to their own tests. It must of course be admitted that the cultural condition of a country is a test of its capacity to be left to look after itself. In this criticism, however, mere personal likes such as " Rationalism " European literature and art; and dislikes such as Metaphysics and " supernatural " religion; and political prepossessions (such as English " Liberalism ") either take the place of, or outweigh, any solid criticism based on an understanding, reasoned, and detached examination, according both to their own and' alien standards, of the leading features of Indian culture whether existing in the past or to-day. Mr. Archer is of course not peculiar in having prepossessions. They affect other such critics. Impartial judgment is rare. For this, one must, as Carlyle said, have the capacity of placing oneself into the skin of other people so that we may think and feel as they do. To do this one must sacrifice at least for the time being all Egoism or Ahangkâra. This I may observe is, apart from the valuable critical result obtained, a useful spiritual exercise.

V

COMPETITION, CONCERT, SACRIFICE

I HAVE spoken of the past and present world as an era of conflict. And so it has been and still largely is. Amidst animals it was a purely animal conflict, as it also was and is amongst man, to the degree that he is still bound up with the animal element in his humanity. Not only has there been conflict but it has been rude and brutal. How else could savage man be made to understand? Even the " civilized " man of to-day must often have his own flesh ground in misery before he can sympathise with the world-suffering. It is said in the Buddhist Tantra that the Buddhas and Bodhisattvas have four methods by which they subdue and save sentient beings of which the fourth is " the stern " or method of downright force. And thus it is said in " The golden rosary of the history of the Lotus born " (Padma

113

Thangyig serteng) that the demoniac
" Black Salvation," the Matam Rutra was
impaled.

Throughout the past and in the present,
animals and men have made their advance
through conflict. Each man and people in
the struggle for existence has lived on,
and overpowered others. Their good has
been attained at the cost of others. Like
the animal, each has lived on the other.
This is the so-called basis of the biological
theories of life commonly current. The
facts are correct enough. The error of
those who exclusively hold these views is
in making past and present fact a rule of
conduct which absolutely justifies such
conflict in the present as in the future, and
thus looks to nothing beyond. An historical
fact has thus been raised into a pseudo-
ethical theory.

Because animals and men have competed
amongst themselves in savage struggle for
existence, which struggle was justified
according to the stage of their evolution :
and because some men may still do so in

accordance with such stage, is no reason why they and others should be enjoined to continue such struggle, and should ignore the rising conscience which speaks of a more spiritual advanced stage to follow. This is to sin against the Light which it is the object of the world-process to unveil more and more to man's power of spiritual vision. On the other hand there is no sin provided there be good faith. Throughout the ages the illuminate Masters of Humanity, incarnations of the Humane Ideal in, and evolved by, man's mind, have taught the unity of all being and have anticipated in their presence the yet unfold future. of mankind. Their teaching has had effect but has been without complete result. For man is not raised at once to the level of these manifestation of his and their common Spirit. And so we still see, particularly in the West, an irresponsible individualism in every sphere of social life with the motto " Each for himself and let the devil take the hindmost : " a principle of selfishness which, if not to-day always openly expressed, is still acted upon by many, both as individuals and as national bodies in their political aggressions. As each individual seeks its own interest, so do the nations. The chief meaning of the late great war is that its occurrence marked the climax and close of an epoch of conflict which at first natural, and then modified by Christian ideals, burst out again, on the loss of those ideals, in a corrupted form, and with the greater vehemence by reason of increased knowledge and the development of scientific instruments of death. The force-principle biologically creative as regards the successful in life's conflicts, and destructive as regards others, had reached that maximum of intensity which perhaps marks the commencement of the close of the first great epoch in man's evolution. Progress is gradual and therefore though as has been said, the red flower of war may die down, it will be sometime before its seed has gone. For my part I do not share the optimism of those who think that we are about to enter the millennium. Man will suffer until he has cast aside all hardness of heart and truly knows himself and therefore others. Here India can help so much if She will. But she must speak with Her own voice. The Western wants no echo of his own teaching.

What will follow in the future? An anonymous Indian writer in a recent number of the " Vedânta Keshari " has well outlined what he calls the " three policies " of individual and national conduct and their relation to the Vedânta. According to the first, each man and nation in order to secure his and their life puts every other to suffering and to the risk of losing their own. This is the competition policy of nature. In the pre-family stage each man fought against each other man. Then each family fought each other family. Then there was the first organization of the Community the object of which was to end both individual and family conflict. Then communities fought with communities, which became larger and larger, until nations fought with nations and empires and confederations with one another. This struggle, open or veiled, between Peoples reacts on weaker societies and by disorganizing them recreates individual struggle among the latter. This struggle can only end with the organization of the whole human family. Mankind should, according to the Vedânta, learn to live without harm to any man or nation, and then he will, as India has done, do reverence to all animate being. To such as have this consciousness, all conscious harmfulness is sin and harmfulness produces suffering. As the Buddha said " Hatred is not cast out by Hatred. Hatred is cast out by Love." The first policy creates struggle between men and peoples, and assists the natural development by the negative force of racial antagonism, rivalry and selection. At this stage men and nations think of and act for themselves and not for the Self Whose body the whole universe is. None is safe and men and nations rise and fall ; and so long as this principle prevails will continue to do so.

The second stage of spiritual advance is that of the " Concert policy " when each lives in concert with every other; a stage in which there is struggle both for individual or national life and for the life of other individuals and nations as well. Mankind is developed into this stage through the cruel disciplines of the first, and by the teachings of the spiritually wise who have never been absent from humanity. For Man has That in him which ever guards him. By the previous struggles the body and mind, as vehicles of the Spirit, have been prepared for the succeeding stage in which by recognition of human unity the positive or co-operative and benevolent forces of nature are brought into play. The circle of Man's interest is widened from himself and family with which it commenced to the whole of humanity and then to the entire universe. Sarvam khalvidam Brahma. " All this is verily Brahman."

The last or third policy is that of Sacrifice in which each gives himself for the good of others who are now known to be aspects of the one Self. This has yet to come. For the second stage has (if at all) barely commenced for most. Meanwhile, as the writer I have cited has acutely observed, the sacrifice must be a conscious sacrifice. If a nation sacrifices itself ignorantly, as the weaker nations are doing, it will fall into a state of individual struggle and then disappear. There is, I may add, no merit in the lamb or the goat who goes in ignorance to its slaughter. In every stage there must be strength and power; a will which determines its end; a will for self; a will for self and others; or a will for others at the cost of oneself. Be ever strong. Meanwhile and until the world as a whole has advanced beyond the era of conflict each people must at least defend itself against aggression and show that manliness without which our common human nature is disgraced. Without such defence the guardians of the great Eastern Tradition are in peril from (to use the words of the late sociologist Mr. Benjamin Kidd) " the dark, efficient and terrible West."

120

The Vedânta of the "barbarous" Indian people teaches that the Universe is the Self appearing to the limited self or Man. All being is one. It teaches that when this is known, man will not harm or live at the cost of another. To harm another is to harm oneself. As Shiva in the Kulârnava Tantra says, man "should do good to other beings as if they were his own self." (Âtmavat sarvabhûtebhyo hitain kuryyât Kuleshvari). Each fraction of the body of the Lord should, whilst preserving itself and holding to its duty, help the other to preserve the harmony of the whole. Hinduism has provided for this organization within India and amongst its followers by the wonderful Varnâshrama Dharma. Though the evolution of the world has hitherto not called for it, the Vedânta also supplies the fundamental principles upon which international relations may be built. Where can be found a finer saying than " To do good to others is the highest religion ? " Paropakâro hi paramo dharmah. This is true civilization and India has evolved it.

VI

CULTURAL ATTACK ON INDIA

NOW-A-DAYS one hears a great deal of the principle of self-determination by peoples : ' that is each people should be allowed to work · out its own development without outside interference from others. It has been rightly said that this is also the principle of Svadharma which was proclaimed by Shrî Krishna on the banks of the Sarasvatî river in Ancient India. It is an essentially Indian principle that each individual and people has and have his and their own law (Svadharma) governing their development and that they should be free to follow it. Whilst general Dharma (Sâmanya Dharma) is affirmed, a particular Dharma (Vishesha Dharma) is recognised. Svadharma, as my friend Professor P. N. Mukhyopâdhyâya well puts it, is the individual's particular current in

122

the great stream of the flow of cosmic evolution. India stands for the principle "live and let live" according to the law of self-evolution. All nationalists amongst politically servient peoples have always claimed the right of self-determination for their country. But it is new doctrine in the mouths of dominating nations. The Editor of the "Hibbert Journal" writing recently in a London Weekly says: "What is wrong with Germany is simply that she has never learnt to mind her own business and leave other nations to mind theirs. She claims the right to impose her own culture on the rest of the world without consulting it." What European nation however has minded its own business and left other nations to mind theirs; least of all those peoples who have planted themselves all over the earth? The Editor of the "Hibbert Journal" says that if civilization had been grounded from the first on the law of "minding one's own business" with less said about "doing good to others" there might not have been so much wealth, but what there was would be worth more. We should be doing each other more good than by what is called social service. There would be less idleness, less inefficiency, less ugliness, less dirt, less shoddy and, above all, less humbug— less, in short, of everything which darkens the future of the earth. However this be, the Western has not, in general, admitted any such principles as regards Africans and Asiatics, peoples whom he regards as inferior races, to civilize whom, with some profit to himself, is the so-called " white man's burden." What however he objects to is the administration of his own " civilizing " medicine to himself. Whatever may be done elsewhere he now objects to any external interference and aggression as between Europeans themselves. It is quite easy to understand the objection. But if an Asiatic may be "improved" and "civilized" through the domination of a "superior"' people, it may be asked why should not an European Power dominate for its good one of its fellows. On the other hand, if we strictly apply the rule that each people should mind its own affairs; what if it minds them badly? The principle stated gives no right of interference. All European Nations have in fact been acting on the principle of interference with other's affairs. Whilst they in fact interfere for their own profit it is possible to give other grounds for their action. Thus it will be said that there is no indefeasable title to any part of the earth's surface. It belongs to those who can rightly use it. Only those can best use the earth who represent the highest state of evolution at which the human race has arrived and with whom power in fact resides. Therefore uncivilized or less civilized races may be displaced. The dispossessor in more modern times, assuming the role of trustee, combines self-profit with the duty of uplifting his ward to the level of the trustees' own civilization. Thus India is alleged by Mr. Archer to be barbarous and the duty of leading Her in the direction of civilized ideals is said to be incumbent on its Rulers, a more advanced and progressive people. Each of the leading European powers however considers itself to be highly civilized and therefore any attempt by one to impose its culture on another is resented as uncalled for impudence. Such an one however who might seek to impose it would justify himself on grounds similar to those which are admitted to apply as regards "inferior" races. He would claim that his culture was so superior to the rest as to justify its spread and predominance.

It may be that to-day we are witness to the commencement of a great change in the relation of the earth's peoples to one another ; but as regards the past, from the dawn of history until the outbreak of the great war, the principles governing the relation of one European people to another, or to Asiatics and Africans was force and gain. If it was profitable to dominate another people, and if it was possible through the latter's weakness it was done by all the European peoples. Until quite recent times no one thought of alleging that what was undertaken to gain profit for onself was done with the object of benefitting others. It might *in fact* benefit them which is another matter.

Is it possible to apply and will the principle of non-interference be applied even to-day ? Will true savages and barbarians be allowed to manage their own affairs on the principle of self-determination and be left either to work out their evolution for themselves or to go lower and then perish. If the principle of self-determination and Svadharma is not applicable, it is not likely that at any near date we shall see a philanthropic nation prepared to undertake the education of a backward people without profit for, and perhaps at cost to, itself. On the other hand, there will be many claimants for this " burden " if the carrying of it produces a profitable wage. Probably the exponents of the new morality would say that whatever be the profit to the uplifter it must, in order to justify his dominance, be shown that it is also in some substantial degree for the benefit of the subject people. Profit to the governors must be combined with benefit to the governed. In some cases the dominance may be complete, in others less so by way of Protectorate or still looser control according to the degree of difference existing between the respective cultural advancement of the two peoples. When however there is a general cultural equality between two peoples, then the attempted dominance of one over the other, whether for the simple and ancient motive of territorial and economic gain, or the more modern alleged motive of cultural improvement, would doubtless be condemned.

Let us leave it to those who have formulated the doctrine of non-interference to work it out honestly, consistently, and without any false hypocrisy. What seems clear however is, that if in the future one nation interferes with another, such action will be sought to be justified on the grounds of the imperfect civilization of the latter. It is for this reason thet Mr. Archer and others, endeavour to show that India is barbarous, unprogressive, mediæval, superstitious, ignorant, unspiritual and so forth. Therefore She must be made a ward of a

Civilized Power, of what some people now call a " Culture Nation," as if India was not that. Those who have hitherto allowed such charges to go against them without reply have shewn less perspicacity than those who have made them. In days, which though past are not old, superior force was considered sufficient justification for dominance and there was no need to seek any other. The times have changed ; and it is now considered necessary to satisfy, or at least allege to, the public conscience that political dominance or control is necessary in the interests of the servient people themselves. Upon this matter the spiritual, intellectual and social state of that people is of primary importance.

VII

AN EXAMPLE

THE· institutions of a coloured people, particularly of a politically servient one, are very likely to appear inferior to those without understanding and subject to prejudice. Though there is an answer, it is not unnatural to ask why, if a civilization is of value, it has not kept its people free ? Why, if it possesses an uplifting religious doctrine, does it not raise them from political subordination and the lack of the virile side of morality which such subordination implies ? We must distinguish between Ideas and the human channels by which they are given expression. These latter may be in decay or weak, or their development may be impeded.

The extent to which from early times Indian civilization has been the subject of cultural attack and scolding abuse is a noteworthy fact. All Asiatic civilizations have had their share; but my reading of this literature disposes me to the conclusion that India has suffered much more than any others. Even in 1830 (to go no further back) Sir Thomas Strange ("Hindu Law") thought it necessary to say "It is the duty as well as the interest of Britain to foster those whom it has become the *unworthy fashion to undervalue and abuse.* It were at least a more magnanimous course *parcere subjectis.* Nor can it be a commendable one to irritate by *insulting* them."

There are and have, been both in the present and past those who, without accepting the principles of Indian civilization, have striven (not always successfully) to be just to it. There has always been a smaller band of what Mr. Archer calls "Orientalizers" and "India-worshippers." That great man and Orientalist Sir William Jones said : "It is impossible to read the Vedant or the many fine compositions in illustration of it, without believing that

131

Pythagoras and Plato derived their sublime theories from the same fountain with the sages of India." Though he did not live in a time when the political aspect of the cultural question was dominant, there is no reason to suppose that, if he had, his greatness of mind and judgment would have been affected by any considerations not strictly germane to a criticism of the great philosophy and religion which he thus praised. The celebrated French historian of Philosophy Victor Cousin wrote : " When we read with attention the poetical and philosophical monuments of the East, above all those of India, which are beginning to spread in Europe, we discover there many a truth and truths so profound, and which make such contrast with the meanness of the results at which European genius has sometimes stopped, that we are constrained to bend the knee before the philosophy of the East and to see in this cradle of the human race the native land of the highest philosophy." Freidrich Schlegel wrote : " Even the loftiest philosophy of the

Europeans, the idealism of reason, as it is set forth by the Greek philosophers, appears in comparison with the *abundant light and vigour of Oriental idealism* like a feeble Promethean spark in the full blood of heavenly glory of the noon-day sun, faltering and feeble and ever ready to be extinguished. *The Divine origin of man is continually inculcated to stimulate his efforts* to return, to animate him in the struggle and incite him to consider a re-union and re-corporation with Divinity as the one primary object of every action and exertion." The lines I have italicised indicate " uplifting spiritual concepts " if mankind has ever known such. Professor Max Muller (by no means given to an uncritical admiration of things Indian and who has in several matters misjudged them) said of Schopenhauer's well known saying—" in the whole world there is no study so beneficial and so *elevating* as the Upanishad. It has been the solace of my life, it will be the solace of my death : "— " If these words of Schopenhauer required any endorsement I should willingly give it as the result of my own experience during a long life devoted to the study of many philosophies and many religions."

These are the sayings of the greater men but the world is not made up of such. The bulk of criticism of Indian culture has been hostile and a good deal of it ignorant, abusive and unfair. A missionary author whom I have already cited has recently said: (' Christian Thought and Hindu Philosophy ' by the Revd. A. H. Bowman) —" It is not many years ago that the whole literature of Brahmanism was considered *a mass of intellectual and moral rubbish.* To-day the verdict of Western Scholars has completely changed. Indeed, the danger is lest now we may have gone to the other extreme." There is some exaggeration in this statement. I do not know of any Orientalist Scholars who are over-apprecia- tive of India though there are an increasing number of laymen both English and others who are commencing in a just spirit to value its culture. Nevertheless the passage

134

cited errs on the right side in so far as it indicates the unfavourable character of the general past verdict of the Western world. The change is by no means so complete, as the reverend author supposes. Moreover, political reasons have in recent years accentuated the cultural attack. Those who have read the previous sections will have understood the reasons.

Here two facts may be noted. The first is that there must be something peculiar in Indian civilization which is the cause of this animosity : and the second is the proof such attacks afford of the living force of this civilization. No one now goes into moral hysterics over the absurdities or iniquities of Phaenician, Carthaginian or Babylonian civilization. They are dead and gone, but India lives. Up to now India has presented itself as one of the " immortal " peoples, to use the word of (I think) some French writer whose name I forget. Suffering racial and social division, politically disrupted, with a great variety of languages and scripts, governed for centuries by stangers, She has yet held together so that we can still speak of "India." This I think is due primarily to certain religious and philosophical concepts held in common by Her people—and as regards "Hinduism" in its technical sense —the wonderful organization called Varnâshrama dharma.

An English author has spoken of that "hideous blot India": a criticism which at least marks it as distinct from the rest of the "unblotted" world. That distinguished thinker Professor Lowes-Dickinson, in an essay which seeks with justice to define the character of Indian civilization, profoundly remarks that it is so unique that the contrast is not so much between East and West as between India and the rest of the world. Thus India stands for something which distinguishes it from all other peoples, and so she calls Herself a Karmabhûmi as opposed to the Bhoga-bhûmi of all other peoples. For this She has been wonderfully preserved until to-day. Even now (and in this consists one cause of the extraordinary interest which India arouses} we can see the life of thousands of years ago. Standing on the Ghats at Benares or by any village well we are transported into the beautiful antique world. One of the greatest (amongst several) services which England has rendered India consists in this—that She has not only aroused this country to new life, but She has during such process also largely helped to preserve Her archaic customs and ancient thought until to-day. For social and religious institutions are the body in which the spirit of ancient ideals is conserved. India is now about to be drawn into the world-whirlpool wherein She must herself struggle to preserve herself. Until now England has been a protection and a shield. For had India been drawn into that whirlpool before commencing to recover her strength, She was likely to have altogether disappeared. She has been and will be preserved up to that point of time when, whatever may happen to India Herself, She is able to communicate Her ideas to the West and

137

up to the time when the latter has reached a stage when it is receptive of them.

The author, whom I have just cited, finds the uniqueness of India to consist in Her religion of eternity and in this he is right ; though, as I show later, Indian doctrine is not, when rightly understood, one-sided but has a "time-religion" also. One form of Vedânta—that of the Shâkta—effects one of the most complete syntheses of the life of the world and of spirit that I know. It is perhaps a misunderstanding on this point which may account, in part, for the repulsion which many Westerns feel towards Indian religion and philosophy. The missionary author whom I have cited quotes Dr. Matheson as saying :—" It is not too much to say that the mind of the West with all its undoubted impulses towards the progress of humanity has never exhibited such an intense amount of intellectual force as is to be found in the religious speculations of India.........These have been the cradle of all Western speculations, and wherever the European mind has risen into heights of philosophy, it has done so because the Brahman was the pioneer. There is no intellectual problem in the West which had not its earlier discussion in the East, and there is no *modern solution* of that problem *which will not be found anticipated in the East.''* Upon this the author who makes the citation observes " We may think this language too strong but we shall never again depreciate the intellectual value, the philosophic subtleties, the religious purpose of the sacred books of the East.

This prophecy has not proved correct. Mr. Archer's and other criticisms belie it. On the whole, however, it rightly indicates the general tendency where political motives do not intervene. In the Administration Report of the United Provinces (1913—1914) there is the following happy and yet unhappy statement: " It is satisfactory to note that the vernacular Christian literature has *almost* freed itself from vituperation and abuse of other religions." Progress has also been made in a higher class of literature towards a better understanding of Indian culture. It is being found that some of its philosophic teachings harmonise with the canclusions and generally accepted hypotheses of modern Western natural science and psychology. Again, what is called Occultism has made great strides in recent years. Even so-called "scientific" men have been constrained to accept against their will occult phenomena which have for ages been known and recognised in this country. The doctrine of the Vedânta is being widely spread. When Western thought has worked independently it has been in the same direction. A recent philosophical work ('Religion and Reality'—J. H. Tuckwell) rightly says "In our main conclusion we have long ago been anticipated by the religious philosophy of India. In the West our philosophy has been surely but slowly moving to the same inevitable monistic goal. In Professor Ladd of Harvard we have a notable Western thinker who by a process of careful and consistent reasoning, concrete in character,

140

has also arrived at the conclusion that the ultimate reality must be conceived of as an Absolute Self of which we are finite forms or appearances. But it is the crowning glory of the Vedânta that it so long ago announced, re-iterated and emphasized this deep truth in a manner that does not permit us for a moment to forget it or explain it away. This great stroke of identity, this discernment of the ultimate unity of all things in Brahman or the One Absolute Self seems to us to constitute the masterpiece and highest achievement of India's wonderful metaphysical and religious genius to which the West has yet to pay the full tribute which is its due."

But this increase in appreciation of India's culture rouses to stronger effort those who are opposed to it. From the religious side it is natural enough that Hinduism should still encounter opposition from other forms of religion. Philosophers will also continue their age-long debate. Lately, however, a political motive has worked strongly at the back of hostile criticism both in this specific class of literature and in the Press. The motive is to show that, notwithstanding claims and appreciations to the contrary, India is unqualified for the political advancement which, rightly or wrongly, She seeks. No one says bluntly now-a-days "We want a country and therefore we will take or keep it." What is said is "in the interests of Humanity, its Liberty and therefore Progress it is necessary that we should take charge, or keep control, of this Country (whatever it may be) and see to its well-being, raising it to the high level of spiritual, moral, and intellectual culture which we ourselves possess." So some German people professed that it would be for the well-being of Europe if its Kultur were spread therein. The principle had previously been acted upon by all European powers as regards so-called "backward" peoples. It would be as absurd, as it would be unjust, to say that all who put forward these pleas are consciously dishonest. On the contrary, so far as India is concerned, action is I believe largely taken on a belief sincerely held. I say so because ignorance of the true character of Indian civilization is such, and it has been so misrepresented, that the bulk of Western people may well believe that they are also serving both the interests of themselves and this country by cultural dominance. It may be that in some cases and in some particulars they are doing so. Criticism of this country is not altogether ill-founded. But if their belief be either wholly or partially wrong, the Indian people are largely to blame for this result, because the English-speaking section of them have been indifferent to the defence and exposition of their culture, where they have not actually neglected, depreciated, or condemned it. It is however, I believe, true to say that there is hypocrisy in some in over-stressing the supposed altruistic aspect of their action, and the attacks made on Indian culture are often either unscrupulous in spirit or inaccurate in fact. What indeed can be less so than the charge that India is barbarous, without religion and morality, and so on, and the constant harping on alleged evils without reference to the excellences which Indian civilization possesses. Here as in other things the wish is father to the thought. We find therein such arguments as that the doctrine of Karma, Reincarnation, Pessimism, Absolutism and so forth are such sapping influences on moral and intellectual character as to render this country unfit for self-governance. Such critics are, as likely as not, without interest in such philosophical questions considered in themselves. Most would be hard put to it to define accurately, for instance, what Karma is. Others who know more have written erroneously of it. But it is obvious that if it can be established that India on this and other account is not civilized but barbarous, that is an argument against Her capacity for political autonomy. If Her face can be made ugly, religiously, morally, intellectually and socially and in every other way, then the British people will not like the look of it. In the meanwhile do not

144

let them be deluded by the idea that She has real civilised worth. She is barbarous. If other Western critics, judging the matter without political bias, have approved any form of Indian culture, steps must be taken to discredit them and to show they are all wrong or interested. They are either, as the "Times" charges, seeking a "cheap popularity" or as Mr. Archer says they are Orientalists (how many?) making the most of a subject which, meagre in worth though it be, has cost them years of study; or they are "Theosophists" or gullible, or cranks and so forth. It is necessary in particular to deny the alleged spiritual character of Indian civilisation. It would never do to admit this. For spirituality is honoured of all men and where it truly exists, there are other excellences. For this reason too "The Times" approves Mr. Archer's work as establishing that Indian culture does not provide "anywhere any great moral or spiritual concept capable of *uplifting a nation.*" It follows, of course, that others must provide these concepts and take in

charge the business of " uplift.'' Similarly,
the leader-writer of an Anglo-Indian
Calcutta Daily, after drawing attention to
the fact that a British Statesman to whom
he referred had the " Christian outlook on
politics," stated that in India " the Tantric
view of life and its problems still insidi-
ously survives," as an argument against
political change. What the writer meant
I cannot say unless it be that as the word
' Tantra ' makes many people shudder, the
association of the word with Indian political claims would give them a sinister
colour. Similarly a correspondent in the
same Journal, after stating that to grant
self-government to India would be to
subject the Englishman to the control of
races " who are not his peers in the sense
of their having attained to the same plane
of civilization and culture " and denying
that the Indians are " a very highly civilized people " says :—" Is it sound and far
seeing statesmanship to subordinate to the
rule of Tantric worshippers " races who
profess a religion (to wit, Christianity)

" which exterminated the cults of Isis, Mithra, Astarte, the Eleusinian and other mysteries of classical times." Whether such writers are politically right I do not here discuss. I am only concerned with the motive and truth of their criticisms so far as it affects their value. They continually talk of their superior civilization : and it may be that in some matters it is superior. But what as regards others ? Mr. Archer belongs to this class.

Claims have been made for the essentially spiritual character of the Indian mind. Mr. Archer first says " The glory which is claimed for India by serious Western thinkers—in words re-echoed a thousand-fold by Indians themselves—is that of a high spirituality, an unique genius for grasping and expounding the realities behind the phenomenal world and the innermost meanings of life." But it is just on this point that Mr. Archer is most markedly dissentient. For he says " It is precisely on the religious side that the character of the Indian people, as I read it,

147

is conspicuously defective." "India's real distinction lies, not in evolving, but in killing, the germs of sane and virile spirituality." "The Indian people have always gravitated towards the lower rather than the higher element in religion; towards the form rather than the substance; towards the letter rather than the spirit. That is why I hold it the very acme of paradox to claim for them an exalted spirituality." Only a "few fanatics" would say that India "has evolved a noble pure progressive religion in intimate relation with high racial and individual morality. Higher Hinduism, he says, is so contaminated by the lower that "except in small reforming sects" it can be scarcely said to exist. By Higher Hinduism he evidently understands Theistic movements similar to, and influenced by, Christianity; a common notion of English writers who naturally and with greater ease understand these movements than orthodox Hinduism. The latter, he finds, is based on an "enervating" metaphysic and certain false notions of

Pessimism, Asceticism, Karma and Reincarnation. In particular it preaches "the unreality of the world, detachment from terrestrial interests, the unimportance of the life of the moment compared with the endless chain of past and future existence : all doctrines which lead to the enfeeblement of volitional individuality." "It presents speculation in the guise of dogma." Its cosmology, physiology, psychology are found to consist of "baseless classifications and ingenious guesses." "But to mistake groping for seeing, guessing for knowing— that is the very unspiritual habit into which India has fallen." The Indian people have not manifested an "unique religio-philosophic genius." On the contrary "the genius which the Indian people, from the Brahmin caste downwards, has displayed to great perfection is a genius for obfuscating reason and formalizing, materializing, degrading religion." "Great thinkers she may have possessed but she has not extracted from their thoughts a rational, ennobling, or even a morally helpful religion."

149

It is somewhat of a surprise to learn from this book that it is thought to be part of the business of Census Officers to pass judgments on the religions of this country ; for Hinduism is said in the (1901) Census of India (cited as an authority by Mr. Archer) to be " Animism more or less tempered by philosophy " or more briefly " Magic tempered by metaphysics." These smart sayings are, however, Mr. Archer thinks too favourable ; for " to my thinking the animism and the magic are much more palpable than the transformation and tempering." " The ' sprituality ' manifested in the lower Hinduism is that to which anthropologists have given the name of ' Animism '." " Hinduism as a popular religion consists in the cult of a monstrous folk-lore oppressing and paralysing the imagination." It is " the lowest professed and practised by any people that purports to have arisen above savagery. Beside it the devotion of the Russian or Spanish peasant is rational and enlightened." " Hinduism *is* the character of the people and it indicates a melancholy proclivity towards whatever is monstrous and unwholesome." It is not a "morally helpful religion." If nevertheless he finds in the Hindu writings many admirable ethical doctrines " it is only because Hindu philosophy is after all too human to be logical." "Hinduism, though it has much talked of righteousness, has never claimed moral teaching as one of its functions." It is true he says that "there are vices and stupidities among the nations of the West from which the Hindu is comparatively free " but even this is not to be counted to his credit—the reason being that it is " rather because they do not come his way than because he rises superior to them."

As for metaphysics which, as is well known, is associated with the Hindu religion, it is true that India " has displayed an unequalled diligence in thinking about the unthinkable ; that being an exercise agreeably compatible with physical immobility and living upon the alms of the faithful." Its philosophy " denies all value to life " and has led the people " not

151

towards the study of nature but away from it." It is an effect of climatic influences. " Only in a hot country is it possible for a human being to spend months, years, or even a lifetime in sitting cross-legged and contemplating his own navel. Only in a hot country could the opinion arise that this 'was the best way of ascertaining the truth as to the nature and constitution of the universe." Its metaphysic is " enervating " expelling all volitional individuality. But any kind of metaphysic even the best is " a man-made illusion." It is quite a mistake to suppose that " familiarity with metaphysical conceptions—perhaps even the capacity of arguing with some subtlety a metaphysical point, is necessarily a proof of great mental capacity." He is sceptical " of the value of thought in a region where there is no possible test of values." Such speculations " are all efforts to know the unknowable and think about the unthinkable." It is conceded on the other hand that India can claim priority of date in some of her philosophical speculations and that India may have had great and subtle thinkers. The appraisement of India's contribution to metaphysics he would leave to the experts; whilst he in fact forestalls them with his own criticisms.

In short the spiritual genius of the Indian people everywhere expresses itself in forms "which not only the Western world but China and Japan have for ages outgrown." "The Western mind has decisively outgrown the Eastern : has embraced a wider range of experience and touched greater depths and—I do not hesitate to say— deeper depths of thought." "The ordinary daily practices of the (Indian) cult are sufficient to place it beyond the pale of civilisation." "Wherever you turn you meet repulsive performances of piety." Hinduism is "anti-rational." "It is in short the great anachronism of the modern world." "Hinduism has not been cleansed for thirty centuries." "It is true that corruptions have crept into other religions which have relapsed into something like primitive fetichism, and that attempts at filtration hae been only partially successful." But "Hinduism on the other hand is a wholly ufiltered religion—a paganism which has rsolutely declined filtration. It is this tendency towards pollution rather than purification that assigns it its place—incomparably the lowest—in the scale of world religions. Until Hinduism has somehow got itself filtered, India . cannot reasonably claim fellowship on terms of equality with the civilised nations of the earth."

Mr. Archer is not alone in this class of criticisms. He has the countenance of some learned Orientalists. Dr. A. E. Gough described the Upanishads as " the work of a rude age, a deteriorated race, and a *barbarous* unprogressive community." " It is no more spiritual than the old observance of prescriptive sacra." " There is little " as he says " that is spiritual in all this." "In treating of Indian Philosophy a writer has to deal with *thoughts of a lower order than the thoughts of the every day life of Europe.* The great difficulty lies in this,

154

that a *low order of ideas* has to be expressed in a high order of terms, and that the English words suggest a wealth of analysis and association altogether foreign to the thoughts that are to be reproduced. The effort is nothing less than an endeavour to revert to a ruder type of mental culture and to become for the time being *barbarous.*" So when the sage uttered his wonderful generalization "That thou art" he gave expression to a thought lower than, the thoughts of the every day life of any Western Dick, Tom or Harry. Another English Professor went a step, further when he told a young Indian friend of mine upon his return to India : ." Not to waste his time over Indian religion or metaphysics *for there was nothing in them.*" If Dr. Gough found that that the former contained thoughts of a "lower order," the other man of learning deemed them to be of no value at all. If I remember rightly, my friend was counselled to seek the satisfaction of his soul's needs in the Science (doubtless useful in its way) of Numismatics.

With such views among some orientalists
it is not surprising that others with less
opportunity for knowledge go astray. Sir
Harry Johnston (who according to Mr.
Price Collier in "The East in the West")
p. 214 "at least cannot be accussed of not
knowing India" described the Hindu religion
as "a mixture of nightmare nonsense and
time-wasting rubbish fulfilling no useful
purpose whatever; only adding to the
general burden of existence borne by
Humanity in its struggle for existence."
He added that "So long as 200 Million
Indians remain attached to these prepos-
terous faiths with their absurd and useless
ceremonials and food taboos, so long, if for
that reason alone, will the British be
justified in ruling the Indian Empire with
some degree of absolutism." Another tourist
(whose name I forget) applying the £. s. d.
test wrote: "For an Englishman to get
a plain statement of what Brahmanism
really means is far from easy. The only
wonder is that people *who have to live on
nine pence a week*, who marry when they

156

are ten years old, are prevented by caste life from rising out of what is often, if not always, a degraded state *have any religion at all.*" The journalist, Mr. Harold Begbie, in a work (" the Light of Asia ") published by the " Christian Literature Society for India " speaks of Hinduism (to summarise a longer criticism) as " a weltering chaos of terror, darkness, and uncertainty. It is a religion without the apprehension of a moral evolution, without definite commandments, without a religious sanction in the sphere of morals, without a moral code, without a God, except a Being which is a mixture of Bacchus, Don Juan and Dick Turpin. It is the most material and childishly super-stitious animalism that ever masqueraded as idealism : not another path to God but a pit of abomination as far set from God as the mind of man can go ; staggering the brain of a rational man ; filling his mind with wild contempt for his species and which has only endured because it has failed." The publishers of this " Christian Literature " are evidently no believers in the more modern so-called "sympathetic treatment" of Indian culture: which, to use the words of one of its exponents, while finding something precious in Indian civilization finds also much that is false and unwholesome. I have never but once come across offensive criticism written of Christianity by a Hindu; and that was the case of a man who published a short lived " comic " paper in Calcutta modelled on a French anticlerical journal, the illustrations of which he seemed to have borrowed. "Christian Literature," of this kind serves at least the purpose of contrasting this form of Christian aggression with the doctrine of the Vedânta and Gîtâ that all religions should be respected.

To return to Mr. Archer.

As regards Art he is of opinion that India has not been lacking in talent and abounds in noteworthy works; but he is strongly opposed to the view that it is a supreme expression of the spirit of man, superior or even equal to European art. He desires to show the " anti-rational bases of the unqualified and unmeasured eulogies of the Indian genius." India " is a hotbed of imagination." " Hindu (as distinct from Mahomedan) art habitually tends to extravagance and excess." If for instance one compares the Javanese Boro-Buder sculptures with the reliefs and friezes at Mamallapuram and Badami " the difference almost amounts to that between fine art and barbarism." The broad shoulders and thin waist of the typical Indian heroic figure " are due to the fact that the ideal of strength was based on the proportions of the lion or tiger. Such an ideal is very naturally formed by a people in a state of semi-savagery and adherence to it might not unfairly be interpreted as showing that the semi-savage state has not been far outgrown.". India, it is said, thus " goes to the jungle for its ideas instead of to the gymnasium and the council hall ; " which I may add in modern days does not always provide models of masculine beauty. " There is more spirituality in (for example) the ideal head of Homer, seamed by suffering and furrowed by thought than in the whole pantheon of Buddhist or Hindu sculpture." Hindu sculpture "carries to excess all the faults noted in the Amaravati relief and adds to them the undesirable characteristic of constantly dealing in grotesque monstrosities." "Within the temples it is just the same colossal contorted forms looming menacingly through the gloom, everywhere a riot of violent, often sensual, imagery, nowhere one touch of nature or one point of rest" except in the "pot bellied Falstaff of Hinduism" Ganesha. "The monster gods of India are originally ogres; figures in which cowering savages embodied their conception of the destructive powers of nature. Kâlî is set "in a ravening attitude like that of a barn-storming player of the good old days tearing passion to tatters." Sophisticate them as you please the monster gods of India are survivals from a low stage of spiritual development."

Mr. Archer then passes to the Hindu epic and drama in which "we seem to see the over-strained over-elaborated overcrowded sculptures and in viewing the sculptures we seem to hear the vast labyrinthine multitudinous epics." " The Indian imagination suffers from habitual and ancestral over-fatigue." " There is an insensitiveness to normal and wholesome stimulation." " The epics keep the Indian mind stagnant." " The Greek epics would make ten times better Bibles than the huge accumulations of sacerdotalised folk-lore from which the Indian populace derive their notions of the heroic and divine." Then he objects to the stories of asceticism, the generation stories, the spectacular, sensational and passionate, the stories of magic and so on. Similar ideas, he says, doubtless prevail elsewhere but not so extravagantly. The character· is dehumanized such as the saintly Râma who is too saintly and the long suffering Sîtâ whose heroism is " too often like that of Alkestis and Griselda excessive to the verge of immorality."

Then there is the " self-defeating, the enervating, the exhausting extravagance of

11

hyperbole, the wildest monstrosities and folk-lore incapable of awakening any feeling, other than scientific, in a civilized person or person aspiring to civilization." " The Mahâbhârata is in no way behind the Râmâyana in crudity and extravagance :" " It is in many respects the more barbarous of the two." There are " limitless insensate conceptions of heroism, expressing itself in terms of frenzied ferocity," " contortions, convulsions " " of a turbid flood of primitive and barbarous legendry." The passion for hyperbole is blended with an " amazing and amusing euphemism."

It is somewhat of a relief to pass with the author to the Drama where he says the imagination can move healthily and at ease instead of " passing through epilepsy to paralysis." Yet still " the Hindu Drama remains a curiously undeveloped art form ;" meagre as compared with the literature of the West or Far East. " It is the drama of passivity where the characters are the passive puppets of supernatural wire-pulling." " A people which thus leaves out

162

of its drama the element of will, probably does so because the element of will plays no efficient part in its life."

As for architecture no doubt the giant temples of the south are marvels of massive construction and have often a sort of titanic impressiveness. But they look as if they had been built by demoniac Râkshasas. "Of unity, clarity, nobility of design they show no trace." "It is a disease of gigantesque barbarism." When we pass further north we still find the same ponderousness, the same absence of anything like lightness and grace. "They are less barbarous perhaps than the Gopuras of the south but scarcely more beautiful." There is a "self defeating wastefulness in Hindu architecture" which provides "incredible marvels of insensate over-elaboration." Mahomedanism however begets things of beauty. Mr. Archer who does not seem to admire anything except his own rationalistic civilization (whatever it be) says "I am no admirer of Islam; but the glory of its architecture is a patent, palpable fact which proves what India can do when it wakes from the hallucinations of Yoga and the multitudinous nightmares of its indigenous cults."

Indian painting is then brought up for judgment. Apart from the Ajanta frescoes it is said to be a late and post-Mahomedan development. But just as "monstrous" is the epithet for Hindu sculpture, "miniature" is a reproach against painting. It is allowed that there is wonderful illuminative richness, extraordinary draughtsmanship, great beauty of decorative detail (remarkable gifts on the part of a barbarous people) but, as one might expect, there is a drawback to all this in the shape of "a total inability to escape from a laborious convention, to attain freedom and breadth of design, to suggest to the imagination anything more than is presented to the eye." There is a "certain hard limited cleverness." "Though they may be great by Indian standards by world standards they remain small." "The arrest of development in Indian art seems to be closely paralleled by the arrest of development in Indian civilization." "There is however no question that India has splendid artistic capacities," but what she wants is restraint; "for a self-satisfaction was from the first her besetting sin." In other countries artistic movements germinate, ripen, culminate and decay, but in the extraordinary climate of India "they do not ripen but are checked before they have even approached maturity." Mr. Archer once more writes foolishness about "Reality." Others "have fallen under India's illusion that art inspired by transcendental truth must be the greatest art in the world." But Indian truth if it is true is said to be destructive of art "because it is only in so far as India ignores her own truth and accepts provisionally the real existence of the visible universe that she possesses any art at all." He concludes with the "radical inferiority of Indian art." "Europe even in virtue of its works of the second and third order is incomparably richer than India in products of artistic genius." Certainly Abanindranath Tagore's " Buddha as mendicant " has great nobility of character " but the type is European." We must, it is said, attribute all this inferiority to the " general undervaluing in religion and philosophy of will and endeavour." " Life is conceived as a shoreless expanse in which generations rise and fall as helplessly and purposelessly as waves in mid-ocean. The individual life is everywhere dwarfed and depreciated." " India has contributed only one great character Gautama Buddha to the world's pantheon ; " but this limited concession is rendered nought by the sceptical remark " and he perhaps never existed." " If a claim be put in for Asoka it may possibly be allowed (Mr. Archer relents) but then the old mood surges up— " but after all how featureless he is ! "

Then Mr. Archer states that European history, literature, and Art swarms above everything with great characters but " when we have named the Buddha and Akbar " (who it may be noted was so kindly disposed to the Hinduism which to Mr. Archer is so great an offence) " we have exhausted the supreme personalities whom India has given to history." Where are the Indian Charlemagnes, Alfreds, Columbus, Luther, Cromwell, Richelieu, and Napoleon? Where, he again asks, are the fictitious characters Hamlet, Falstaff, Shylock, Lear, Quixote, Alcestis, Tartuffe, Don Juan, and Mephistopheles? Where are the Raphaels, Titians and others? " At whatever point we institute a comparison we find India deficient in the record, at any rate, of strong, energetic, dominant personality." " There is throughout a depression of will and energy."

Music is then bid to appear and though Mr. Archer says " in the absence of technical knowledge I can at best speak vaguely " he cannot resist a depreciative criticism on this point also for fear apparently that he might not be complete. Mr. Archer is decidedly " Pûrna " on his theme. " In music, it seems to me, we have the irrefragable proof that the Western mind has decisively outgrown the Eastern." "The delicate tinklings of Indian melody cannot be compared with the titanic harmonies of Handel and Haydn, Beethoven and Wagner."

Mr. Archer himself overcome by his excess of depreciation winds up: "I unfeignedly regret in conclusion the controversial and even depreciatory tone of this Chapter." But why? If the facts be as stated, why regret the statement of them, if a statement be at all considered necessary? It seems however that India's art strangely enough "contributed to the spell she cast upon me." India must indeed be a Râkshasî. But Mr. Archer resists this spell because he has been aroused by the claims made for India that in art, as in other things, India is supreme, and sanity is essential for India's salvation; and so he has thus written to cure Her of Her pride.

Mr. Archer then proceeds to deal with "the insensate racial vanity and the bacillus of arrogance," as displayed in social institutions, "the inhuman snobbery" of caste (so unlike the class snobbery and injustice to the poor of the West); the priesthood, (existing in Europe also), marriage (as to which " our habits are not like those of India mere crystallizations of barbarism "), Sati, infanticide, (so rare to-day that their mention is evidence of an untempered desire to defame), widow-remarriage, sea voyage, and the like. As for " progress," he says, that " the country in its inmost heart resents and despises it." The conclusion is stated by Mr. Archer in connection with the caste question in the following query :—are the people who adhere to such customs justified in claiming an independent and equal place among the nations of the world ?

I have neither the space nor time to meet in detail all these criticisms. Indian culture cannot be disposed of, as Mr. Archer has done, in a few summary Chapters. As regards Indian Art I refer the reader to three writers on the subject who have understood it—Mr. Havell, Dr. Coomara-swamy, and Shri O. C. Gangooly. Indian music which, like medicine, went from India to Europe and has also influenced both Chinese and Japanese music, is now being studied by Western writers who have found it worthy of their research and is being encouraged by the All India Music Conference now in its second year. It has proposed a National Academy of Music at Delhi which has Princely support in the person of His Highness the Nawab Sahib of Rampur. There are other smaller institutions which evidence a rising regard for this form of Indian art. There is much that is absurd in Mr. Archer's criticisms but some of it is not without ground ; though it is weakened by his excessive language and generalizations. In some matters of taste I not unnaturally, being a Western as he is, prefer what is our own. The glories of the great Gothic Cathedrals, the wondrous expressions of Christian worship in the ages of faith, and the noble simplicity of Greek architecture appeal to me more than any Hindu Temple. For me as for him Indian music, beautiful as it is, has not the majesty of Beach and Beethoven, the romantic brilliance of Chopin, the heroic grandeur and sensuous magic of Wagner. But what of that? Western and Eastern music move on different planes. Naturally what is our own in literature or art and culture generally appeals to us best. We have produced it and like our own child. This can be admitted without unnecessary or excessive and, let me add, offensive, depreciation of the culture of others. These comparisons in matter of *taste* seem to serve no useful purpose. Let each mind feed upon what it likes best; and do not let ourselves intrude on the peace of its enjoyment. I will therefore in the succeeding sections mainly and shortly deal with some of the fundamental concepts of Indian religion and metaphysic which are the root of, and are expressed in, other forms of Indian civilization the Arts included.

Meanwhile it may be pointed out that Mr. Archer refutes himself on all points. He is not a logical thinker and has evidently been carried away by his feelings.

171

So after this plethora of hostile criticism we come across the following passage :— " There are in Calcutta, Bombay and elsewhere a certain number of emancipated and highly cultivated families with whom social intercourse is a privilege and a pleasure. The difficulty in their case is that *one is apt to feel like a semi-barbarian* upon an abode of *ancient, fine spun aristocratic culture.*" " Awe " he adds " is perhaps not quite the feeling with which these grave Orientals regard *our Western crudities.*" Just so. Even Mr. Archer feels himself a semi-barbarian in the presence of high examples of Indian culture. For it is Indian culture of which he speaks. He would not of course feel a semi-barbarian in the présence of his own. We then ask where does this *ancient* fine spun aristocratic culture come from? Is it not an inheritance from the Indian past the glories of which Mr. Archer denies? Is it possible, for what is essentially an unspiritual barbarism, to produce results which make even Mr. Archer abashed? And if, as he says, many thousands have in the past arisen and are now arising from Barbarism and have become so civilised as to make him feel a semi-barbarian, how did they do it? A worthless tree cannot bear good fruit. Why not then say that the tree is a good one and if to-day its fruit is not always what one might expect, it is because the tree is suffering from disease, want of nourishment, or may be from the infirmity of age. In the latter case let us look and see if some young shoots are springing from the base of its age-old and weathered trunk.

VIII

A REPLY

IN criticising Indian civilization there are two simple facts to be first remembered. India in the first place is no exception to the general rule that a country is made up of all manner of men. Secondly, although, as set out later, there are certain general features which we may call Indian, there are on the other hand a variety of beliefs and practices. Hinduism is in fact not so much a religion as a Culture, which has produced, amongst other things, certain fundamental religious and philosophical beliefs on which have been superimposed a number of varying forms of particular philosophies and religions.

Whilst the differences alleged are not always such or as great as they seem, an historical survey of India shows that She has (as one might have supposed) produced all varieties of human character. India which is religious also produced (as an atheistic acquaintance of mine was greatly pleased to hear) the Chârvâkas and Lokâyatas; materialists and sensualists who denied the existence of God, reviled the Vedas and the priests as frauds and cheats; sought enjoyment only in life leaving at death " as many debts as possible." India which produced ascetic fugitives from women also worked out a scientific Scripture of Eroticism—the Kâma Shâstra, wrote sensuously conceived literature, carved recondite obscenities on its temples, and painted similar scenes for the incitement of its passions, which it satisfied in many forms of sensual enjoyment both on this, and (as the Magician), the superphysical plane. The same India which in the person of the Sannyâsî fled from the world to the forest, also glorified that world in sumptuous art. India was meditative and yet gave birth to men of action celebrated as warriors and statesmen, and a people who governed themselves practically and with success.

Those who say that this country has never known Self-government do not themselves know their subject. As M. Barthelemy Saint Hilaire said (" L'Inde Anglaise "), "In no country in the whole world has communal autonomy been so developed " " Dans aucun pays du monde, l'autonomie communale n'a été poussée plus loin.") It was, as Professor Monier Williams said, Self-government in all its purity. This was the primitive communal organization of the village with its headman, Panchayet or Council and its local officers and servants. Well developed also were the relations and functions of the people (Prajâdharma) towards the King with his Councillors and of the King towards his people (Râja-dharma). Some seem to think that because India had not the ballot-box and hustings and other paraphernalia of political Western life, it did not know what Self-Government is. There are also a class of political writers who repeat that India " likes to be ruled " meaning thereby auto-cratic government. Such also know nothing of the Hindu Spirit or History. The Hindu Kings were not autocrats. Their will was as much subject to the general Dharma as were the people. Whilst the people recognised the King, his duties and functions, the King did the same as regards the people. Ancient India possessed a notable substantive law and procedure which, in particulars, has been found even superior to that which we possess to-day. Thus Sir William Markby was of opinion that the English Law of Prescription should be remodelled on the lines of Hindu Law, and the distinguished, and happily still living, lawyer Sir Rashbehary Ghose characterised the Hindu Law of securities " as a model of good sense and logical consistency." The Hindu Spirit politically displayed itself in a form which was worthy of its other great achievements. India has produced men successful in industry and commerce ; though it is often forgotten or unknown that from the date of Greek and Roman civilization until about the close of the eighteenth century India was renowned for

177

12

its artizanship and industries. " The wealth of Ormuz and of Ind " was proverbial. Pliny in fact complains of the drain of gold from Rome to India which furnished the former Imperial Capital with some of its splendours. English experts speaking of its unrivalled beauty and delicacy have described Indian cotton (to take an example) as " the finest the earth produces." Great industrial, artistic and commercial activity is spoken to during the seventeenth and eighteenth centuries by the travellers Pyrard, Jourdan, Roe, Bernier, Peter Mundy, Tavernier. Alexander Dow (History of Hindostan) says that " Bengal from the mildness of its climate, the fertility of its soil, and the natural industry of the Hindus was always remarkable for its commerce." Sj. Narendranáth Law from whose " Notes on the Commerce and Industries of Bengal " (Modern Review) I make these and the following quotations says that the commerce of Bengal continued with unabated briskness up to the middle of the eighteenth century as will appear from Orme's observations made in 1753. In 1678 a loud outcry was made in England against the importation of Indian goods (Baine's History of Cotten Manufacture 7). Heavy duties were imposed. In 1700 an Act was passed against the use of Indian manufactures (Birdwood's Industrial Arts 271.) From various causes, including acts of commercial coercion, the Indian manufactures were by 1813 superseded by the British and by 1837 the people of India became chiefly agricultural instead of being both manufacturing and agricultural. Whilst ever famed for its deep introspection, India was also not without Her men of science with outward-directed mind; limited necessarily as their achievements were if compared with those of our time. Mr. Archer is under the impression that the Hindu's knowledge is obtained by a mechanical " pouring in " from the teacher to the disciple. This is, of course, not so. It seems absurd to have to say that the Hindu, like every one else, admits as a valid source of knowledge, perception (Pratyaksha), inference (Anumâna) and the like and has developed a logic of great subtlety and completeness. Their application to the positive sciences of the Hindus may be found in Professor Brajendra Nath Seal's work of that name. A short and useful summary of " Hindu Achievement in Exact Science " has recently been given by Professor Benoy Kumar Sircar in the " Modern Review." He makes a point to which I have also alluded elsewhere in another connection, namely, that the difference between Asia and Europe in the matter of the so-called exact sciences dates from about three hundred years back, which is the age of experimental and inductive science. It was during this period that the cultural superiority in this particular respect of the Modern West was established ; nor was that superiority great until much later, when during the nineteenth century the application of steam to production and transportation effected the parting of the ways of East and West ushering in " Modernism " with its new world-politics, social institutions, science and philosophy, giving Eur-America its present alleged superiority over Asia. If, however, we compare the Indian contribution to exact positive and material culture with parallel contemporary developments amongst the Greeks, Greco-Roman, Saracen, Chinese and mediæval Europeans the Hindus can make at least an equal and, in some respects, a superior claim to that made by these peoples in respect of scientific culture. In fact, the trend of recent scholarship is towards establishing the Hindu source of Greek science. Much of the credit also given to the Saracen is really due to the Hindus from whom they derived their Mathematics, Chemistry, and Medicine. The Hindus, however, may have been indebted to the Greeks in some cases, as is admitted in respect of Astronomy by Varahamihira. Professor Sircar observes that the pure Mathematics of the Hindus was on the whole not only in advance of some of the Greeks, but anticipated European discoveries of the Sixteenth,

Seventeenth, and Eighteenth Centuries. As Hankel in his history of Mathematics says "It is remarkable to what extent Indian Mathematics enters into the Science of our time." Dr. Morgan says "Indian Arithmetic is that which we now use." The Hindus originated the numerals, wrongly known as Arabic because the Europeans got them from their Saracen teachers, and the decimal system of notation known to Âryabhatta as early as the Fifth Century. Algebra is a Hindu Science despite its Arabic name; for as Cajori says the Indians were "the real inventors of Algebra." Colebrooke has analysed the points in which Hindu Algebra was favourably distinguished from that of the Greeks who, as Cajori thinks, got through Diophantus their Algebraic knowledge from India. Geometry was studied by the Hindus from the date of the Sulvasûtras of Baudhâyana and Âpastamba to Bhâskara in the 12th Century and beyond. In some points the Hindus anticipated Modern Trigonometry devising the Sines (an Arabic corruption of the Sanskrit

Shinjini) and Versed Sines unknown to the Greeks, who calculated by the help of the Chords. Professor Seal says that Vâchaspat, anticipated in a rudimentary manner the foundations of solid (co-ordinate) Geometry Bhâskarâchârya (1114) anticipated Newton by five hundred years in the discovery of the principle of the differential Calculus and its application to Astronomical problems and computations. In Kinetics, the Hindus analysed the concept of motion, gravity, (ascribed to the attraction of the Earth), acceleration, the law of motion and the accelerated motion of falling bodies.

Professor Sircar says that whilst the Hindus may have failed like other races to discover fundamental laws planetary, inorganic and organic if judged by the generalizations of to-day, yet "Some of their investigations were solid achievements in positive knowledge as in Materia Medica, Therapeutics, Anatomy, Embryology, Metallurgy, Chemistry, Physics, and descriptive Zoology. And in these also, generally speaking, Hindu enquiries were not less, if not more, definite, exact and fruitful than the Greeks and Mediæval Europeans." "The Hindu intellect has thus," he rightly says, "independently appreciated the dignity of objective facts, devised the methods of observation and experiment, elaborated the machinery of logical analysis and true investigation, attacked the external universe as a system of secrets to be unravelled, and has wrung out of nature the knowledge which constitutes the foundations of Science." It is quite an error to suppose that the Hindus have had no achievements beyond those in Metaphysics and Religion (in which they are generally admitted to have been pre-eminent): and still more so to suppose with Mr. Archer that they have spent the long ages of their history "in gazing upon their navel."

India in short has produced men and women of great virtue and distinction, together with criminals, sinners and the ordinary men who everywhere make up the bulk of humanity. Those therefore who write against or in praise of India should do so with exactness, discrimination, and the latter with avoidance of mere puffing general statements. Thus shortly before I had written this I came across the following passage " To a Hindu there is no past, present or future. He is always with his God and to him all the universe is always in God " and so on. From writing of this kind (and it is one of a class) one might suppose that every Hindu was thinking at all times of God. Such suggestions are absurd and make the Indian case laughable. The general character of Indian civilization is spiritual but this is not to say that every Hindu is ˙that. In India as elsewhere the bulk of the people are ordinary men and women occupied with the usual thoughts and cares of all such the world over; the better amongst them reflecting in their way and according to their capacity the great thoughts of the highest of their race and thus gaining distinction amongst all the peoples. Some are as worldly minded and material (particularly to-day) as their corresponding class in Europe ; though (for lack of food and other causes) with generally less energy in their materialism than their Western brethren. Some few reach the highest spiritual experience of which the writer cited speaks. As an American humourist said, there is a good deal of human nature in man everywhere. As I walk along the streets of Calcutta a word I overhear perhaps more frequently than any other is "Paisa" or "Ha'pence" which the poor have little of. The middle-class, becoming increasingly indigent, are distraught with the thought of how to find ways and means to educate their sons and marry their daughters. There is indeed a past to which they regretfully look back, a present in which they suffer, and a future which some look forward to with hope and others with fear. Faith sustains some, in other, as in Europe, it is lost. The rich are too often concerned with themselves and the Government honours for which they hunt, and too little with the needs of their country.

Some people are resigned, and some buoyed up by their religious faith; and some are truly spiritual men whose lives and thoughts inspire and maintain their race. We must distinguish between India and the Indian : particularly at the present time when so many have fallen from the ideals of their race.

With all these varieties of men there are differences of belief and practice and degree of spiritual, moral, and intellectual development. When I hear people talk of Indian "Religion" I ask what form of it they mean. The question is disconcerting except to those who will approve nothing but what is their own, and who are out to blame everything. These will find fault with all forms. The so-called "Pantheist" (a misnomer) is said to be given over to "cold abstractionism;" and the Theist to extravagant and misplaced devotion, Buddhism is "atheistic." Monism (advaita-vâda) carries tolerance so far as to be "indifferent to the truth." The sects have so little of it as to be "fanatical." Indian archi-

tecture is demoniacally " titanic." Indian
Painting is too " miniaturist." Râma is
over-saintly. Sîtâ " verges upon the immoral ;" and so on and so forth. At the
back of the minds of such critics is the
notion that nothing Indian is good because
none of it is the same as their own.

Moreover the beliefs and institutions of a
coloured people are apt to be regarded as
inferior. Particularly is this so when that
people is a politically servient one. The
dominant race naturally asks itself why it
is in fact in possession and control, and finds
the cause in its superior civilization. It
asks how can the civilization of the people
which it rules be good ; seeing that they are
subject ? How can its religion have the
power of moral uplift when there is the
lack of that virile side of morality which
subordination implies ?   .

For the purpose of adverse generalizations India is treated as an unity. In this
sense some speak of " Indian religion,".
" Indian philosophy " and " Indian morals "
condemning each en bloc. Political and

religious criticism on the other hand treats it as a mass of irreconcilable differences. Such will ask " What is Hinduism? " These imply that there is nothing to which that name can be given. It is not a people but a medley of various races, so it is said. If this be so, general criticisms cannot be passed. These ask how it is possible to link together " Godless " (Nirîshvara) systems with Theistic theologies ; the monist the qualified monist, and the dualist, the worshippers of the " Idol " and of the " Point of Light " (Jyotirbindu); rituals which in the past have sanctioned human, and to-day practise, animal sacrifice ; and an the other hand believers in the sanctity of all life ; worshippers of millions of " the gods " and Yogîs seeking realization of the " Impersonal " Spirit; strict adherence to caste and sects which combat all caste and so forth. To many a foreigner therefore Indian beliefs and practices seem a " jungle " in which there is no path. There is a path. Meanwhile those who have not found it will save their credit if they avoid generalization on a subject which they do not . understand. As I show later India does possess *a spiritual unity* for it possesses certain common fundamental beliefs. It also displays a wondrous variety of belief and practice suited to the capacities and temperaments of men. One of the most interesting enquiries is that which seeks the Theme of which these are the variations. These Themes will endure whilst their variations may either alter, or pass away.

When in reply to criticism I speak of "India" I mean an Idea apprehended by us as an abstraction derived from present experience and study of the past, which in the Cosmic Mind is a particular type of Consciousness projected with all its variations by Its power or Shakti. The Shakti is both cause and effect and appearing as India is the Bhârata Shakti. Particular men or classes of men in this country embody in varying degrees and well or ill that Powerful Idea. Some even are unfaithful to it.

One of the mistakes which Mr. Archer and his class of critics make is to fail to distinguish between what is essential and vital in the Indian civilization ; and what is mere crust and alien (and even in some cases) evil, accretion. It has been well said that the tree of Indian Dharma is very ancient and it is not therefore surprising if in the course of the ages, some parasites have gathered on its trunk. If he and they were to confine their attention, at least in the first place, to these, they might produce some just criticism and offer some useful advice if either is called for. But Mr. Archer does just the reverse. He attacks the principles of Indian civilization (that is the little which he understands of them) and fails to distinguish between such priciples and what are not their legitimate results,' but abuses due to the weakness and evil of men. A powerful case of a different character might be made against India but he has not the knowledge to make it. Such a case would set forth the principles of Indian civilization in their purity and would thus show how far some of the Indian people have fallen from them in the present time. Such an enquiry might also include an investigation into a matter generally over-looked by those who, like Mr. Archer, speak of the " arrested " development of this coun-try. And that is the influence produced on the pure Âryan culture by the indiscrimi-nate mixing with the earlier peoples which followed on the relaxation of caste produced by Buddhism. When one looks upon some " black Brâhmanas " and " white Shûdras " as they are called, it is seen clearly that we have to deal in the case of the first with the type which is not that form which the principles of this culture first proceeded. But Mr. Archer speaks of all abuses as if they were the legitimate application of principles evil in themselves. Those prin-ciples may be well-founded or not. They differ fundamentally from the "modernism" of the West still in search of sure basis on which to build itself. Men, it may be, will always differ in some of these matters. Difference of opinion, as the Radd-ul-Muhtar nobly says, is also the gift of God.

But this is not necessarily to say that the principles are evil or barbarous. Eastern and Western Civilizations are in fact different but that is not to say that the former is inferior to the latter. In fact who will be so rash as to say that India will not in the future be shown to be right. I speak of general principles. There is scarce a principle which the Western Civilization of the last century has preached which is not called in question and is not on trial to-day. Meanwhile in its past form it threatens to disappear with the smoke of its guns in a War for which all the West was ultimately, though in varying degrees, responsible, because all were responsible for the conditions under which it became possible.

Mr. Archer again lumps together indiscriminately matters which are contrary to the eternal Dharma ; matters unconnected with or unessential to it and often of comparatively recent development ; and matters sanctioned by religion but which have in some degree been misunderstood or mis-

applied and have thus become an abuse. As
instances of the first class we may cite his
charges about female infanticide and Satî.
There have been, in the past, cases of
infanticide limited to particular parts of the
country. But all such acts are condemned
by Indian religion as by any other. Similar
charges have been made against China and
have formed a staple of missionary polemic.
But as Professor Giles has shewn (" Chinese
Civilization ") they are, except as instances
of exceptional aberration, false. This kind
of error dies hard when it serves some
political or religious purpose. Even to-day
there are still many who believe that
Mahomedanism teaches that women have
no souls. Satî, considered not as an act of
truly voluntary devotion, but as a *practice*
which compelled or drugged widows to
immolate themselves was a cruel barbarism.
But it is not sanctioned by the principles of
Indian Dharma, however much some, at
the time of its suppression, endeavoured,
even by the falsification of texts, to show
that it was. On the contrary the Mahâ-

nirvâna Tantra says that woman is the embodiment of the Divine Mother of the universe and that the destruction of women in the Satî rite leads to Hell. Moreover, though cases have very rarely occurred in modern times (I remember to have tried one myself) the rite is so much a thing of the past that to drag it up with infanticide to-day as a charge against India is unscrupulous.

On the second head we may refer, as he does, to the rule against sea voyage. This is a matter upon which Pandits differ and on what do they not? It is not an essential of Indian Dharma. On the contrary Ancient India had a large foreign trade and was in active intercourse through its merchants and sailors with the other countries of the world. The restrictions against sea voyage are of later date and were possibly pres- cribed like other rules with the intention of keeping India together and upholding its Dharma against corrupting alien influence. The rule is now being gradually abrogated. Again the so-called " shutting up " of women

195

by Purdah has nothing to do with Hindu religion. It prevails in certain parts only of India and there in respect of the upper classes only. It was borrowed from the then Mahomedan Rulers, and is still liked by many of the ladies concerned who consider it to be a sign of respectability. In the same way the glamour which attends a dominant race produces amongst the imitative the "have a drink" and "so English" Indian; the type which bans "native dress" from his Club because it is "run on European lines" and brings up his children in "Indian Etons" to segregate them from the common run of Indian folk. One of these, a young man, informed an Indian friend of mine that he belonged to the "upper ten." All such imitative snobbery is alien to the spirit of this country. The education of woman according to modern notions has been neglected, as it indeed was in England until a quite late epoch. This is not the place to narrate the long history of Western women's disablilities or of the low ideas which have been held of their sex.

Woman was to the Hebrews an inferior being. As ·Mrs. Cady Stanton says ("Woman's Bible") "The canon and civil law, Church and State alike taught that woman was made after man, of man, and for man, an inferior being, subject to man." St. Paul and the Christian Fathers approved her inferiority and subjection. Their disdain for her and their contempt for marriage are known. St. Augustine asks himself why She was created at all. She is (to quote some sayings of the Fathers) the "root of all evil" created from a rib of Adam's body not from a part of his soul " " Marriage is good for those who are afraid to sleep at home at night " and so on. In the feudal legislation of Europe woman sank lower and lower. As Mr. Lecky says " woman sank to a lower legal position than she had ever occupied under Paganism, notwithstanding 'the fact that Christianity (and ·in this it was not alone) did introduce into the Roman world some true principles as regards woman. M. Legouvé says (Histoire Morale des Femmes 183) that "under the feudal regime conjugal morals return to brutality." It is not however necessary here to relate ancient history. Mrs. Cady Stanton gives a summary (History of Women's Suffrage iii, 290) of the English Common Law which, basing itself on the alleged inferiority of woman, deprived her of the control of her person and property and made her morally and economically dependent on her husband. Only in 1865, and within the life of every man over fifty, J. S. Mill wrote "The Subjection of woman." Only within the latter half of that period was any advance made to establish her position and rights. It is only but yesterday that the battle seems to have been won. The education of Western woman has only just commenced. In this country also, whatever may have been the primitive condition of the Âryan woman, she was in time brought under subjection. Her inferiority was proclaimed. It was, and is generally, thought to be a misfortune to be born a woman,—as, unhappily, it is sometimes in fact so. She was placed under the

charge of the man. Though some of the
hymns of the Veda were spoken by women
the hearing of the Veda was and is denied
to her as to the Shûdra. In fact the vicious
principle of the inequality of the sexes
asserted itself in this country as in others.
But on the other hand whilst individuals
may have spoken contemptuously of her,
as when woman is said to be " the vessel of
dirt, worms, phlegm and urine" (Shivajnâna-
siddhiyar, i—27) and sexual union is spoken
of as a thing to be abandoned, in the style
of the ascetic the world over, nothing that
I am aware of is to be found in the Hindu
Shâstras which equals the defamatory
statements of the Christian Fathers, nor is
there a scriptural sanction for their inferiority such as that which is implied in the
legend of Genesis. On the contrary many
beautiful sayings are found which give
honour to woman, marriage, and mother-
hood, and Hindu law recognises her rights
of property (Stridhan). In the Shâkta
Tantra in particular, woman is regarded as
a Divinity, as the earthly representative

of the great Mother of all. Over and over again do they prescribe that no injury be done her, that no ill-word even be spoken to her, but that she should be honoured always. The sexual relation also is divinised. It does not lessen nor detract from the truth and beauty of these principles that they have been applied by some in a manner which has led to abuse. The history of India tells of many women great in learning, administration, and battle-prowess from Gârgî, Maitreyî onwards, and there were many more doubtless who are unknown to fame. The reader of Bengali will find an account of some of these in Pandit Hari Deva Shâstri's useful little book on some of the great women of India. It is obvious however that, for some ages past, the Indian woman has suffered some evils and one of them is the neglect to give her the opportunity of that full education which is both her right and need. This is not to say that Indian women were, or are altogether, lacking in culture any more than the Indian peasant is. The late Sir George

Birdwood called the latter the most cultivated peasantry in the world. It is true that
(to borrow the words of Mr. G. K. Chesterton
concerning the Russian peasant whom the
Indian peasant, in some respects, resembles)
the latter knows little or nothing of modern
science, commerce or machinery. He ploughs
with an old plough, is scantily clad, and has
nothing but his faith, his fields, his great
courage in facing a life as rude and hard
as a subject of Alfred the Great, but he is
truly civilised in so far as he shares in, to
the limit of his capacity, the great cultural
traditions of his country. Education and
literacy are not one and the same. No
sensible person objects now-a-days to the
education of Indian women. The discussion
rightly centres round the question what
that education is to be. The views which
generally prevail in India are rather like
those which were generally entertained in
England during the Suffrage Movement
by its more moderate opponents, which
still have some support there; and which
exist over the greater part of the European

Continent. Personally I am in favour of giving the fullest opportunities to women, believing that nature is more to be trusted than man ; but it must be admitted that time has yet to show whether the older views based on the more rigid application of the physiological and psychological differences of men and women, or those of the " advanced " and free school will be found to be the more correct. This is not when examined so much a question of the " inferiority " or " rights " of woman but a difference of opinion upon the question as to the nature of the education which woman should receive. If we believe, as the Shâktas do, that woman is visible Divinity we cannot go astray, or do her wrong so long as that belief is truly given effect to.

Instances of the third class of criticism are the rules relating to caste and marriage. As regards marriage there is a considerable literature which those who are interested may read: The learned differ upon the question whether Shâstric authority supports a state of affairs of which they complain either as regards early marriage or widow re-marriage. Until this matter is settled it is obviously premature to charge the true principles of Indian civilization with any abuses which have occurred. There have been abuses in connection with the first but the present tendency is to raise the age of marriage. If even then it seems early judged by recent Western views, according to which marriage is becoming more and more deferred, it should be remembered that under the English common law a girl could be married at twelve and was in fact in past times married early; that girls attain puberty much earlier in this country than in the colder West; and that the Hindu insists on marriage for all men and women in the world both in the interests of the conservation of the race, and as a safeguard from the sexual errors which abound amongst men, and are now commencing to affect woman, in the West.

Indian Caste, it is claimed, arose naturally under the influences of the unifying forces of advancing civilization to bring about the best possible kind of unity and concord among the many heterogeneous communities ("Hindu Message" II. 383). It is on the question of caste which is, according to orthodox views, a part of the Hindu Dharma, that Mr. Archer, like most other Western critics, shows himself most angered. He says that in India "the most inhuman snobbery is a religious duty" and that caste "has corrupted Indian morality making insensate arrogance a religious and social duty." To speak of "snobbery" in connection with caste is to wholly misunderstand the matter. Sociology shows the existence of caste everywhere as rulers, warriors, merchants, agriculturists, servile population and so forth. These distinctions did not arise from snobbery but from the inherent needs of society and its organisation. Classes, and (in a practical sense), castes exist in the West to-day. Many are of opinion that classes will always exist however much they may shift. Thus Professor Giddings the sociologist says "classes do not become blended as societies grow older; they become more sharply defined." He considers that "any social reform that hopes for the blending of classes is foredoomed to failure." The notion that "all men are equal" either in work, capacity or utility is unfounded. In modern Europe the sociological and economic order has not necessarily anything to do with religion at all. In fact country after country has separated Church and State. This was otherwise at the time of the great Catholic Synthesis, which the ": Reformation," Renaissance, French Revolution, and other modern movements destroyed. In fact, modern Europe is without any settled foundation or aim. On all matters there is a chaotic difference of opinions some of which contain the seed of disruption which the late great war will complete.

The main class divisions in modern Europe and America are between the rich or those comparatively so, and the poor or relatively poor. The man of wealth is the man of worth and power. Those to whom he is not so are either adherents of the old religious ideas, or modern reforming social movements. Of the time when he wrote, Professor Giddings, in his principles of Sociology, says: " Upon a review of some parts of Europe and America, it may be inferred that in a community whose life is a tireless pursuit of materialistic ends—in which money getting is the sum of success —there will be a sharp separation of the successful from the unsuccessful classes and an exploitation of the poor by the rich as wanton and as merciless as that of the weak by the strong in societies of military character. The laws will favour the prosperous, the mercenary spirit will corrupt judgment and religion alike." Whether the present revolution which Europe is undergoing will stay this process remains to be seen.

The ideal Indian scheme of social order is based on religious and philosophical principles which are also the practical ideals of daily life. The original Indian castes spoken of in the Scripture were, as is well known, four. To-day there are practically only two main castes the Brâhmana and the Shûdra ; just as of the four Âshramas only two survive—the Grihastha and Avadhûta. It is in the last or Shûdra caste that the multitude of sub-castes have developed according to the nature of the occupations. The secular occupations of the castes are called Vrittis. Whilst each caste is expected to confine itself¦¡to its own prescribed calling, it is said that some latitude is allowable according to necessity in the case of the three higher castes, which however, if too freely availed of (as we see to-day in the case of Brâhmanas in non-Brâhmana occupations), results in spiritual deterioration. Confusion generally exists in the minds of Western¦:writers on the subject of the castes and those " untouchables " outside all castes called Panchama and Pariah. The question of " untouchability ": (Asprishya) must be distinguished from that of caste. The Pariah is regarded as unclean and in fact his habits are generally so. For this reason (that is for fear of pollution) he is not allowed to use the water wells of the castes. Nevertheless the neglect of the Panchamas has been inhumane; a fact which has led to their conversion to Christianity in the hope of better social treatment. If their surroundings are unsanitary they should be taught and helped to put this right. There is a strong movement to remedy these evils even amongst those who adhere to the caste system as between themselves. The two matters of untouchability in connection with the Panchamas, and of the castes should therefore be distinguished.

The two essentials of caste are the prohibitions against inter-marriage and eating in common. As regards the latter, Hindus do not attach so much importance to this form of social intercourse as do Europeans and particularly the English. It is quite possible to be on friendly terms with a man and to hold him in high esteem without eating with him: and in fact, subject to the two prohibitions stated, the castes mix with one another in a way which is not the case with the European classes. To quote the words of an educated and distinguished negro, the late Mr. Booker Washington, " In all things which are purely social we can be as separate as the fingers, yet one in the hand in all things essential to mutual progress." Moreover where (as in India) there is a rule which is kept there is no humiliation. Even in England the " gentleman " (a term losing its social distinction) and his tradesman, and still less his labourer, do not meet at table. Again in England, and still more so on the continent, interclass marriages do not generally take place. The substantial distinction is that, in the West, class is theoretically flexible, though in fact the rise from one class to another only takes place in exceptional instances. In India caste is inflexible whatever it may have been in the past, in which some think it was not so, as evidenced by the cases of Drona and Vishvamitra. In India again the rule relating to inter-marriage and inter-dining is kept rigidly by those who observe the caste system. In the West a man may dine with his "inferiors" at the risk of a charge of eccentricity and of giving offence to those of the same station if he asks them to do what he does. A man who thus regularly associated with his "inferiors" would probably find that his own class refused his invitations. In the India of caste there is no snobbery at all. For instance, an Indian Lawyer whom I knew, a man of considerable landed property and money, used to take his meals at the High Court with his servant who attended him there—a man of humble position, perhaps earning 13s. and 4d. a month. In England a man may occasionally take a lunch on the moors with the appendage of aristocracy or wealth called a Gillie, but where will we find a "gentleman" of wealth habitually taking his meals with an ordinary common servant? On the other hand the humblest Brâhmana would not take his food with the wealthiest and greatest Mahârâjah. This illustrates con-cisely the difference between caste-exclusiveness and class-snobbery. Where the latter exists in this country, and that rarely, it is amongst those who have adopted English notions, as in the case of the young Bengali (whose father was a rich man) who told a friend of mine that he belonged to " the upper ten." He had learnt the word and the idea it denotes in England. In the same way there is in England a liberty to " marry beneath one " but those who do so may "be cut off with a shilling " and socially " boycotted " unless they happen to possess that open sesame which is wealth. For to the God of Money many make the fullest obeisance. It comes therefore to this that in India we see an ancient system logically and inflexibly applied. In Europe change is theoretically admitted and in some cases takes place in fact. As I write these lines I read that proposals have been recently published in South Africa precluding all coloured persons, Negro or otherwise, from travelling on the railway in compartments reserved for white men or in mail or other notified trains; and marriage between white women and Negroes. Those who think that the reasons which prompt this proposed legislation are sound cannot, without inconsistency, condemn the restrictions imposed as regards the relation of castes, and as between the castes and the pariahs. What is the difference in principle between a rule prohibiting a Negro from marriage with a white woman, or association with white men when travelling (custom excluding relations in other cases) and a rule prohibiting association and marriage between, say, a high Braâmana and a Pariah and his women? In the same way those Indians who protest against distinctions being made against themselves should remember that their caste system assumes the same principle on which distinctions are based.

I am not here concerned to show which of these views is correct but to point out certain common misconceptions and the rational basis on which the rule of caste rests. In this connection an Indian writer (" Hindu Message ") has acutely pointed

out one of the differences of view, here
mentioned, between India and the West.
The former has always attached primary
importance to subjective development; that
is development and strengthening of the
individual Psyche and body according to its
nature (Svadharma). This principle as I
have already pointed out governs also the
inter-state and inter-racial relations.

India has always held that, as between
the soul and its material environment, the
former is of primary importance. Indeed
strong souls are independent of environment and make it subserve their
purposes. The notion, which Mr. Archer
echoes, that man according to Indian
theories " rises and falls as helplessly and
purposelessly as the waves of the ocean "
is born of an excessive ignorance. In no
country in the world has greater insistence
been laid on 'the fact that man is free and
the maker of his destiny. What therefore
has to be strengthened is the organism
which is the bearer of individual character.
If this be done, such adjustment as is

necessary to the environment becomes easier. In India a systematic attempt has been made to preserve and transmit the Guna of the " Ids " of the germ-plasm, as Weismann calls them, from father to son : in the face of opposition from individual emotions and interests. Spiritual growth is mainly dependent on the organism and on the exercise of the Svadharma appropriate to it. This has been kept in mind in the evolution of the Indian social organism.; for the social aim has been self-conquest (Jitendriya) self-rule (Svarâjya-siddhi) and liberation (Moksha) for the individual spirit or Jîva. On the other hand the social aim of the modern West has been largely the conquest of the external environment, which it has sought to effect through a variance of the " Ids " entering into the constitution of the germ-plasm, so as to enable the organism to more and more adapt itself to the environment.

I cannot here more fully enter into this matter which is based on certain fundamental concepts of Indian Philosophy.

Suffice to say that the factors or Gunas of the ultimate material cause (Prakriti) of both mind and matter display themselves variously not only in man but throughout all created being; not only in the bodily matter but in the inner psychical tendency or Sangskâra which gives rise to individual mind. The souls are born into bodies suitable to them and thus the four castes or Varnas were, it is said, created by the Lord (Îshvara) according to the division of Guna and Karma, that is the Svadharma or the particular Dharma of each being. Without the acceptance of this doctrine, caste largely loses its significance. According to the Western view this is not so. The Christian teaching is that a soul pure as it leaves God is by special relation placed in any kind of body, which may be either good or bad, and there commences its experiences for the first time. To the Eastern, as to many Westerns, such a notion is irrational. Caste appears to the Western a hardship because he ordinarily does not believe in the past or future births.

Man's only chance is, according to him, in this birth. The orthodox Hindu holds that the soul is born into a body which is suitable to its previous merit or demerit and acquirements; that man's caste is fixed for a particular birth; but that if it is a low caste he may by fulfilling its duties and by self-development qualify himself in future births for a higher or the highest caste. One caste does not consider itself superior by reason of wealth or social standing. Such snobbishness is a mark of class-distinctions in the West. In India a man is not despised because he is poor and of humble occupation as he often is in the West. The present caste is an＊indication of the measure of merit and demerit in previous births. Subject to caste rules, there is social association. The Brâhmana mind, even as it now exists, has in general a distinctive and high quality which other castes lack. This is due to heredity largely maintained, but obviously not wholly so, seeing the colour of many Brâhmanas to-day. A true Brâhmana should not give

216

way to pride any more than to any other sin ; otherwise he will become a degraded Brâhmana in this birth and possibly of the lowest birth in his next life. It is a mistake to suppose that the caste-system is a " system of group morality." Those who so speak do not know what Dharma means. Sâmânya Dharma or the general rules of morality govern all castes and all men. Each man must be truthful, charitable, just, free from pride and so forth. It is the particular rules called Nishesha Dharma which bind only members of a particular caste. As a matter of fact the high caste of a Brâhmana connotes more rigorous injunctions (Niyama) than those imposed on the Shûdra. The result which (as recently pointed out by H. H. Shrî Shangkarâchâryya at Kumba-konam) the latter can attain by a minimum of Niyama, is only to be had by the Brâhmana through a maximum of the same. The followers of the Varnâshramadharma do not, like adherents of some other religions, hold that those who follow their own religious faith are less fitted for salvation than themselves. Any one who follows the Dharma of his own caste ; any non-Hindu who follows the Dharma of his own religion with faith in its truth and in God will necessarily rise in the scale of spiritual growth and have that material and spiritual happiness to which his actions and knowledge entitle him. It need hardly be said that in fact we do not find these high ideals always kept ; nor do Christians always keep theirs. Fault is not attributable to the Eternal Dharma. The fall of the Hindu is due to his not keeping it. Thus the Brâhmanas who were once respected as the " Guardians of the Treasury of Dharma " have now (in the words of H. H. Shrî Shangkarâchâryya of Karvir Pîtha at the last " All India Hindu Conference ") often " become objects of ridicule and contempt." Those who should live austerely and simply are now in the scramble for place, wealth, and power. It is no wonder that, in the degree in which they are unfaithful to their duties, their claims are resisted. Sir George Campbell in his book dealing with the relation of Blacks and Whites in America, says:—" In India I have had the experience of how communities of people varying in culture, rank, and racial qualifications have lived for centuries amicably together side by side: and this has been possible in India only through the organisation of caste." The well-known educationist Dr. William Miller of the Madras Christian College said that the solidarity of man was more markedly recognised in Hinduism than in any other religion (" Hindu Message," II. 383).

An American Author Mr. Price Collier (" The East in the West " pp. 222, 223) after pointing out that in ancient India poverty was no disgrace but birth and caste counted, says " Now India is being inoculated with the economic lymph of the West. What a man accumulates and holds counts. This is new to India. This situation adds to the existing discontent. It is easier to be good than to be rich and vulgar, but many, none the less, are being influenced to prefer the latter. Their own miseries were not enough. They have now this new source of discontent, the poison of the West ; the standard of money." The same author says (p. 229) that " the European Christians in India are a caste by themselves who will not hear of much social intercourse or marriage, while Christians refuse to meet African Christians even at the sacrament. Much more strongly do they persist in ostracizing them socially." One hears the same tales about communion and other services for natives in India.. On the other hand Professor C. H. Pearson said " The Roman Catholic Church has habitually treated Black and White as equals before the altar " (National life and character 210). I myself have seen in this country a separate cemetery for Indian Christians. Even when under the soil they must be kept apart. I was told that this was because their graves were not kept clean. I do not know which is more pitiable, the fact or the explanation. And yet we hear talk of the absurdity and iniquity of Indian caste. Let us be honest. If we condemn all exclusiveness let us get rid of it amongst ourselves, where it exists in some of its worst forms as the money-standard or a base form of racial prejudice. If we hold to the principle (and something may be said for exclusiveness) let us say nothing about its application in India.

I am not concerned to advocate the caste system. This is a matter for Indians themselves to decide. If they really want to get rid of it, it will disappear, for certainly no one else will hold them to it. But if they do not, it is because it still fulfils some useful purpose in their social organism, notably in defending it from disintegration under European influences. For the contrary reason, some* Westerns advocate it as the means of breaking up the Hindu social structure and with it Hindu religion. I believe that, with the removal of all danger of aggression from outside influences, the caste system would largely modify itself in a manner favourable to the views of those now opposed to it. Even some of the orthodox do not deny that the caste system has its drawbacks, and a dark side. But they claim that it has a bright and beneficial side also. After all, this is the case with every human institution. To me it seems that some of the evils connected with caste are not necessary to it. Thus the mere fact of social distinctions need not destroy the sense of human brotherhood. I know of a case where an Indian servant did things for his sick English master which were contrary to his caste rules, but which the necessities of his master called for, and which the servant's devotion to him accorded. But in practice it may operate badly.

There are without doubt abuses in all these matters. There are also some barbarisms both in the pejorative sense, and in the sense of incomplete development, according to Western ideas. Whether these latter are always right is another matter. But what country in the world is without them in the eye of another? The missionary is apt to place before the Indian an idealized picture

222

of " Christian " Europe : for the actual facts
tell against the Christianity which he
preaches to the Indian people as being a
more potent influence for good than their
own religion. The facts are now becoming
known and some who have been there for
themselves have begun to complain of
deception. Those Easterns who, now that this
war has ended, will read the books which
each of the contending parties have written
against the other, will find a store of material
with which to confound the pretensions of
each. Meanwhile any intelligent Indian
who has passed a few years in Europe can
make a case against it of barbarism and
wrong in the form of crime (let the criminal
statistics be compared) vice (intemperance,
sordid prostitution, white slavery and sexual
perversities previously unknown in this
country of which Elphinstone wrote " Their
freedom from gross debauchery is the point
in which they appear to most advantage
and their superiority in purity of manners
is not flattering to our self-esteem ") cruelty
to children and animals (in Europe, societies

for their protection are necessary—kindness to and love of children are a marked trait of the Indian people and so is their respect for animal life, notwithstanding some modern cruelties amongst the low such as the carters and Goalas of the towns. In Europe also there is unnecessary killing of animals in " sport " and horrible crimes in connection with vivisection); lack of cleanliness (the Anglo-Indian taught his home-people the daily bath): evil customs and social injustice (such as regards the latter the grinding and "sweating" of the poor); vulgarity (which scarce here exists); irreligion; crude religion, and many a superstition; political aggression and so on; all of them the more odious because parts of an organised system which is predominantly to-day (as contrasted with ideals of the Christian past) a worship of mere material success. All this is not to deny the presence of great qualities and virtues amongst some and the truly spiritual endeavours which these make towards the general betterment of Humanity. In truth if we were all sane and modest in our self-appreciation we should discover quickly that no people or country is free from blame. We should then effect good to others and escape the charge of hypocrisy against ourselves. If the merits of all peoples were balanced, India would appear high in the scale. Men are not yet Man. Some have been and are so. The rest are still candidates for Humanity.

IX

BHÂRATA DHARMA
AND THE COMMON PRINCIPLES OF
INDIAN CIVILIZATION

WHAT then are the common religious
and philosophical ideas to which I have
referred? As in the case of the terms
"Civilization" and "Progress," so very
varying, and sometimes vague, notions are
held as to the meaning of the word
"Religion." In its most fundamental sense
Religion is the *recognition that the world
is an Order* or Cosmos of which each man
is a part and to which he stands in a
definitely established relation; together
with *action* based on and consistent with
such recognition and *in harmony* with the
whole cosmic activity. The religious man
is thus he who feels that he is *bound* in
varying ways to all being; just as the
irreligious man is he who egoistically considers everything from the standpoint of

his limited self and its interests, without regard for his fellows or the world at large. The essentially irreligious character of such an attitude is shown by the fact that, if it were adopted by all, it would lead to the negation of Cosmos, that is, Chaos. It has thus been noted (B. Swift " Ludus Amoris ") that the primary cause of probably every organic degeneration is a fact of profound moral significance. Disease begins in the attempt of one isolated cell to set itself up independently of the rest, with the result that all its neighbours become its prey. The benign feudalism of health, in which all the members obey a central control, disappears in disease. It is in short in the infernal egoism of cellular life that all organic disease springs.' In fact there is an accurate parallelism between anarchism in the social community and in the physical organism. Life and morality are harmony. For the same reason all religions are agreed in condemning selfishness and in holding that, in its widest sense, it is the root of all sin and crime (Adharma). These acts are wrong conduct on the part of the individual limited self (Jîva) productive of suffering. The Vedânta goes further, holding that all ignorant notion (Avidyâ) of such a self, whether issuing in good or bad action leading to happiness or pain, binds to the world of birth and death (Sangsâra). According to the ideas here discussed this Order or Cosmos, that is existence according to Dharma the Universal Law, is not conceived as arbitrarily produced and governed by some merely extra-cosmic God. The order or Dharma is inherent in, and manifested by, all beings and denotes their true nature and qualities; in fact that which constitutes them what they are. Morality is the true nature of man. The general Dharma (Sâmânya Dharma) is thus the universal law, just as the particular Dharma (Vishesha Dharma) varies with and is peculiar to, each class of being.

To this general concept the common faith of India adds others. The universe is held to be rooted in desire for enjoyment in the world of form; that is desire which seeks for itself the fruits of its actions. Desire manifests in action (Karma) which may be either good (Dharma) or bad (Adharma). Desire governed by Dharma is legitimate on the path of worldly enjoyment (Pravritti Mârga). Man's three ends are then Law (Dharma), Desire (Kâma), and the Means (Artha) by which lawful desires may be given effect. These are known as the Trivarga of the Purushârtha. But desire should be controlled lest it stray into sin: and so that man may become more and more the master of himself. Those who seek the fourth Purushârtha or Liberation (Moksha) and are on the path of Renunciation (Nivritta Mârga) generally live lives of increasing asceticism. Both kinds of action bind the individual soul (Jîva) to the world of forms: and necessarily so, because those souls which desire embodied life get it, whether their activity in such life be good or bad. But whilst action with desire (Sakâma Karma), whether good or bad, binds to the universe of form which as such is the worlds of birth and death; yet there is this difference between the two, that good action leads to happiness and bad action to suffering; not merely, if at all, in this birth, but (since the soul survives physical death) in future states of happiness and suffering and in future births on earth. For, according to views accepted throughout India, the soul is not born once only but many times both in the past and future; the conditions under which it manifests on earth being (according to the general law of cause or effect) the result of actions (Karma) of previous births; just as present actions are the cause of conditions in future births. These multiple reincarnations are called Sangsâra or "Wandering" in the Worlds of birth and death. The law of Karma is the law of action according to which man has made himself what he is and makes himself what he will be; being thus the master of his destiny in the Sangsâra and having the the power to transcend it. The world, as being limited, is transitory and liable to suffering. There is however a state of eternal, blissful, unchanging Peace beyond all words and understanding called Liberation or Moksha or Nirvâna, which is known as the fourth end and aim of man (Purushârtha). This can be realised by the practice of morality, acquisition of purity of mind through spiritual discipline (Sâdhanâ) and by direct knowledge (Aparoksha Jnâna). There is thus a moral law (Dharma) which, in its essentials, is the same as that held by all other peoples. Man is enjoined to follow that law; the sanction of morality being ensuing sorrow and happiness and the necessity of right action as a preliminary condition of direct and eternal Spiritual Experience (Moksha). The universe thus exists for a moral purpose, namely, as providing a field upon which man suffers and enjoys the fruit of his actions, and wherein man may attain his supreme end which is liberation (Moksha) from the suffering worlds of form and thus the attainment of Eternal Bliss. True civilization consists in the upholding of Dharma as the individual and general good and the fostering of spiritual progress so that, with justice to all beings, the immediate and ultimate ends of Humanity may be attained.

The aforegoing statement very shortly expresses the *General* Indian Religion or Bhârata Dharma. Excluding Religions foreign to India such as the Semitic Mahomedanism, and Christianity, and Persian Zoroastrianism, the three chief Branches of Indian Religion are Brâhmanism or "Hinduism" (to use a popular term), Buddhism (now practically displaced, except through its influence, in the land of its birth), and Jainism. As Professor Rhys Davids has said "Gautama's whole training was Brahmanical. Buddhism is the product of Hinduism. He probably deemed himself to be the most perfect exponent of the spirit as distinct from the letter of the ancient faith." He was a Yogî who taught the principles of the Jnânakânda; given to meditation, laying stress on the destruction of the thirst for worldly things and on compassion (Karunâ) for all beings, just as Krishna does in the

Bhagavadgîtâ. It is noteworthy here that he is an incarnation (Avatâra) of the Hindu Religion and that his Avatâra succeeds that of Srî Krishna. He taught Dharma, Karma, Sangsâra, deliverance from Avidyâ in Nirvâna, practised Dhyâna and experienced Samâdhi. Buddhism is not, as this Professor says, atheistic though one understands why an European might call it so. It was possibly owing to the later developments of Buddhism which Shangkarâchâryya combated, that his Avatâra was said in Puranic times to have been for the purpose of misleading and destroying men. Professor de la Vallée Poussin rightly says " A mon avis c'est un abus que d'accuser les Bouddhistes d'athéisme ; au moins ont-ils pris pleine conscience d'un des aspects du divin " (" Bouddhisme " 70). Nor is Jainism "atheistic." The state of the Siddhânta is that of Godhead., It does not however identify what is a state with a solitary Being. Its first Tîrthangkara Rishabdeva is said in the Bhâgavata Purâna to have been an Avatâra of Vishnu ; and

the 22nd Arhat of the Jainas, Shrî
Neminâtha is, I am told, described as a
cousin of Shrî Krishna. As regards the
Jainas and the Vedânta I may refer my
readers to the address of the President-elect
of the Syadvad Jaina Mahâmandala in
December 1903.

The General Indian Religion or Bhârata
Dharma is the doctrine and practice *upon
which all these three branches are agreed*,
that is, the doctrines of Dharma, Karma,
Sangsâra, Purushârtha, Pravritti, and
Nivritti Mârga and their implications
above stated, as also what Mr. Archer calls
" Asceticism " and " Pessimism," the true
meaning of which however is stated later.

The divisions of the general Bhârata
Dharma as Brâhmanism, Buddhism, and
Jainism have other doctrines and practices
peculiar to themselves, and are each
subdivided again into various Schools and
Sects with peculiarities of their own. As
it is not possible to speak in terms of all
these varieties of Indian belief I write
from the standpoint of those worshippers of

the Brahmanical Branch of the Bhârata
Dharma who are called Shâktas. Like all
other Indian Schools they accept the
common principles of the Bhârata Dharma
and present on this basis a particular
version of the monistic (Advaitavâda)
Vedânta of the Brahmanical branch of the
Bhârata Dharma.

Though Mr. Archer's understanding of
the subject is incorrect, he has rightly seized
upon Karma, Reincarnation or Sangsâra,
and the theories and practices which he
calls " Pessimism " and " Asceticism " as
fundamental doctrines of the general
Indian religion ; though he of course adds
that " they are not symptoms of high
spirituality or idealism in the people which
has evolved and lived upon them." To
refute all his statements on these matters,
this short essay would not suffice. I am
only here concerned (and that only in a
very general way) with the notion that
these doctrines and practices are the cause
of the generally " barbarous " condition of
the country ; that they are not and cannot

be the foundations of a " pure or moral " religion ; and that they have so moulded the Indian mind for evil that before this country can be admitted into the circle of independent peoples it must throw over these principles and adopt something more wholesome and rational in their stead. For owing to these doctrines and the Vedânta the Indian people are said to lack will-power, to be deficient in energetic dominant personality ; to be without desire and power to " progress ; " to have a weak grip on life which is deemed of no value ; to be dreamers holding the world to be unreal and cowardly fugitives from it.

Philosophically speaking the charge of "Pessimism" amounts to this. The Hindu, like the true Christian, says that the world is a passing thing, and still more so is his life therein. However fortunate that life may be for a few, it is for the body of men mingled with suffering. For some it is practically little but suffering. Therefore perfect lasting happiness cannot be had in the world. Both of these are obvious facts of present experience. But all men seek happiness. Some Westerns in modern times have thought that it is possible to abolish unhappiness, sin, crime, and disease and to make the world an Earthly Paradise. May it be so. The Hindu believes that in the recurring cycles of time there is a perfect age or Satya Yuga along with imperfect and evil ages. But he (whether rightly or wrongly) does not believe it to be possible that the world can be made perfect as regards all beings at one and the same time for all the length of its existence. And if it could, he asks what then ? For he denies that any form of material or intellectual happiness can suffice to stay man's longing for that Eternal state of Bliss which is his true inner nature and is theologically called God. If this be Pessimism then all the great religions are pessimist. But he is also, like the Christian, optimistic. For both say that there *is* a release from suffering and an Eternal Peace. It is true that in the degree that Europe has become " modern " and " pro-

gressive" it has ceased to be Christian,
either in the Church sense, or in that of
Christ Himself, whose Yoga doctrines
taught that true and lasting Bliss is only
to be had in the union of the world in his
Christ-Nature and of both in the "Father."
In truth much of this Europe is not honest
with itself and is not Christian at all, how-,
ever much it may use the name. Nevertheless it has never been said that Europe
was pessimistic until it took to these new
ideas within the last half century. England
in particular was once called " Merry
England." But when ? Before the " Reformation" when the ideas which Hindus
hold in this matter, as also as regards
" Asceticism," were fully dominant. But
there is in fact a great deal of sadness in
India. Any people who are inherently
great and have achieved much, but have
fallen and are subject to foreign rule must
be sad. If they were not they would be
ignoble. And then they are materially
miserable through poverty and disease.
Probably few English readers are aware

that as I write this there are over 30,000 deaths *a week* from plague and over 10,000 deaths from malaria, not to count other diseases, such as diabetes and consumption which is in the towns commencing its ravages. We speak of the mortality on the battle front. But what of this? Again the country is very poor. Though portions of it may be better off a large part of it never knows what it is to be sufficiently fed. Everywhere there is a lack of food. Though it is of course possible that there is a strain of melancholy native to the Indian as to other highly sensitive peoples, it is to the material circumstances we must first look rather than to philosophical theories of " Pessimism." Literary men moreover are often apt to take " bookish " views. " Pessimistic " utterances are to be found in both Indian and Christian literature. They do not necessarily represent the outlook of all the persons whose race has produced them. The Catholic Liturgy speaks of man weeping and wailing in this " Vale of Tears " as it calls the world ; a pessimistic utterance if there ever was one. Nevertheless one may see in the Churches prosperous sleek men and worldly women reciting these words about the " Vale of tears " and then going home to enjoy life thoroughly ; commencing with a Sunday lunch with the customary round or sirloin of beef, horseradish sauce and Yorkshire pudding. Whatever their Scriptures may say, they find the " Vale of tears " to be a happy one which they are loathe to leave. Death sorely tests the sincerity of those who hymn their desire to meet their God. Many would defer this visit. There is not the same amount of material happiness in India. But many doubtless are not too greatly depressed by the melancholy sayings of their Scriptures if they know of them. The vital impulse is nearly always everywhere insurgent in some degree against these sad reflections. As a matter of fact Hindus hold that the world is a duality (Dvandva) of both good and evil. When it is spoken of as evil, this is relative to heavenly and eteral bliss.

If the evil aspect of the universe is sometimes emphasized it is with the view to stimulate man towards sustained effort to win his ultimate end and not to tarry on a way fraught with dangers.

Mr. Archer then demands whether there is any token of spiritual genius in " Asceticism." That depends of course on our point of view. It does not accord with his theory that India should learn to " want more wants; " nor where it is adopted will commercialism do " big business." Most will agree, in theory at least, that desires should be controlled, because, without some restraint, the strength of natural passion is likely to lead to sin and crime particularly when we fan the flame of desire by " wanting more wants." Ordinarily however Asceticism is understood rather as referring to more rigorous control amounting to austerity (Tapas), positive self-denial, and mortification of the flesh ; sometimes associated with the notion that the carnal and material world is evil. As regards the last the world is what we make it, as the old Buddhist Krishnâchâryyapâda said. The nature of Asceticism varies according to the degree of its practice and the reason for it. Hinduism requires a certain amount of Asceticism even for those living in the world, such as occasional fasting, just as the Catholic Church does. Neither is excessive. Those however upon the path of renunciation are naturally given to stricter, though not irrational, Asceticism, whilst some (such as a class of Hathayogîs and others) have pushed their practices to great extremes. The same happened in the West in the early days of Christianity and the Catholic middle ages. Professor Hopkins, the American Orientalist, who writes superciliously of Indian religion says that Asceticism is not part of Christianity. This extraordinary statement about what I suppose is his own religion, or what at any rate ought to be known to him, is a gauge of the value of his opinions on the religions of India. Jesus has said in His

Yoga doctrine that men should leave.all,
follow Him and take up the cross of self-
denial. So far from " wanting more wants "
they are not to lay up the treasure " which
moth and worm corrupt ; " they are not to
save for the morrow, but to be " as the
lilies of the field ; who toil not neither do
they spin." And so we find hundreds of
men and women, who in the belief that
they were following Him, abandoned the
world and practised extreme austerity ;
Simon Stylites standing on a pillar, Hein-
rich Suzo torturing himself throughout the
years, Joseph Labre keeping himself dirty
and verminous, and the Blessed Lidwine
of Schiedam drinking the water mixed
with blood, pus, and scales of skin with
which she had washed the limbs of lepers
and other suffering diseased. In all this
exaggeration one can discover the usual
western coarsening of the teachings of
Jesus. Mr. Archer brings up " the filthy
and disgusting creatures daubed with
ashes " and so forth. As a matter of fact
most of these are quite clean, the ashes

being applied after the morning bath. Some classes of religious mendicants seem to outward view dirty; and a number of persons exhibit a doubtful, when not fraudulent, Asceticism " for ha'pence. Some are truly spiritual men. Mr. Archer misunderstands the doctrine of detachment when he says it is not profound at all (what Indian doctrine is so to him?), but " merely the exaggeration of a common and somewhat pusillanimous rule of prudence" which is "anti-social,""incompatible with rational ethics," " hedging against destiny " and the like. As in so many other matters he is here beyond his depth. Detachment does not necessarily mean remaining away from the world, but is compatible with every action therein, including all forms of social service. It means that what is done is so accomplished without selfish purpose and not for the fruit. A man who does good because it will be advertised, because he will profit by it, because he will get social credit, or because he will go to heaven, is not superior

to him who does all this detachedly for
good's sake and without hope of gain for
himself. One is reminded here of the well-
known Hymn of St. Francis Xavier and of
what St. Bernard says of the "mercenary"
worshipper. To quote the words of a seventeenth century work "Non diligititaque
Deum qui a Deo non quaerit nisi Deum"
(Amor Pœnitens I—ix—5). Even those who,
like the western monk, leave the world, do
so because of their dispassion (Vairâgya) and
not because according to Western notions and
in Bookmaker's language they are "hedging" on anything. Seeing that men are
of varying worth and animated by various
motives it would be hazardous to deny that
some of these may have been actuated by
fear of the world or other weak motive.
When all is said the instances of true and
rigorous asceticism anywhere are rare. Man
is so prone to pleasure and fearful of pain
that we need not worry ourselves over the
thought that the world is in danger from
asceticism. It was never less so than in
the present age. Let us however encourage

the simplification of life even at the cost of running counter to the trader's philosophy.

Let us look at the matter broadly and freely and then we shall see that as a matter of fact there is no religion which more justly and logically balances the claims of the life of the world and the life of spirit than does Hinduism. Its principles are opposed to all false Asceticism. This is seen in the Purushârtha, the Âshrama, and the distinction of life upon the two paths of enjoyment (Pravritti Mârga) and renunciation (Nivritti Mârga). The Trivarga of the first are Morality (Dharma), moral desire (Kâma), and the means (Artha), namely, wealth and so forth, by which lawful desires may be lawfully realized. Man in the world is encouraged to seek all these. In the first two Âshramas life was lived as the continent student (Brahmacharyya) and as the married householder (Grihastha). Save rare exceptions all were called upon to marry. The fourth Purushârtha is Liberation (Moksha) to which man is

exclusively bent in the subsequent forest
life (Vanaprastha) and as the mendicant
(Bhikshu), who, without aught of his
own, and wending to his death, sought
union with the Source of all. In the
first two stages man was on the path of
enjoyment; that is lawful enjoyment
worshipping God; in the last two when
household duties were done and commencing old age wended to death, entry was
made on the path of renunciation and union
was sought not with Spirit as embodied in
the universe, but as transcending it. This
was the round of life for all, except for
a few highly developed souls who might
enter the path of renunciation at once
without first going through the stage of the
householder. How supremely beautiful and
balanced this ancient ideal was, none can
know but those who have studied it and
fathomed the profound principles on which
it rested; principles which harmonized the
World and God in one Whole. This glory
has to-day largely passed like others.
Nevertheless it remains a wonderful vision

which only a truly civilized people could have seen and practised.

This blending of worldly life free from "Asceticism" with its underlying Source is also profoundly effected in the Shâkta consciousness of the unity of the Activity of Forms and of the Formless Peace from Whose Power (Shakti) they issue. As the Kulârnava Tantra says, Yoga and worldly enjoyment are then one (Yogo bhogâyate) and *the world itself is made the seat of liberation* (Mokshâyate Sangsârah). What modern western doctrine surpasses these principles according to which man is taught that he need not flee the world, for therein he may, in himself, harmonize' the Ultimate Reality and Its Appearance? For such, one's country and one's family, and the whole world are but forms of the Mother-Power (Shakti) and service of them is service and worship of Her. This doctrine is a wonderful synthesis of the conflict between Spirit and Body. Then when all is realised as the Supreme Consciousness, desire therefor is burnt out.

Without ascetic rigour it has passed away.
The statement that Indian doctrine is " a
flat negation of the value of life " is flat
nonsense. Life is supremely valuable both
as the finite expression of the Infinite Being
from which it comes and as affording the
opportunity (the only one) through which
man may reach It. Over and over again
the Scripture speaks of the value of human
birth which is so hard to get (Durlabha) and
which man has only attained after millions
of births of upward striving. Constantly
does it warn him to avail himself
of this opportunity to rise higher, for
otherwise he becomes a " self-killer." Life
has value both in itself and as the stairs
(Sopâna) up which man mounts to his end.
It is therefore of course real. Like many
critics of Indian beliefs Mr. Archer talks
foolishly of Reality. The Indian (we are
told) does not believe in the " reality of the
world." In fact he is said to be only
artistic at the cost of the betrayal of the
principles for which India stands. Mr.
Archer apparently therefore thinks it would

be dangerous to trust the Hindu with so real a thing. He might not take it seriously, to the danger of himself and others. Through his " fatalistic " doctrine of Karma he would not have the will to set things right; and his "asceticism" and "pessimism" might tell him not to bother himself any further with the matter. Is it necessary to say that the world produces the same sense of reality in an Indian mind as it does in any other? And Indian philosophers too notwithstanding their " enervating metaphysic " give common sense their support. Of the three standards Nyâya-vaisheshika, Sânkhya and Vedânta, the first two expressly contend for the reality of the world. But it is also " real " in the Vedântic schools, in one of which only (the socalled Mâyâvâda Vedânta) we hear speak of the " unreal " world. But in what sense?

The term " real " must be understood according to its definition. Whilst to others a thing may be real although it changes, in this form of Vedânta the truly real is that which was, which is, and which will be, changeless in all these " three times." And this is God only, " as it was in the beginning as it is, and as it ever will be world without end," to borrow Christian parlance. When therefore the Vedânta says that the world is not " real " it means *in this sense* ; but not in any other. It is real to us whilst it lasts and its material cause or Mâyâ Shakti is an unexplainable (Anirvachanîya) mystery which, whilst not real, is also not unreal. The Western also admits that some day this universe must pass. No Theology that I am aware of teaches that the world has the same reality as God. Shangkara the great Vedântic doctor of this school expressly refutes the Idealism of those Buddhists who were alleged to deny the reality of the objective world, saying (as he does) that the outside world is everywhit as real as the inner mind which perceives it. Both are the creation of the Lord (Îshvara) and exist as a real parallelism on our plane and as an apparent dichotomy of that supreme Consciousness in which there is neither without nor within. It is doubtless said that the world is a " Dream " : but to whom ? Not to man in the waking state, but to the Lord, the projection of whose Consciousness as Divine Imagination (Srishtikalpanâ) it is. But no school is so philosophically fallacious as to hold that there can be an object without there being some Consciousness to perceive it.

Lastly there is the doctrine of Karma and Sangsâra, which missionaries commonly regard as their greatest obstacle in the way of the Christianisation of India, and which Mr. Archer has discovered to be also a political obstacle. Other English writers, with solicitude for the welfare of this country, also deplore the alleged ill-effects of the doctrines of Indian philosophy on the Indian people ; and some few of the latter, re-echo these lamentations. These doctrines are said to be one of the causes of the enfeeblement of will, absence of energy and disinclination for " Progress " which stand in the way of the full application of the principles of

Western political "Liberalism" which appears to be Mr. Archer's creed.

The doctrines are, it seems, a chief cause of their indolent notion that "life is a shoreless expanse in which generations rise and fall as helplessly and purposelessly as waves in mid-ocean, the individual life being everywhere dwarfed and depreciated" to cite Mr. Archer's words. Moreover the acceptance of these doctrines is one of those things which convince him that India is not spiritual. These theories he says are " shallow " and the second in particular is " an untutored savage fancy borrowed probably from aboriginal tribes." " The theory is an empty one and there is little proof of spiritual genius in having evolved it (the aboriginal authorship is momentarily forgotten) and still less in having clung to it for three thousand years." This implies some considerable obstinacy in the Indian people. I am sure of this, that they would only be too glad if the doctrine could be shown to be untrue, for the thinking and spiritually minded among them have a horror of repeated birth in the suffering worlds. What however they would say is :— "Show and prove to me any truer doctrine than mine." Their reason compels them to reject the theories which Christianity or other creeds and persons offer them. Nor, whether their theory be right or wrong, are they foolish in this refusal. The philosopher Hume, and if I remember rightly Cudworth also, considered the Re-incarnation Doctrine the most rational theory of immortality. For as Professor William Knight wrote " Pre-existence (a doctrine which assumes several forms) has fewer difficulties to face than the rival hypotheses."

I am not here concerned to establish its truth, or to refute the errors of Mr. Archer and others as regards it. It may be admitted that it has its difficulties. And what theory has not? Indians whose doctrines are criticised would do well if they asked their critics to state *their own* theories first, in which case it may be found that they involve still greater difficulties. Cardinal Newman, an admittedly subtle mind, said in his Apologia that there was not a Christian dogma which was not infested with intellectual difficulties, and that speaking for himself he could not solve any of them. Theories with such abundance of difficulty cannot, it will be said, be rational. It may seem, even to those who are not its adherents, that there is a truth underlying this reincarnation doctrine, whether or not its Indian form of Karma and Sangsâra fully, and in every respect, correctly expresses it. Further it is obvious to any impartial thinker that from the point of view of reason there are less difficulties in the Indian doctrine than in any other.

But whether the theories are true or not they are certainly not " shallow." Professor William Knight says that "if we could legitimately determine any question of belief by the number of its adherents the *quod semper, quod ubique, quod ab omnibus* would apply to metempsychosis more fully than to any other." Once practically the whole civilized world embraced it, as the greater number (nearly two-thirds) of the Earth's peoples now do. It has been known since the dawn of history and has been held by both primitive peoples and the highly learned. Whilst the doctrine seems to be a native and ineradicable growth of the oriental world, it appears since the spread of Christianity rather as scattered instances in the Western world. It is said to have been held by the ancient Egyptians, (though this is disputed) by some of the Greeks, notably by Empedocles, Pythagoras, Plato and the Neoplatonists, and was taught in the Mysteries ; it was also held by some of the Latins, and by the Gauls, the Druids, and followers of the Edda. It occurs in primitive Christianity ; such as (to take a notable instance) in Origen. In fact some contend that the Christian Gospels when rightly interpreted assume it. (See " Reincarnation in the new Testament " by J. M. Pryse). It appears sporadically again in Europe in the Middle Ages. What however resisted this belief was the Semitic Judaism (I do not speak of the Kabbalists) and its two Semitic offshoots, Christianity and Maho-

medanism. Christianity, an (historically)
aggressive and persecuting religion, either
largely drove it out of Europe or prevented
its adoption there. Mohamedanism worked
with the same effect in those parts of Asia
which underwent its influence. Nevertheless in Europe the doctrine has never
entirely disappeared and in recent times
has gained a number of adherents. Those
who are unaware of the extent to which the
re-incarnation doctrine has received
approval or adoption from Western thinkers
should read Mr. E. D. Walker's book on
" Reincarnation ;" itself based on the larger
standard treatise of the Revd. W. R. Alger,
" A critical history of the doctrine of a
future life." Amongst those who have held
or written favourably of this " shallow "
theory may be counted the grand Italian
philosopher Giordano Bruno, burnt alive by
the Church as a heretic ; the German
philosophers, Schelling, Fichte (younger)
Leibnitz, Schopenhauer, and the great poets
and writers Goethe, Herder, Lessing ; the
English Christian Platonist Dr. Henry More

and others; and the philosophers Cudworth and Hume; the French and English scientists Flammarion, Figuier, Brewster; and the Modern Christian Theologians Julius 'Muller, Dorner, Ernesti, Ruckert, Edward Beecher and W. R. Alger. There are many others whose names may be found in the works cited as also large numbers of poets, the Seers of their race. A recent work is that of the metaphysician Professor McTaggart who in his Essay on Pre-Existence argues that the Immortality of the Soul involves its pre-existence. The case of the Revd. W. R. Alger is remarkable. In the first Edition of his Work (1860) he characterised the theory as a "plausible delusion unworthy of credence." But after fifteen years of study he, though starting with this unfavourable conclusion and with all the natural prepossessions of a Christian clergyman, gave in the last edition (1878) the final result of his ripest investigations in endorsing and advocating the doctrine.

Mr. Archer's allegation of its "shallowness" is only one, amongst many, instances of the unreasoning prejudices with which he judges this country's beliefs. Not to mention other great names, let us take that of the world-renowned Buddha only. Neither he nor they were " untutored savages " or shallow thinkers which they must have been if they adopted and preached what was in fact a " shallow " theory.

Neither however this nor some other Western critics understand these doctrines: since they have not sufficiently studied the principles on which they rest. For the Karma doctrine is distinctly metaphysical. It is not a mere empirical generalization but has a strong rational basis. It is not to be identified, as some Western writers do, with the physical law of causality. The gist of the criticisms made is that it is opposed to the freedom of the will and to morality. Both these statements are as wrong as any can be.

All Western Idealists, as does Brâhma-nism, posit a Self unchanged in the midst of Its changing experiences. Therefore the Karttâ (Doer), the Karma (action done) and the fruit or result of the action (Phala) must be distinguished. Karma being distinct from the Karttâ cannot dominate the latter. That is, the Self is not co-ordinate with, but distinguished from, the action it determines. We may compare, in this connection, Kant's distinction between what he calls the Intelligible and Empirical characters. The Self is in fact according to Indian notions as free as it is according to Western Indeterminism. To talk as some do of the " inexorable " or " fatalistic " law of Karma, as though it reduced man to a machine, is to have misunderstood the elements of the subject. All Indian schools admit the possibility of liberation. If Karma were inexorable how could it be possible to gain liberation ? Liberation is thus the proof of man's essential freedom. What however the doctrine says is that when man does an action he must take the consequences (Phala) of it, and this whether he remembers it or not. Lack of knowledge or memory, for instance, of an injury suffered by a child at the moment of birth does not prevent the consequences of injury ensuing. If through precedent actions our present condition is unfavourable, we are called upon to make good Karma to maintain our moral state and lay the seed of future good conditions. And though this may be in cases difficult, owing to the load of evil results we carry, it is not impossible; for the Self which performs the action remains always free. In the same way it is said in Christianity that however unfortunate be the conditions in which, according to this theory, a man is placed at birth, through no antecedent action of his own, he has yet sufficient free will to surmount by its exercise all temptations. So far then from Karma being fatalistic it is the doctrine according to which *man is master of his destiny.* He has made himself what he is and makes himself what he will be, notwithstanding unfortunate conditions which are due to his previous actions and which, according to the Christian theory, have no cause but the arbitrary, and in its result, as the Hindu would say, unjust will of God.

261

Leaving this point, it is sometimes said that the ethics of the Karma doctrine fail to draw that vital distinction which exists between good and bad action. This also is quite wrong. Wholly unselfish good action (Nishkâma Karma) does not bind, and with true spiritual knowledge leads to liberation. Selfish, though good, action, that is action done with desire for fruit (Sakâma Karma) leads to happiness in this world and in Heaven. Action which is both selfish and bad leads to suffering in this world and in Hell. There is thus the most emphatic distinction between all three. What Hinduism says is that liberation from the world cannot be had, even by good actions, if done with the desire to get benefit for oneself in the world. How can a man be free of the world who binds himself by his desires to it? As long as man has any selfish, even though legitimate, desire he cannot attain the highest state. It has been also charged that there is no room in the doctrine for social service and philanthropy. This is possibly based on an erroneous interpretation by

some Indians who, like some Christians, are
ignorant of the true meaning of their Scripture. Thus it is sometimes said that it is no
use to alleviate the lot of a suffering man
because he is working out his Karma and
this would be to interfere with the operation
of Karma. But how does the objector know
this? Is he the Dispenser of Fruits so as to
know what has been awarded? Because a
man's bad Karma has brought upon him
suffering, it does not follow that it is to be
unmitigated suffering. It in fact may be
his Karma to suffer subject to certain relief.
Moreover, and this is the principal point, a
man who refuses help to others, whether for
such reasons or otherwise, stores up bad
Karma for himself. Instead therefore of
putting forward futile objections, let him
devote himself to social service, and philanthropy. The principles of the Vedânta
which accepts the Karma doctrine require
this; for he who serves another serves the
Self. The Vedânta gives profoundly based
reasons for all charity and brotherliness.
Dealing with this absurd charge that the

Vedânta is defective in morals Dr. Deussen says "the fact is nevertheless that the highest and purest morality is the immediate consequence of the Vedânta. The Gospels fix quite correctly as the highest law of morality ' Love your neighbour as yourself.' But why should I do so, since by the order of nature I feel pain and pleasure only in myself and not in my neighbour ? " " The answer is not," (he says,) " in the Bible but it is in the Veda in the great formula ' That thou art ' (Tat tvam asi) which gives, in three words, metaphysics and morals together." So it is said—Paropakâro hi pàramo dharmah (" To do good to others is the highest religion.") It is true that in Hinduism, as in Catholicism, numbers have left the world. Perhaps, as an Indian friend of mine has said, it was Shangkarâchâryya who gave a predominantly ascetic and other-worldly character to conduct, wishing by his Maths to preserve the teaching of Hinduism against the incoming Moslems. I think we may go further back and find the cause in Buddhism which, being in this

less balanced than Brâhmanism, over-
stressed the way of renunciation. For my
part I do not admit that the true Indian
recluse or the true Catholic Monk or Nun are
useless. The objection is too materialistic.
All humanity is raised in their persons
which shed a spiritual influence upon the
striving world around them. Nevertheless
there is nothing antisocial in the Vedânta
as such, nor in the Gîtâ, the "cream of the
Upanishads," which teaches the doctrine of
selfless action in the world. So too the essentially practical Shâkta version of Vedânta
holds that "the world is the seat of liberation." The truth is that this and other
difficulties are largely "discovered" simply
because those who raise them have wished
to find them.

Let us now leave philosophy and look at
the facts. Are the Indian people wholly
inactive and without will or hope? What
is this political movement in India which
has roused Mr. Archer to write his book?
What are the "social reform" movements
which Mr. Archer and others approve; some

perhaps because activity is thus, in part at least, drawn off from what they think to be inconvenient political directions? What are the movements (retrograde as he and they would call them) manifested by the Brâhmanism which still to his disgust " rears its head? " What are the religious movements to restore and revivify Hindu religion which he calls " aggressive anti-rationalism," though Hinduism in its essentials is one of the most rational of religions ? The position for instance assumed by Shangkarâchâryya is that even Veda would be no Veda if it were irrational.

Some will say that this activity is due to Christianity, others that it is due to Western secular influences. If so the Karma doctrine, in the case of those who still uphold it, has not stood in the way. But still more strange is it that long before Western influences were at work in this country, and for thousands of years, India has lived and now survives under the load of this supposed soul-deadening, will-weakening, anti-social doctrine of Karma and Sangsâra and still obstinately (as Mr. Archer complains) "rears its head." Whence has it drawn the strength to do so? Notwithstanding this alleged lack of volition it is evidently difficult to destroy Her resolution to be Herself. Another Western journalist has offered the "explanation" that "Hinduism has endured because it has failed." Others will think that it is not necessary to have recourse to senseless paradox, and that the attention of the writers has been given to "progress" in the common Western and material sense, and even to hustle, fuss and self-advertisement, rather than to the strong silent will, and unobtrusive action, which have sustained this country throughout the ages.

X

BRÂHMANISM

BRÂHMANISM which is to-day in India
the most important branch of the Bhârata
Dharma is based on Veda (a profound but
only superficially understood concept) and
is sub-divided into several sects who interpret the Vaidic texts in differing ways,
worship God under particular aspects, and
whose rituals in some respects vary. There
are, as I have often elsewhere pointed out,
matters of substantial agreement; nevertheless there are others of difference such
as (for example) the identity or otherwise
of the individual and supreme Spirit, with
consequential differences as to the nature
of the state of liberation (Moksha). Some
of these differences hardly affect the
question here discussed but there are others
of importance in this matter, in so far as,

whilst all forms of Hindu belief provide an answer to the criticisms which have been made against them, it may be contended (as I do) that the form I here shortly describe meets them more strongly and effectively than others.

India has appreciated, as one of her people has said, the " dignity of objective facts " and daily sense experience. She would have been very silly if she had not done so; nor do such facts allow themselves to be ignored. But experience is not limited, according to Indian notions, to sense-experience. There is spiritual experience which is recorded in the Vedas and which has been attained in varying degree by the spiritually wise. This considered as authority (Shabda Pramāna) is the instrument (Pramāyāh karanam) for the attainment of supersensible (Atīndriya) truths. These truths, though attainable only by Veda, are yet not inconsistent with reason. For as man is made of a piece, what is irrational cannot be spiritually true. No country has placed greater reliance on reason than

India has done. "A reasonable saying should be accepted even from a boy."

The Tantras of the Shâkta Âgama, accepting and based on the Vedântic texts, teach the identity of the individual (Jîvâtmâ) and Supreme Spirit (Paramâtmâ) and proclaim that "All this (the world) is verily Brahman," though in a different manner from those who hold that the universe is Mâyâ in the sense in which that term is used in the transcendental (Pâramârthika) section of Shangkarâchâryya's interpretation of Vedânta. It may however be argued that these two doctrines belong to differing fields of experience and therefore do not conflict with, or cross, one another. I have explained this and other technicalities elsewhere. Here I very shortly deal with the matter from its practical aspects as constituting the principles on which Indian civilization is based. For that civilization has a religious basis and a spiritual aim and organises society so that this end may be attained. For this reason it is necessary

to enquire into matters which may seem
alien to the subject to an English reader.
Indian thought always touches the root of
things.

According to Shâkta teaching, the
Universe is a manifestation of the Power
(Shakti) of the Supreme Consciousness or
Self which is theologically called Shiva
" the good and auspicious " or God, who in
His aspect of manifestation of Power is
known as the Great Devî, or Divine Mother
of all. The two are one. Consciousness
(Shaktimân) and Its power are one. They
are twin aspects of the One : Shiva being
the static changeless aspect of Spirit or
Consciousness, and Shakti being the kinetic
or changing aspect of Consciousness, in
which it veils and negates Its infinity into
finite forms. For creation is the negation
(Nishedha-vyâpârarûpâ Shaktih) or limit-
ation of the infinite All (Pûrna). The
Infinite Consciousness thus *finitises* Itself.
He and Her, or Consciousness and Its Power,
as transcendentally resting in Themselves
(Svarûpa-vishrânti), are the Perfect or

271

Ideal Universe, the formless state of supremely blissful Love (Niratishayapremâspadatvam ânandatvam) in which the Self experiences its Self (in Whom the whole universe is) as pure consciousness. Consciousness manifests through its Power, that is, It presents Itself to itself as the limited universe. This manifestation is due to the ripening in consciousness of the subconscious impressions (Sangskâra) left by past experiences and which evolve into mind and matter of present worldly experience. This is the imperfect and finite universe of forms in which Shiva, without loss of His own natural and changeless Beatitude, enjoys and suffers as man and all other sentient beings. God, though of His own nature blissful, yet *as* and *through* man suffers and enjoys. Consciousness or Spirit involves Itself in matter and then gradually evolves Itself therefrom. This process is the Evolution of forms through plant, animal, and human bodies, which in greater and greater degree admit of the manifestation of Consciousness or the immanent Shiva. The difference between man and animal is not of kind but degree. But with man entrance is made into the world of conscious morality. Shiva is thus the Soul of the World and the world is Himself as Power (Shakti). Man who is spirit, mind and body is divine. He is divine not only as spirit but as mind and body. For these are divine power, there being none other. Man is a " little Brahma Spheroid " (Kshudra-brahmânda) that is, microcosm. Everything which is outside is within him. As the Vishvasâra Tantra says : " What is here is there. What is not here is nowhere " (Yadihâsti tadanyatra Yannehâsti na tat kvachit). There is no need to throw ones eyes into the heavens to find God or Shiva. Man as spirit is God. Man as mind and body is the Power (Shakti) of God. Man is thus God and His Power. As God's power, man and the universe are real. The world is real though it changes and does not last for ever. The world is the experience of Shiva in the form of all beings and His experience is never unreal.

Effort is real. Effort is possible because man is the free master of his destiny. There is no fatalism. Man has made himself what he is, and he will be what he now makes himself. What is to be the manner of his striving? It must be according to morality (Dharma) with a view to make good Karma and with the consciousness (in the highest) that man is one with the Active Spirit in its form as the universe. To those who have this outlook (Vîrabhâva) on life, every physical function and thought is a religious rite (Yajna). Every being or thing is the great Mother in that form. Whilst life should be lived with simplicity and restraint, there is no need of asceticism, though those who really wish for it may adopt it. Thus, whilst in some forms of ritual there is fasting before worship, it is said that Kâlikâ is angry with those who thus worship Her. " For if Shiva and Jîva are one, why give pain to Jîva ? " There is no need to renounce anything except ill-thinking and ill-doing which bring ill-fruit. For what can man renounce when all things and beings are seen to be the Mother? To renounce them with such consciousness is to renounce Her. To cherish wife and children, to feel for and help fellow-man, to serve one's country or race is to serve and worship Her. The service of them is service of the Self. What is the end of effort? Full self-realisation—a Spirit vehicled by mind and matter so that man is truly in conformity and harmony with the active immanent Shiva and the developing world-process; and then the realisation of man's final end in unity with the formless and transcendent Spirit thus gaining final liberation from the world of forms. True progress is the gradual release of Spirit from the bondage in which It has been seemingly involved. True civilization is the organization of society, so that the individual man and his community may attain his and its immediate and final end, that is enjoyment and liberation (Bhukti and Mukti). For the general good was the object of the Indian social organization. And the community has governed itself. There is in this doctrine itself no depressing Pessimism for Ânanda or Bliss is seen in all ; there is no asceticism for those who feel no call therefor, since the doctrine is one of enjoyment (Bhoga). There is no Fatalism or lack of will, for man is known to be master of his destiny and alone responsible for his past and future. It cannot be charged with being " Anti-social " for life is fully lived in the world in the knowledge that man and his fellows and all beings are kindred expressions of the one Mother-Self. Whether its teachings be accepted as true or not it must be conceded that this is a grandiose and all inclusive doctrine.

In another book of Mr. Archer, criticising Mr. H. G. Wells " God the Invisible King," he says that the latter " has come a good deal in contact with Indian religiosity ; " and that " this craving for something to worship points to an almost uncanny recrudescence of the spirit of Asia in a fine European intelligence." He adds " It is possible that an epidemic of Asiatic religiosity may be one of the sequels of the war." He says " It has sometimes seemed to me that the one great advantage of Western Christianity lies in the fact that nobody very seriously believes in it. ' Nobody ' is not a mathematically accurate expression, but it is quite in the line of the truth. You have to go to Asia to find out what religion is. If you cannot get so far, Russia will serve as a half way house : but to study religion on its native heath . . . you must go to India. I cannot believe that anywhere between Suez and Singapore there exists that healthy Godlessness that lack of any real effective *independence of any outward power* which is so common in and around all Christian Churches. In the land of " Om " anything like freedom of the spirit is probably very rare and very difficult. The difference does not arise from any lesser stringency in the claims of Christianity to spiritual dominion, but rather I imagine from a deep-rooted divergence in racial heredity. We Western Âryans have behind us the serene and splendid rationalism of Greece and Rome. We are accustomed from childhood to the knowledge that our civilization was founded by two mighty aristocracies of intellect, to whom the religions of their day were, as they are to us, nothing but more or less graceful fairy tales. We know that many of the greatest men the world ever saw while phrasing their relation to the *Deus absconditus* in various ways were utterly *free from that penitential suppli-catory abjectness which is the mark of Asian salvationism.* And though, of course, the conscious filiation to Greece and Rome is rare, the habit of mind which *holds up its head* in the world and feels no childish craving to cling to the skirts of a God is not rare at all." This interesting passage invites a lengthy comment. It is true that large numbers have no serious belief in Christianity. With much of the attitude here revealed many a Western will have a fellow-feeling. All classicists will salute the glory that was Greece and the grandeur that was Rome, and it is in the

English temperament to dislike all abjectness, religious or otherwise. But I must
pass on with the observation that Mr.
Archer has here again misunderstood his
subject. Many of his criticisms on Mr.
Well's " Veiled Being " and " God-King "
are effective, but will not be so as applied to
the logically developed metaphysical
Indian concept of Îshvara and Parabrahman which are the supposed sources of
Mr. Well's theory. If, however Mr. Archer
understood the Doctrine which claims to be
the highest thought of India, he would
know that it teaches that man is *not*
dependent on any outward extra-cosmic
power but on himself and Self ; that it as
completely affirms, as any other doctrine,
the claims of reason and the freedom of the
human spirit, and that it is " utterly free
of any penitential supplicatory abjectness."
If such a charge can be made at all, it is
against some of those who profess
Christianity, and those kindred forms of
Indian dualistic beliefs which make man
a supplicant before, and dependent on,

some Power which is not his Essential Self. In fact, the Christian charge against these high doctrines is that they are not penitential or supplicatory but err through that blasphemous overweening *pride* which makes man himself (in his essence) Divinity. Mr. Wells speaks of him who has not accepted his " God-King " as a " masterless man." "But is it really," Mr. Archer asks " to our Western sense, a misfortune to be a masterless man? If any one is irked by that condition, the Roman Catholic Church holds wide its doors for him." According to Shâkta Vedânta, man is his own master. The self makes homage to the Self. World-enjoyment is the self's and Liberation is Its peaceful nature. The heroic-man (Vîra) does not flee from the world through fear of it. His doctrine is not anti-social, for life is fully lived in the world in the knowledge that all men and all other beings are kindred expressions of the one Mother-Self. Nor does he cling to any other than the Self. He holds the world in his grasp and wrests from it its Secret.

There is no fatalism or lack of will, for man is known to be the master of his destiny and alone responsible for his past and future. Escaping from all the unconscious driftings of an Humanity which has not yet realised itself, he is the illumined master of himself whether developing all his powers on earth, or seeking liberation therefrom at his will.

But the "Rationalist" may say that all this is only the metaphysical dreaming of the Indian people. Well, what do Mr. Archer and those of his way of thinking offer them in its stead? They are "to want more wants" and at the same time to cultivate "higher mundane ideals." Why? Let us suppose that, as is not unlikely, man in the process of "wanting more wants" should turn from "higher mundane ideals" and elect for the more popular lower mundanities for which Western civilization offers so luxuriant a provision. It is then said "Appeal should be made to loyalty to Humankind" with a capital letter. But what is Humankind that we should be loyal to it ? Since the first men fell from natural harmony they have been each others enemy, except where religion has taught them better. Mr. Archer says that all that is needed is " to kindle a sentiment (one might almost say) to awaken an instinct of loyalty to *something* higher than our personal and family interest : *something* not ourselves that makes for or rather demands righteousness." He here perilously approaches the contemned metaphysic. What is this " something ? " How does a " something " demand ? If it does, why call it " something ? " How do we know that it exists ? What warrant has Mr. Archer for this affirmation and, in particular, that it is not ourselves ? Why not suppose that it is the conscious Higher Self ? What is it that it should make a demand and why does it do so ? Why should we obey the demand and what will happen if we do not ? All such half-baked thinking ill-qualifies for a criticism of the great Philosophies of India which say that there is a Supreme Spirit who is manifested by all beings bound by righteousness (Dharma) as the Law of their nature and that there is an ordered and just universe. It is this Supreme Spirit which, one with the Inner Self of man, is higher than the personal interests which are the expressions of the limitations in which Self binds itself through Its power. Loyalty to Humankind is called for, because it is the manifestation of the one Spirit which is in and manifests as all men. Its sanction is the happiness and suffering which follow in harmony with, or resistance to, the world-order and therefore world-peace which is a reflection of the Serene Ground of all that is. What is the proof of all this? The world-experience of every man who knows that ill action leads to suffering ; and the higher spiritual experience which is had by those who are Masters of our Race and Incarnations of the Soul of the World.

XI

SELF-EXPRESSION

ONE may argue as one will as to the greatness of Indian civilization, but the fact will remain that the Indian people have been, and still are, a subject people governed by foreigners; a fact which, it will be contended, is inconsistent with the possession by them of true morality. For on the world-path (Pravritti-Mârga) a free and independent spirit which looks to itself to do the work of the self and does it with courage, vigour, and adherence to racial ideals is morality. In short, a complete and free manhood is true morality and those who are politically and culturally subject, by that very fact have it not. Freedom, again, is the sign of true spirituality. That glorious word Svârâjyasiddhi involves in its fullest sense the effective rule of the self by the Self in all the planes spiritual, mental and material; for this autonomy is not, as in the Western sense of the word, merely material and political, but freedom of the soul ending in Liberation itself.

Mr. Archer and others attribute the lack of this-world morality evidenced by the present subjection of India to an arrested development, or to the vicious principles on which its civilization is founded and to the false ideals it holds. In the same way, some lay to the charge of the Christian religion which preaches "peace on earth to men of good will" the present Carnage and its wealth of Hate. In either case the fault lies not so much (if at all) with the principles, but is due to neglect and wrong application of them, and to the failure of those who profess to hold these principles to state them rightly, and to make them effective to-day. In judging, moreover the cause of the present state of India, it must be remembered that all peoples pass through periods of rise and decline, of activity and rest, according to the rhythm which governs the whole universe. India has been for some-time past in a cycle of depression which may mean either Her approaching death—India's final Pralaya; or merely a state of inertia, corresponding to the Nitya Pralaya which is one's daily slumber (Sushupti), from which she will rise refreshened in the morning of a new day. If it be the first, then India has been preserved until such time as the West and a new Eastern civilization are ready to receive the truths which She has taught. If it be the second (and the stirring of life may be put forward as showing it) India will, in the essentials of Her civilization, remain, in whatever way her external social structure may be re-formed to meet the needs of the time. In either case these essentials and in such sense " India " will endure until the World-dissolution. I here, however, speak of India as the particular expression of those ideas as existing in fact to-day.

Before a conclusion in the first sense is reached, we must ascertain the cause of the present conditions and see whether they are removable. It will be time then to consider whether Her civilization is at fault. Those present conditions are attributable both to causes which were in operation before the arrival of the English and to causes which have since arisen. The first cause is the decline or inertia which rendered India open to the Mussalman invaders, and the second includes the same together with other special causes which have come into play by reason of the introduction of the western civilization of India's present rulers through whose influence, on the other hand, this country is again showing signs of a freshened vitality.

What is wanted is Power (Shakti). It is wonderful to see how throughout the world, in East and West, this idea of Power is spreading concomitantly with the consciousness of man's essential Divinity. If there be one people whose doctrine (whatever be their practice) preaches self-reliance, it is India. For She alone has taught in its fullest form the doctrine of the Self. If to-day all are not self-reliant in fact, it is due to bodily weakness, ignorance and want of appreciation of these truths. It is curious to note how the so-called " progressive " nations of the West have been self-reliant in fact, notwithstanding a religion which, preaches humility, self-abasement and dependence, and how India has been lacking in self-reliance despite the fact that what claims to be the highest form of its religion teaches that man is the master of his destiny, that he is essentially one with the Cosmic Power (Prapancha-Shakti) and that complete autonomy (Svârâjya-siddhi) is his goal. The Shâkta Dharma is a perfected type of this doctrine of the worship of this Mother-Power.

Power (Shakti) is physical or material and psychic or mental, and spiritual. This Shâstra teaches that man is a Magazine of all power. In every man there is this " Inner Woman," as a Shâkta Sâdhaka aptly called Her. The problem is how to make Her awake (Prabuddhâ). With the mass of men we must commence with the gross physical vehicle (Sthûla deha). The first fact we notice is the weakness of the body. This is due to the great poverty of the mass of the Indian people. And so food is lacking. Food is Power, for it is the material source of both physical and psychic Power. Annam is Brahman. Salutation, therefore, to Annam. Ill-nutrition induces disease. As I write some 30,000 deaths have taken place in a week in India from Plague and some 10 to 12,000 weekly from Malaria, due in part at least, it is said, to disturbance of natural drainage caused by railway embankments and to the silting up of rivers. The Sanitary Commissioner with the Government of India in a review of the plague epidemic between July 1898 and June 1918 states that more than a million and a quarter deaths from this disease have been recorded in India. Consumption, too, is rapidly spreading. An English doctor recently told me that it was " decimating " (I use his own word) the student population and poorer homes in Calcutta to-day. In varying numbers these deaths have been going on for years past. Effects breed again their causes, and we therefore see lack of

289

attention to those principles of hygiene and sanitation which the ancient Smritis and customs prescribed, as does Western science to-day. (The connection between poverty and disease is shown by the fact that it is nearly always the poor who suffer. If food be wanting and if the body be unhealthy, the mind becomes weak. For the mind is fed by food. Without health and strength of body there is listlessness, sadness, and lack of will and energy. Let India be fed, and then let us see whether these will disappear.) It is not, as Mr. Archer and others suppose, Karma and Transmigration, Asceticism and what not which are primarily at fault, but lack of food and the spread of disease. Then in the renewed body mental power will generate.)

The mind is the soul and the body is dependent on it. If the people's soul be lost, then all is lost. It is not yet lost but it is yet not wholly out of danger. When in 1834 Macaulay's Educational Minute decreed that India was to receive through English education the civilization of the West, it was then, it has been said, that ancient India was first to any great degree moulded by foreign invaders and a new India was born. Professor Seeley wrote that " never was a more momentous question discussed. " We were led to stand out boldly as civilizers and teachers. Macaulay's Minute remains the great landmark in the History of our Empire considered as an institute of civilization. It marks the moment when we deliberately recognised that a function had developed on us in Asia similar to that which Rome fulfilled in Europe." To an Indian, self-conscious of the greatness of his country's civilization, it must be gall and wormwood to hear others speaking of the " education " and " civilization " of India. India who has taught some of the deepest truths which our race has known is to be " educated." She whose ancient civilization ranks with the greatest the world has known is to be " civilized." And yet this policy of English Education was necessary in the sequence of Indian history ; otherwise, it would not have been initiated and carried out. If the Indian spirit and traditions are not maintained, if Indian vitality ebbs, then the Indian people must fall into tutelage. This resolution "to civilize" and the work done thereunder has been in several aspects for the benefit of India. But like all else it has had its evil side and dangers. For as the Hindu proverb runs, there is nothing wholly bad nor yet wholly good. It was good in that it gave new life and a widened outlook to this country. The evil has lain in the fact that the Power of the West, working in a weakened Indian body, tended to overlay and suffocate the Indian soul. A class arose, and still, to some extent, exists, which finding everything Western, to be good, neglected its own ancient heritage; which lost soul-life, became imitative and lived upon the borrowed ideas of others and not upon its own. This way soul-weakness lies. We can never be strong through others' souls, great though they be. Life may be roused from without, but action must proceed from the inner source which is the own Vital Self. We may awake a sleeper but he must talk and walk of his own power. Each hemisphere can learn from the other and the West can bring to India with profit to Her the knowledge it has gained during the last century when India was wrapped in a crust of inertia. But the true function of English Civilization is to act as a blister to rouse India from this inertia.

"What a pessimistic view" some one said to me. The remark is characteristic of the ordinary Western standpoint which regards the function of the West to be not the arousing of the ancient spirit of Indian civilization to new life, but the supplanting of that civilization by its own. To me there is no ground for pessimism but rather for rejoicing in the fact that other cultures than my own will survive. The whole world will benefit from a variety of vital self-active cultures, just as it will lose by the suppression of any which are of worth, and will suffer by imitative cultural automatisms. I believe, with India, in Svadharma. Live and let live. Each to his own. "You are always speaking in terms of difference" said another to me. Yes I do so speak; for difference is a present fact and I deal with facts. Difference is in Nature itself and I want no cultural or other Kidgerees. But I also believe that there is an Unity behind all these differences, the varied expression of the One Self. And if we recognise and act on that belief, we shall each hold to our own self-expressions without hate or oppression of others. It may well be that as the world goes on, the differences between civilizations may lessen. For all we know they may some day disappear. But meanwhile the duty of each is to perfect his own type in accordance with Svadharma, so that he may become a fit part of the future cultural unity which may be. The reason is that in this material world, as in that of spirit, all types when perfected are closer to one another than they are in their undeveloped and imperfect state, and a good cultural whole can never be made up of indifferent parts. I have, therefore, my moments of angry wonder as I see the increasing vulgarization of the fine and (in an Eastern sense) aristocratic life of India, the betrayal or neglect of past traditions and culture, the senseless imitation of foreign ways simply because they are foreign and the many shams and falsities of modern Indian life. Not the least thing which this country can learn from the British and the Irish (with else which they can teach) is the necessity of faithfulness to racial ideals. They look to, and are true to, themselves. They are not always looking up for the next cue to others. Little that is foreign is adopted. But such adoption as there may be is fully self-determined and not accepted in servile dependence upon others. How many Europeans have been even in partial degree "hinduized" (if that term can be applied to any) as compared with the thousands who have been anglicised? This does not necessarily show that English civilization is *per se* superior to Hindu civilization, but that the British are for the moment more vital than the Hindu. To a Western, true to such ideals, it seems inconceivable that a race should adopt with avidity a foreign language, neglecting its own; as also foreign ideas and customs, neglecting and even, as some seem to do, condemning its past cultural inheritance. And yet such has happened and many have become, as I have elsewhere said, the mere mind-born sons (Mânasaputra) of the English. This is the reason for the obvious poverty of much of the political thought in this Country which, though cast in the thought-mould of the English, who are masters of political thinking, should nevertheless be original, inspired by Indian ideals and have an eye to the particular Indian need. Like everything else it should take count of the past history, the inherited character and aptitude and the wants of the Indian people. I once asked a leading Indian why he thought in this way, and his apt answer was " Because I have had an English education." That is he could not (naturally at least) think otherwise. Politics has

been accounted in the West something
soiled, and in truth they often are,
for the politician has not seldom a professional living upon, instead of serving, his
fellow men. It was high wisdom in India
which enjoined that the Brâhmana caste
should live austerely and not seek wealth.
As acutely pointed out by Sj. Bhagavân
Das in an address recently (November 1918)
given at Benares, Ancient India partitioned
Honour, Power, and Wealth between the
Brâhmana, Kshattriya and Vaishya respectively. Politics however need not be so
As the Author cited says, the first cure is
the application of the Indian principle that
Âtmavidyâ, or the Science of the Spirit,
governs all civic affairs. Political as all
other activities are thus spiritualized. The
next is the cultivation of a freely-moving
Indian culture. I say " freely moving,"
for each must have freedom to develop
himself and to determine the essentials of
the culture, which, in its general lines, he,
as an Indian, will naturally and without
compulsion follow. All institutions tend

to crystallise. What has been a product of growth becomes an obstacle to it.

The cultivation of these Indian principles will spiritualize the individual, and therefore the political and other institutional forms, which are the outward expression of the collective life of which he is a part. Mere forms and change of form effect little. All depends on those who work them. The application of these principles will require and attain an ethical as well as an intellectual value in those who control the social organisation. Thirdly where the seed of Indian culture is held and fostered, what grows from it will be an Indian plant. In every sphere, political and economic, the outward form will be an expression of the Indian Spirit which it subserves. And being Indian, the forms will be suitable to the needs, and advance all the interests, spiritual, intellectual and material, of the Indian people. India has had in the past Her political, economic, industrial and educational organisations articulated in a true and coherent social organism which, like all living organisms, was self-maintaining and self-renewing, not something borrowed and mechanically operating from without. Is it to be said that India which evolved such an organism for Herself in the past is incapable of devising another for Herself now? If so Her days are numbered for She has ceased to be creative and is merely lingering on under the impulse of those immense forces which made Her what She was.

If so the most She can offer, and that is valuable, is a contribution to those spiritual forces which in the West are seeking to establish themselves amongst their peoples. She will then, at least, in Her declining days get the benefit of these same principles as applied by others and pass through the infirmities of old age and death in greater peace and comfort. But let us not think of this. To think of death is to begin to die, and that is why in the ageing the thought of death so readily comes uppermost. We are not really dying until we have relinquished our hold on life.

But the Indian reader may say: "This is all very well; but what is your practical solution. General Principles, however good, are not enough. How shall we apply them?" The question itself is that of a soul which is sick or invalid. The living and healthful no sooner put a question than they answer it. Life always solves its own problems. A truly living organism adjusts itself to its circumstances. This book is not concerned with such political solutions, and even if it were, the answer, to be both true and useful, must come from the Indian People themselves. If they do not know their needs, or in what way to remedy them, how can others do so? A foreign people, however excellent their intentions may be, (and in particular cases in fact are), must act on their own principles, and can only learn so much of what India needs as one man can learn concerning another who is, except for a common humanity, entirely alien to him.

· But even a stranger, and of course still more so an Indian himself, can learn much in the way of solving every Indian Problem by studying the Indian past and the Character existing to-day which is most in conformity with the Principles which produced the already gone or disappearing social organism. From these an analysis will discover what were its fundamental principles and their practical application. How very few have done this? What the English-educated, with rare exceptions, mainly study, are the principles of Western Civilization and its institutions and in particular, those of the English who rule them, to whom they look for a gift from their (the English) store. It is the same with Law. I am not aware of a single attempt to construct a system of Jurisprudence based on essential Indian Principles. One may find a study of Austin, Bentham, of Savigny and of the American jurists but not of the Smritis and the principles on which their injunctions proceed and of the institutions based 'on them. There are of course books on specific aspects of Hindu Law, but I speak of a synthetic work on Indian jurisprudence. I will only say this with conviction, that if the Indian people steep themselves in their culture, and if those who have lost, regain their Indian Soul, that Soul will give an Indian answer to every Indian problem which the Indian Soul suggests to itself. The Soul which replies will be spiritual and endowed with that will to maintain itself from which all success follows. To think the thoughts of another is to be his Chhâyâ or shadow which is dependent on, and follows, him. We ourselves alone can give what our nature craves. In short India should have her *own* solution of political problems, and can have it, if She be vital enough to really *will* to achieve it. Will achieves all, either immediately or in time.

So again, in religion and philosophy we find the Chit-system applied even to the Upanishads ; which some hold to because some Western or other has given them his approval. One may legitimately set off against one Western's depreciation another Western's praise but if the doctrine of the Upanishads is true, it is so because it is true, and not because even a Western philosopher of world-repute may think so. This same dependent spirit is observable in smaller matters, as in the case of a Bengali friend of mine who was invited by an anglicised countryman to come and taste " puffed rice " from America, which turned out only to be the common and despised country Murhi, yet not so fresh and good ; but then it " had come from America." So, again, the ancient custom of taking sour milk (Dahi) which some looked upon as an old folly was respected as a scientific practice when Professor Metchnikoff discovered the Bulgarian Bacillus: and so on and so forth, for " puffed rice " is to be found in religion, literature, philosophy, art, science, institution and manners. To use the recent words of Mr. Lawrence Housman " India must decide whether She wishes to be Herself or a reflection of others. Is the movement of India for the Indian people to be accompanied by a subsidiary move·

303

ment for India to be peopled by Indians *coloured to European taste.* Is India now trying to find Herself, or somebody else— Her own soul or another's."

It is in the Indian cultural inheritance that the mass of the Indian people will gain mental power. The same is true of spiritual power. I am wholly against such as themselves hold to Indian religion not because it is believed to be true, but because it is Indian. This is to prostitute what is most sacred in man's nature. Honesty is an essential of true religion. I am, however, equally against those who, without belief in Christianity and without desire that their children should become Christians, hand them over to Christian Mission schools simply because they are cheap, or because such education brings other worldy advantage. The result is that spiritual mess in which the mind of some English-educated Indians flounders to-day. This is the worst of all Kidgerees. One thing is clear and will be admitted by all, that there is no true power unless it be based on

and supported by religion, Hindu, Mahomedan, Christian, Positivist or whatever
else it be. A Christian may still be an
Indian provided that, in holding to the
essentials of Christianity, he does not also
think it necessary to become a "Sahib."
India has many forms of religion, and
some of the dualistic systems bear marked
resemblances to Christianity, differences
though there also be. Indian Religion is
too often identified with what is but one
form of it, namely that based on Advaita
Vedânta. Again the facts and principles
of Indian Sâdhanâ, that is, worship and
spiritual disciplines, are either ignored or
misunderstood. For my part I see resemblances (in some Indian principles and
ritual) with, in particular, the Catholic form
of Christianity. I have dealt with this in my
"Shakti and Shâkta." I have therefore
wondered why the Christian missionary so
often merely attacks Hindu religion, and by
destroying the Hindu religious sense "throws
the baby out with the bath," instead of
rather seizing upon those general principles,

305

doctrines, and practice which either agree with, or are friendly to his own faith, thus making these the basis for the Christian structure which he wishes to see built. Such a method, together with a really saintly life, may effect something where declamation against " heathen darkness " will produce nothing but a well-justified resentment. Further we can see to-day, particularly in Southern India, Christian communities following caste and other rules of the Hindu social organism. It may be said that the Semitism inherent in Christianity makes it antagonistic to Aryan principles and culture. It must however be remembered that, though the predecessor of Christianity was Judaism, and the Old Testament might well disappear, so far as many to-day are concerned, without producing any sense of spiritual loss, Christianity is a New Dispensation. It bears, in its orthodox form, some traces of its Judaic origin, but these are becoming of less and less moment for the mind of to-day, though the fierce old books have recently been put to the use of encouraging some war-passion or other. Moreover, as I have already pointed out, Christianity as held by an Indian, free from the tutelage of Western ecclesiastical authority, may receive a new interpretation and so take on an Indian colour. It is I believe the knowledge of this which makes some missionary organizations so chary of letting Indian Christians really manage their own affairs. So even an Indian Bishop may be given an European Co-adjutor to see that he does not " go off the lines." The peculiarly absorbent character of Hinduism is, amongst the Missionaries, much feared, and from their point of view rightly enough. As regards the Europeanisation of Non-European races a recent pronouncement of the Catholic Vicar Apostolic of Nigeria is very noteworthy (reported in the " Catholic Herald of India," 26th Feb. 1919). Lecturing in aid of the West African Mission in St. Mary's Hall, Belfast, the Right Rev. Dr. Broderick, delared that " the idea that was fostered by Rome in regard to the evangelisation of the

African was a peculiarly national idea. It was Africa for the Africans. It had been pointed out by St. Francis Xavier, and it had been his Lordship's experience also, that for the most part the pagan who adopted European civilization adopted none of its virtues. To ensure, therefore, that the Africans would still be Africans, the Catholic Church was endeavouring hard to establish an African priesthood and an African sisterhood, trying in every possible way to utilise the brain power that undoubtedly was to be found in the possession of the natives." The Hindu religions however have that in them which meet the needs of every capacity and temperament. *Prima facie* they are best for those whose ancestors have evolved them. Even those who hold the contrary must, if reasonable, admit that to have some religion is better than to have none at all. Before they are rejected let them be examined. If they are then found to fail in giving knowledge and inspiration, some other should be adopted or devised. A recent missionary book ('Goal of India " by W. E. S. Holland) quotes the prayer with which the Indian National Congress opened its sessions, which, beginning with " Oh most gracious God and Father " proceeded with Christian wording and sentiment to speak of " Providence," " Thy unworthy servants," Thy Holy name, spirit and will, " glorify Thy name " and so forth and then winds up with " Amen." " Why " the author asks " do they not acknowledge Christ and come over to the Christian Church ? " His answer is incorrect. The real answer is not that the author and users of this prayer believed in the institutional Christianity of the missionary but the language of Western religion was imitated just as political agitation and the cultural forms of thought of the West are imitated. It is true, however, that though the English-educated Indian does not as a rule accept any of the Western creeds of Christianity, many have been largely affected by its spirit and even forms. Those even are sometimes to be found who unjustly depreciate their own people on that account. So an English-educated Bengali told a friend of mine that Hindu boys were not fit to become Boy Scouts, because the latter had to eschew impure thought, and a Hindu boy would think of the Linga. This offensive and ridiculous statement was a suggestion from a missionary-environment. Those Hindus who worship the Linga see nothing indecent in it. It is the missionary and some other Westerns who do so.

It was Svâmî Vivekânanda who said that when India becomes English, She dies. If this be so, all intermediate steps towards such a result spell weakness. When the sufficiently nourished and healthy Indian has sought for mental and spiritual power in his own cultural traditions and has failed to get it, it will then be the time to discuss whether his want of success is due to his alleged Barbarism, or to the faulty principles of his civilization or not, and if so in what respect and degree.

There is now and has been for sometime past a re-action towards Indian culture due to a rising racial consciousness, and, lately, to the exposure of some of the weaknesses of Western civilization by the Great War. There are many who now say " Physician, heal thyself." It is now also perceived by some that the effort towards political independence will bear no real fruit, if in the process, the Racial Soul is lost. In other words, the cultural question is of equal importance as the political one. It is possible that, in this reaction, everything western may be in the near future as unduly disparaged, as it was formerly, by some, indiscriminately appreciated. High praise is now more frequently given to all things Indian. If it be held that this is sometimes overdone, it is a fault on the right side. Anything is better than servile imitation of, and submission to, other's judgments. But it is just this reaction towards independence of spirit which we happily see in India to-day of which Mr. Archer complains. He constantly speaks of the " insensate arrogance "

311

of the Indian people and of their overweening pride in the civilization which he calls
'Barbarism.' He denies that they, or any
other people, are a " Chosen People."

To have a better idea of oneself than the
facts warrant is not an infirmity of the
Indian people only. So an Englishman is
apt to regard a "foreigner" (even a
Western) as something inferior. A quite
amusing and recent instance of this occurred
in the case of an English lady on a visit to
Germany just before the War. The lady
complained to a friend of mine of the
annoyance caused by the rules imposed by
the German Police. On being told that
they existed for all foreigners (Auslander)
she exclaimed indignantly " But I am not
a foreigner. I am an English woman." So
strong was her notion of the inferiority of
the foreigner, that she could not imagine
that under any circumstances, even in the
heart of Germany, she could be deemed to
be one. Most Englishmen entertain a high
idea of their country and its civilization
and the claim is even heard that they are

the "moral leaders" of the world. Their greatness has been voiced in much English literature and is with some an Imperial Cult. We have all heard of German claims though "Deutschland ueber alles" is mistranslated. It does not mean "Germany above everybody else" but the nation's interest above that of the individual. Yet even in the midst of complaints against Teutonic vauntings, an English author has recently published a book under a title which could hardly be found in any but political England, for it is called "Christian Imperialism." Therein its author, Mr. A. C. Hill, an enthusiastic believer in the imperial destiny of Britain, seeks to show that the growth of Her Empire has "on the whole been ruled by a religious impulse." A more absurd and inflated claim it would be hard to imagine. England acquired Her Empire not from "religious impulse" but to serve Herself, whatever be the spiritual ends which She may have thus unconsciously forwarded. He then glorifies the British character as that of a race (*pace* Mr.

Archer) "Chosen of God for a high mission;"
holding that British theories of life "have
been stamped with the seal of Christ's
approval;" "that no nation has been more
keenly sensible of the moral value of
Christianity;" that the "literature of
England is an Epitome of Life as it has been
known to all thinking men" and so on and
so forth. One cannot, of course, place too
much stress upon the opinion of any individual author, but there are many others who
have vaunted England's greatness and in
some things rightly enough. Thus Mr. Hill
(though his own claims are pitched in a
high key) thinks that he has been surpassed.
For his assertion of "a superiority on our
part" is coupled with a condemnation of
the popular Evangel of Mr. Rudyard Kip-
ling "as being too reminiscent of the
swashbuckler." Much may be learnt from
Novels which, though works of imagination,
reflect contemporary life. The distinguished
novelist the late George Gissing ("Crown
of Life" 51) gives the following picture of
noisy patriotism, inflamed by the bottle.

" Piers, have you ever felt grateful enough for being born an Englishman ? I've seen the world and I know : the Englishman is the top of creation. Let all the rest of the world go hang. I've seen something of other races and I don't think we have any right to despise them. ' I don't exactly despise them ' replied Alexander ' But I say that they are compared with us—a poor lot ! a shabby lot ! We (English journalists) guard the national honour. Let any confounded foreigner insult England and he has to reckon with *us*. A word from us and it means war, Piers, glorious war with triumphs for the race and civilization. England means civilization : the other nations don't count. We must be armed and triple armed. It is the cause of civilization. I stand for England's honour, England's supremacy on sea, and land."

In the same work written in 1899 another character is made to say :—" We ought to be rapidly outgrowing warfare. Yet we're going back—there's a military reaction— fighting is glorified by everyone who has a loud voice and in no country more than in England."

Another, a lady character. says (p. 193) : " Our work in the world is marked out for us. We have no choice unless we turn cowards. Of course we shall be hated by other countries more and more. We shall be accused of rapacity and arrogance, and everything else which is disagreeable in a large way ! We can't help that. If we enrich ourselves that is a legitimate reward for the task we perform. England means liberty and enlightenment. Let England spread to the ends of the earth. We must not be afraid of greatness ! We can't stop, still less draw back. Our politics have become our religion. Our rulers have a greater responsibility than was ever known in the world's history and they will be equal to it."

Then there are those who, going beyond the " Nation," sweep their eyes with wider gaze over " Race." These speak picturesquely of "The Race," the "Beak of Power," the " Drivers of men " and so forth. Major

Woodruff of the U.S.A. Army in his work on the effects of tropical light on white men says that the white skinned, blue eyed, Aryan, born to government and command, ever leaving his primeval, overcast and foggy home ever commands and governs the rest of the world, and ever perishes because of the too-white light he encounters. The dark types who labour for the white will not perish, but will ultimately inherit the earth, not because of their capacity for mastery and government, but because of their skin-pigmentation which enables their tissues to resist the ravages of the sun. A widely popular novelist voicing this modern glorification of the Race makes one of his characters say "And I look at the four of us at table — Captain West, his daughter, Mr. Pike and myself — all fair-skinned, blue eyed and perishing, yet mastering and commanding, like our fathers before us, to the end of our type on the earth. Ah well! Ours is a lordly history, and though we may be doomed to pass, in our time we shall have trod on the faces of all peoples, disciplined them to obedience, taught them government, and dwelt in the places we have compelled them by the weight of our own right arms to build for us" ("Mutiny of the Elsinore" by Jack, London, p. 161, published in 1915). One might suppose, from some criticisms, that this type of view was confined to Germany. This is not so. The Race-Worshipper, Imperialist, and other similar types are found in all the peoples of the West. The Anglo-Saxon people are a great people. They have maintained their greatness, and have to-day reached the height of their power largely by the strength of their race-consciousness and adherence to racial ideals. They will be greater still when they also recognise all other greatness which is not their own. There is a worship of Race which has in it the same truth as worship of the Motherland and of the natural Mother. It may however, like all else, become corrupted and voiced in a blatant and offensive form, but is even then, to me, greatly preferable to the hypocritical cant which conceals under a pretended interest for others a real contempt for them and a restless and selfish search for its own good. If there be (as Mr. Archer says) arrogance in Indian it does not weakly exist elsewhere.

The English, as other peoples, have good cause to be proud of many achievements. Though Patriotism always tends to exaggerated claims, there can be no question of the greatness of their race. Facts are the proofs. But the sense of racial superiority which they and other Westerns have as regards the Eastern (justified in some degree by their energy and the actual fact of dominance) is likely to, and does, lead to an inordinate self-appreciation, narrow exclusiveness and obtuseness of understanding, when estimating types of culture different from their own. It has often been pointed out by Indian writers that the Western is wont to take his own standard to be the measure of excellence and all which falls short of it is considered to be either bad or of little worth or absurd. There are but few who will judge another culture in a detached spirit. This obtuseness, and lack of insight, bred in the spirit of race-pride is, it has been rightly said, the source of great cleavages not only between Western and Oriental peoples but between the former themselves. On the other hand, it may be conceded that there is racial vanity in India as elsewhere. There are, for instance, a considerable number of people who without reason give themselves airs; for instance, those who are always talking of their great Shâstras and yet never read them, and those who, being in a futile way materialists themselves, have western materialism always on their lips, as if all Westerns were benighted in spiritual darkness. As Indian writer ("Modern Review") after referring to some observations by an English author to the effect that the present War was the outcome of the prevalence of Western civilization and materialism, said that he did not do so to enable every Indian worldling (and to-day there are many such) to vaunt Indian spirituality; adding "a man is to be judged not by the ideals of the best men of his country, dead or living, but by the ideals to which his own life bears witness. Most of us are as materialistic as most Westerns, with this difference that we are feebly and languidly materialistic on a small scale, whilst they are strongly and energetically materialistic on a large scale. But the real question is, are we living up to it ? It should also be considered whether we are as ready as Western idealists are to admit our faults and reform ourselves." There are, on the other hand, in this country, as in the West, truly spiritually minded men, for without some spirituality, no civilization, even inefficiently, endures. It is the fact that there are " chosen " peoples just as there are exceptionally endowed individuals. Greece was a chosen people for her wonderful art and philosophy ; India for her religion and profound metaphysic ; and other peoples have been, in various ways, distinguished.

XII

SANGSKÂRA AS THE ROOT OF INDIAN CULTURE

ACCORDING to Hindu ideas a child is not born with a mind which is *tabula rasa*. On the contrary the mind bears within it the history of countless past experiences in previous births, which have left certain impressions on, and tendencies in, it. These are called Sangskâras. These constitute the disposition of the soul or mental body (Antahkarana). The Sangskâra covers both, (what are called in Europe,) instinct and innate ideas. Just as there is an individual, there is a racial, Sangskâra, that is, certain common tendencies shared by all men of a particular Race. It is by its manifestation that we know whether a man is an Englishman, an Indian, a Frenchman and so forth. It is the Sangskâra which forms the essence of a man or people. For it is the quintessence of past thoughts and acts, their result in the most generalized form. It is therefore that which really counts. The Sangskâra, when embodied in a particular man, explicates into the particular character, disposition, thoughts and acts of that man. The Sangskâra is thus the seed (Bîja) of a man or collectivity of men. It is the root of Type. This general Racial Soul is, in the realm of mind, that which persists, just as, in the realm of Life, we have the continuous germ-plasm, and in the realm of matter, a substratum for chemical and physical changes. There is always something continuous, absolutely or relatively, from which varieties issue. The present collective Indian Sangskâra has been acquired through an immense period of time, and though throughout these ages there have been changes, there has yet been an uniformity more marked than that of the peoples of Western Europe. An orthodox Indian to-day, uninfluenced by English education, living a truly Indian life, is very like the Indian of the past. It is the same man born over again. But the modern English man and woman, though of course of the same general strain as their ancestors, are yet more dissimilar. A modification of Sangskâra has taken place producing a somewhat different type of character and outlook on life. The picture we see of fat and jolly "John Bull" is scarce to be found either in physique or character, amongst present day Englishmen.

The same process is slowly going on in India under the influence of Western education. A modified character is being produced itself productive of Sangskâra which will in time give birth to other similar or further developed forms. How is the Sangskâra acquired ? By action or Karma. Particular actions, and by this term is included all thought-activity, produce like results. The Chhândogya Upanishad says " As a man thinks so he becomes." A man who is always thinking of money and the pleasure of possessing it, becomes a miser. It is for this reason that all moral systems are particular as regards the formation of right

habits. Their upholders know that a single
wrong act (not greatly important in itself)
may lead to another, and this to yet others,
tending to the formation of a habit which
may itself become so confirmed as to be
almost ineradicable. Let us suppose that
the habit is one which so prevails in the
West, namely over-drinking. When that
particular man dies, his soul or mental body
bears on it an impression produced by its
past acts, and a tendency to reproduce these
acts, when, on rebirth, an opportunity is
given to do so. This impression, tendency,
or disposition is Sangskâra. The soul is born
again with a tendency towards this bad
habit, which nevertheless can be controlled
and repressed from actually manifesting
itself. So again, Indian civilization has
hitherto been of a spiritual character. And
this is because the Indian child, himself or
herself the product of a long line of ancestors
taught to take a spiritual view of life, was
trained from early infancy to be devout,
reverential, and upward-looking in his or
her thoughts, and obedient to a discipline

which has been framed to secure a spiritual
result. If however the state of affairs, such
as it now exists in some English-educated
families, be extended throughout India, then
this particular Sangskâra will be suppressed
and in lieu of it we shall have a type which
is lacking in reverence, intolerant of control,
independent to the extent of disobedience,
realistic, concerned merely with the here
and now, sceptical of, or denying, the existence of God, and so on. Such a Sangskâra
if developed in successive bodies is strengthened until a character may be produced of
such a demoniac nature that self-destruction
follows. Sangskâra, let it be noted, is not in
itself, that is as Sangskâra and considered
apart from its manifestation in bodies, a
particular thing, thought, or act. It is
something general, an essence of various
past particularities, which gives again
future birth to them. It is true that a particular Sangskâra potentially contains and
gives birth to particular beliefs and action.
But we may distinguish between the essential part of a Sangskâra, that is as general

tendency, and the particular acts which are the fruit of it. Thus a religious Sangskâra which, when manifested, displays itself in a particular Hindu or Christian form may be considered from the point of view of the general disposition and of that which is the particular fruit of it. Thus, if for example, a Christian missionary were desirous of wisely proceeding to forward his faith among the Indian people, he would in the first place take care not to injure the general religious disposition and tendency, the faith and devotion which spring from the Indian Sangskâra. Above all he would not shock or chill that disposition and devout character by ridiculing its particular manifestation and thus sowing the seeds of a scepticism which might ultimately recoil on himself. On the contrary he would take every care to foster this general part of the Sangskâra and would direct the attention to the particular manifestation, leading the Indian away from it and in the direction he wished his mind to go. In short he would say " Keep your religious feeling, but direct it in the way I show you, and not as your people do." Now let us take a case of less interference with the past experience. A Hindu "Reformer," believing generally in the teachings and practice of the Hindu tradition, is however of opinion that in some matters, belief and conduct have gone astray from the right path and have become incompatible with Indian truth. He is dealing with an Indian child. The latter's Sangskâra may tend towards the adoption of not only what the "Reformer" accepts, but also of what he rejects. The latter, if wise, will foster the Sangskâra in every way, except in the particular he desires to modify it. Thirdly take the case of the Orthodox Hindu. If the Sangskâra of the child works in the same direction as his own he will simply foster it. Lastly assume the case where there is a resolution to supplant altogether Indian culture by another. Such an attempt will meet with some difficulty because of the natural resistance of the Sangskâra which is the result of centuries of past experience. It is not easily pushed away, nor can it be wholly destroyed by another. But perseverance will do a great deal. Let the first generation which is naturally weak—(for when a foreigner gains rule over another people that people must be weak)—be dazzled by the pomp and power of their Rulers. Let them and succeeding generations be told that this Power and all the good things which accompany it are the fruits of a superior civilization. Let the teachers constantly harp upon the inferiority of the ruled, upon the inferiority of their religion and philosophy and art and of their social institutions. Let the first be called a crude superstition, or idle speculation, and the second interesting as an antique relic but not otherwise of value. Let art be called barbaric and so on. Let this be repeated in season and out. Further let the education be of a foreign type in which all that is specifically Indian is ignored. Then let it be made clear that the way to " get on," to get appointments, emoluments and success is to make oneself as like one's Rulers and their Race as possible, and in any case make an English education and a degree following thereon indispensable to State and professional employment. In this and other ways the Sangskâra, acquired through centuries, is so repressed, by another that the Indian character and outlook is partially and temporarily lost. But a Sangskâra is a wonderful thing. The work of Ages is not to be done away with even in a century. And so we see something which disconcerts the lay or religious missionary, namely a recrudescence of the ancient Sangskâra, wherever it is given a chance of display. This is the " Call of the Blood."

The above illustrates what has taken place in India amongst those who are subject to foreign influences ; for, of course, the great mass of the people, who are without foreign education, are largely, though not wholly, untouched by western influence. The Indian Sangskâra has been prevented, or hindered, from developing itself. It has been overlaid by foreign influences. All that is primarily required is to remove these hindrances when the ancient Indian spirit will manifest itself by itself. This is self-expression.

But it may be said by the advocates of " Progress " that they do not desire this, at any rate without qualification. India they fear would then be stagnant. They need have no such fear. Nature will, and always does, take care of herself, if men will only allow Her to do so. India in the past evolved for herself ideas and a social organism, with its customs and practices, which were the expression of Herself and suitable to Her needs. As long as She remains a living organism She will do so again. All that is required is to free the Sangskâra from the superincumbent foreign mass which, being unassimilated, is threatening to choke it. This Sangskâra is the Bîja or Seed of Indian Culture. From it all else grows. I have no partizan interest to serve. Whether India should go in one way or another is for Her to say. Personally I should like to see what is of value to me preserved. But after all, it is not what one likes but what is good for others which counts. It may possibly be that India, if free to develop herself, may produce a future very different from Her past. The demand here made is that She be free to develop *according to Her nature* and *its wants.* India might thus abandon Her present forms of religion for Christianity, Buddhism or Mahómedanism. On the other hand She might adhere to her own present Dharma and its social organism, or again She might adapt herself to new forms of life and thought, consonant with some of the economical and industrial and intellectual principles of the day. Possibly all religions may stress, in future more than they have generally hitherto done, the active aspect of the one Brahman. None of these matters now concern me. I only wish to see India's Spirit, enshrined in the collective Sangskâra, given free play, having confidence that if She regains *cultural freedom,* that is the *full right and opportunity of self-expression,* She will produce in the end what is good and suitable for her, and what, having regard to Her great past, will also be great and thus of benefit to Humanity at large. No good result will be got by the adoption of Mr. Archer's suggestions in " India in the Future " to give up the illusion of a glorious past, which he says does not exist, and to conform Herself to the Western spirit and ways. Life is not thus fostered. The main thing for which man should strive is self-expression. " *Be oneself.*" He should always be true to his nature and express himself, and not others. The one is the path of life and the other of death. This injunction *to be natural* is the essence of Taoist morals. It is also taught in Hinduism, which preaches Svadharma which has been well described by Professor P. N. Mukhyopâdhyâya as the individual's particular current in the great stream of the flow of cosmic evolution. As the Gîtâ says, better is it to follow one's own Dharma than that of another however exalted. Nietzche asks " What saith thy conscience?" and answers " Thou shalt not become what thou art not. Never be virtuous beyond thy nature." As with some other sayings of his, this seems paradoxical and immoral. It is not so when rightly understood. What is meant is that one should strive to be good according to one's nature, not aiming at once at what is beyond one's capacity. This is not possible of achievement and will lead to failure, which encourages despondency, and discourages further effort. If we endeavour to perfect ourselves within the limits of our nature, that is to the extent immediately possible, we shall, when we have attained success in this, be on a level to make a further true advance.

What then is to be done? In the first place all ideas and practices which are foreign and *unassimilated*, and which merely cloak, and thus form no part of the racial spirit should be cast off. The Indian Spirit will then regain its liberty. It should then be strengthened and fostered by the food suitable to it: that is by the food it naturally seeks, and not the food which others think is good for it. Then it may assimilate any food, foreign or indigenous, that it pleases. Foreign matter is not necessarily bad in itself. On the contrary much of it is good and necessary for India. This country cannot, even if it would, shut itself up in a glass case and cry " contamination " when anything approaches it. The West possesses a fund of knowledge from which it must draw, and practices which may be of service to it. But the point is this :—these must not be worn as it were a garment for the body, but they must be eaten and assimilated and thus form part of the body itself. Every nation has thus been indebted to another. But vital nations do not merely borrow and copy. They assimilate, and what is assimilated becomes our own. As I have said elsewhere, Greece is said to have borrowed in her artistic beginnings from Egypt. But She assimilated what She thus took, and made it into Herself,—something so different that the model has ceased to appear in it. And so with India ; let her take what is useful from the West and make it her own. A

new Sangskâra will develop which will be
a variation on India's ancient theme. But
let her not merely copy, for this way a
sterile automatism lies.

For these reasons what is called "National
Education" is of the highest importance.
There are some who are contemptuous of it.
They ask "how is knowledge national?"
Is 2+2 any the less 4 in India than in
Europe and so on? They profess in fact
not to understand what "national education" is. And perhaps such is the low ebb
of vitality in some quarters in this country
that some do not. These objections have
an air of smartness but display considerable
misunderstanding.

National education means to bring up an
Indian as an Indian, and not like an
Englishman or any one else. Is there anything hard to understand in this? If one
were to ask an Englishman whether he
understands what is meant by "bringing
up his boy as an Englishman" he would
laugh. Of course he does. There may be
a few who have sent their children to

Germany or to French or Belgian convents or Austrian schools, such as Feldkirch, but the vast mass would say " We are not concerned to criticise the foreigner. What is our own is best for us. I want my boy to be in English surroundings amongst English boys; to learn the ways and manners of his country, to receive the knowledge which is given to a gentleman and to become an English gentleman himself. Foreign ways and habits are not ours." The Race-consciousness of the British and Irish is very strong, and for this reason they are what they are, mounting in the case of the English to the pitch of exalted Power at which they now are. That Race-consciousness tells them what to do, and they are not therefore always solving intellectual problems, or putting up theoretical difficulties. In India I have heard it said that an exclusively Eastern education will not do. If this means that all Western knowledge should not be shut out, it is indeed sense. But the advocate of National Education also is not

337

without it. What however he desires is an education for Indians under the general control of Indians. He wants that education to be given from the Indian standpoint. Whilst he desires to see taught, all Western knowledge of an objective scientific character, he also wishes that Indian religion, philosophy, art, and literature should not be neglected as they have been in varying degrees up to the present time. Take History. Why should an Indian boy study the History of the English in England and in India and be taught nothing, or next to nothing, of the country as it was before the English came? Why should he learn European and American philosophy and be ignorant of his own? Why should he learn to draw and paint after Western models, however good of their kind (and in India they are generally not that), neglecting the artistic principles and examples of his country? Why lastly and above all should he not be taught his own particular form of Indian Religion? Only those can deny the necessity

338

of all this who regard Indian culture of such little present worth that it may be discarded altogether. But those who take this stand cannot claim any form of independence. If, according to modern views, the relative values of a culture are in such a case any test, then a people whose culture is inferior and incapable of development into what is of worth are not fit to manage their affairs. National or racial education is necessary for the conservation of the Racial Spirit. It is also necessary if real education is to be given at all. What is " to educate," but to " educe," to draw out? What can be drawn out but that which is potentially present in a child? That which is present is the Indian Sangskâra. It is that which must be drawn out, fostered and strengthened by every educational food, foreign or Indian, which it can digest. But at first and for the weak state in which some are, an Indian dietary is the best. I asked once my friend Mr. Havell, late Principal of the School of Art, why he did not get a good selection of photographs of

Western Art including the Italian Masters for the Art Gallery. His answer was what I have given above. He said " I admire these Masters as others do. But my boys will merely copy them and lose their artistic selves. The weak must take one diet. The strong can eat what they like without injury to themselves."

In conclusion I mention an objection which is made to every form of development of Race-consciousness. Disraeli in " Sidonia " said " All is Race." Some still believe it. Others are dissentient. They think that national and race-consciousness are mere representations to-day of the ancient savage tribal consciousness and thus something to be rid of. They see that it leads to divisions among men and to strife. The goal therefore is Internationalism. Nietzsche put it well when he said " Is there a single idea behind this bovine nationalism ? What positive value can there be in encouraging this arrogant self-conceit, when everything to-day points to greater and more common interests—at a moment when the spiritual dependence and denationalisation which are obvious to all are paving the way for the reciprocal rapprochements and fertilizations which make up the real value and sense of present day culture?" Internationalism may be in some future time. So far from desiring to foster quarrels of any kind I would see them all disappear. But my belief is firstly that a true Internationalism can only be founded upon good elements, and that good elements can only be had by, in the first place, developing each Race-spirit to its utmost. In other words the development of the individual man must be according to his own law (Svadharma). When he is perfected in this he will be a true citizen of an international State if such there ever be. Moreover, many are in so backward a condition that such an idea as Internationalism is incomprehensible to them. If prematurely forced into its practice they would ruin the internationalistic idea. For its success the best elements in man are required, namely knowledge, charity, tolerance and the service of Humanity at

large. Man must learn his own true
interests and those of his family first before
he can truly serve the interests of his race,
and he must learn to serve his Country,
Race, and Nation before he is capable of
serving Humanity at large. With all the
present talk of Brotherhood how few
practise it ! We must then work at first on
a lower round of the ladder. There are, and
always will be some, in every country, who
stand on a higher rung. Such will lead the
rest of their fellows there in due time.
Secondly there is a special reason
applicable to India. I believe that the
principles of Indian civilization are of
great value. Without belittling those of
others, I think that it will be to the benefit
of the world at large that it should have
the help of the Indian people infused by
the Indian spirit, and not servile imitators
for whom we Westerns have no place. We
have no need for disciples in matters in
which we are the masters. In order that
Indian culture should take its place in the
world it is necessary that the Indian Spirit,

which has produced that culture, should be fostered. This is for the world-good, and for this end, whatever be our race, we should all render our service, and thus be Friends of the World. (*Jagadbandhu*)

*

XIII

SOME CONCLUSIONS

INDIA is now approaching the most momentous epoch in its history. To answer the question why this is so would lead me into the subject of practical politics which I do not here discuss. The country will also be subject to the play of monster economic forces. Already and for sometime past, Indian markets have been in increasing degree linked up with those of the West with results to Her poor already showing themselves. For the first time in Her history she will be thrown into the World-vortex, political, economic, cultural and social, from which her past form of Government has (I believe providentially) preserved Her. Will She have the strength to keep Her feet in it; I hope She may. The next question is, will She keep Her feet and remain Indian ; that is, will She preserve the essentials of her grand civilization. Again that is my hope. But if so, it will be because She has had the will and the strength to guard and uphold Her Indian Self. Our Western civilization is a great Eater. We consume. What is called a " higher standard of life " has hitherto meant with us that we consume more and more. Industrialism instead of satisfying, has increased our Western needs. " We want more wants ;" and if our own store has not satisfied, then we have gone to that of others. It has been well said by Mr. Lawrence Housman that " in the pursuit of wealth every country had become in more or less degree non-self-supporting from within, dependent on power to control or to influence favourably, to its own interests, outside conditions. And the more it was dependent for its prosperity, or for its sufficiency, or supply from without instead of from within, the more it was involved in the larger international struggle for existence which has ended in the bloodiest and most devasting war known to human history ;" the final accounts of which, I may add, have yet to be rendered. India must then be on Her guard to preserve Herself unless She is content to be assimilated to others and to thus lose Her Racial Soul. Where can She gain strength to save Herself, *as Herself*, except from Her own cultural inheritance. The universal assertion and adoption by all peoples of the noble and essential principles of Her spiritual civilization would lead to a world-peace.

The East has been the home of all the greatest spiritual teachers. India has taught that the Universe is in its ultimate ground Spirit ; that what is material is the expression of the Eternal Spirit in time and space ; that Man is essentially either that self-same Spirit, or a part of, or akin to it ; that the Universe is governed by a Just Law which is the very nature of its true expression ; that all Life is sacred ; that Morality is the law of humanity, which is the master of its destiny and reaps only what it has sown; that the universe has a moral purpose, and that the Social Structure must be so ordered as to subserve it; and many another sublime truth which is the warrant of Her high civilization, which may yet bear fruit not only in India but throughout the world, thus justifying her claim to be the Karmabhûmi.

Every man and every race can only continue to truly live by being himself, by being itself, otherwise he and they are nothing. But this race will not perish if it continues to worship the Mother-Power greater than the greatest, manifest in the littlest, seen in Shâkta worship not as an image of sorrow, but joyous, crowned with ruddy flashing gems, clad in red raiment, (*Lauhityam etasya sarvasya vimarshah*) more effulgent than millions of rising suns, with one hand granting all blessings and with the other dispelling all fears. Hinduism has deeply perceived that fear is an essential mark of the animal and of the animal (Pashu) in man. The fearless win all worldly enterprises and fearlessness is also the sign of the illuminate knower.

In any case India must in order to live be faithful to Herself as each must be faithful to himself. As the Indian scripture says, " The greatest religion is Truth," which means all honesties. According to the natural scheme of things each whether " Orthodox," or " Reformer," must act as he sincerely believes for the benefit of his country. None are doing wrongly who act according to their conscience and judgment, sincerely thought out and held. All honest endeavour works for the World-ends of Îshvara the World-Lord, whatever be the difference in aims and means. Sincerity may be a link to bind all. None have the right to forsake their duty as they sincerely conceive it to be, because they may fancy that what they work for will not happen. How can they know this with certainty—And even if they could, it is the design of Îshvara that what He wills to be shall only come about after every obstacle thereto has been surmounted. For these obstacles are part of His wisdom. Never should we think of failure. Those who do, have already begun to fail. But if we look at things largely, we shall know that to fail is nothing if we have striven to succeed : that effort and its result, limited though it be, is achievement. We are all (though free) in the service of the World-purpose, the organised expression in time, space and matter of the undying spiritual Self. Reverence, therefore, to the highest Self by whatsoever name men may call It—a Self which is both immanent in the universe of forms which are Its Power and yet form-lessly transcends it.

But there are some in this country who, in this period of transition and scepticism due to foreign influence, believe in none of such things and who are as materialist, though often less usefully so, than any Western. Modern Western civilization, great though in several respects it be, is, in so far as it is divorced from religion, poison for Eastern peoples. Such persons in fact think that India has suffered through its religion.

She would, they think, have "got on" better without it. Such have learnt nothing from recent and present events which, like a flash of lightning, make clear the dangers amidst which men have walked in darkness. If, notwithstanding warning, those who have hitherto been the custodians of these great traditions neglect or reject them, they will themselves perish and will deserve to perish, or they will suffer a worse lot, namely a lasting deprivation of the high place in the world which the greatness of their forbears had sought to make for them. They may just exist, but as what and how ? As against such a possibility the Indian may derive encouragement from two facts drawn from his history. The first is that Hindu civilization, which itself survives to-day, has absorbed other cultures. This is in itself, evidences of adaptability to circumstance. It is because "it has swallowed up every civilization and every religion which has mixed with it" that an American writer (Mr. Price Collier in "The East in the West" 177) justifies what he finds to be the British attitude in refusing such intimacy of intercourse as would entail the mixing up of one civilization with the other. Only thus he says can the British retain their individuality and thus their control. The second point is one of which a friendly critic ("The Leader") has reminded me. "Reform" movements in India justify the changes they advocate not by reference to Western precedent but by appeal to ancient Texts. The impulse to such "reform" may doubtless have arisen from the impact of the West on the East, but it does not necessarily follow that the changes proposed are, in themselves, opposed to true Indian principle and practice. It may be the evidence of a striving from the very Heart of the Hindu Consciousness to persist, by adapting itself to the new environment which has been thrust upon it. Firm as is my conviction that what has true value is never lost, and therefore that the basal ideas of Hinduism are imperishable, here or hereafter, uprising according to Indian notions world after world as the eternal Veda, I yet clearly see that the Ârya Dharma is to be now submitted to an attack greater than it has ever experienced in all the Ages. One cannot be certain what the immediate future may be. We must distinguish between the present Indian People and their cultural ideas, which may and will pass over into the West, whatever happens to the race which evolved them. We must distinguish between the question of the rejuvenation of the present Indian People and the persistence of the spirit of the ancient culture. This is eternal and will live in any case in newer races on the exhaustion of the Âsurî-Prakriti, or the present egoistic cycle.

It is obvious to all that East and West are being gradually linked up in a way which has almost entirely destroyed the isolation of the past. There can thus be no purely separatist culture. As a result a Common Human Consciousness is arising which is working for a common moral end, in disregard of all racial and geographical barriers. As I have said cultural conflict may in the future give increasing place to co-operation, which is to many still but an idle, where it is not a dangerous, dream. If so, the future world-civilization will be in a form which is the resultant of the interplay of the forces, spiritual, moral, and intellectual, which have contributed to its making. I am concerned with the present which is the only thing which counts, since it makes the future. The survival and well being of the present Indian people will foster the spread and acceptance of their culture.

Will they survive as a specific living Indian organism substantially such as we have known it? There are some peoples among them who are said to be disappearing. Those who are the custodians of the Indian tradition may surrender themselves to other cultures. The dissolution of the social bonds, which hold that organism together, may be so loosened that it may cease to be such. It may be that, as with the ancient Greek culture, Indian Religion, Philosophy and Art may linger on amongst a few adherents of the ancient tradition, amidst the millions educated by their Western or

353

westernized Governors, (of British or Indian blood) adopting their thought and ways, serving them as the subordinate instruments of their giant industrial undertakings. If so, " India," as the organism we have known it, will have gone. On the other hand, whatever be the material changes which the future may bring, however much the present organism may be altered, its spirit may yet survive with sufficient strength to infuse the new body, which it may then attain, with those root ideas which, as the seed of Indian Being, are that which truly counts. From the Indian seed will rise again another Indian plant. None can yet say what the future has thus in store. It behoves however all who value those ideas to bestir themselves for their conservation.

In any case the chief religious and philosophic concepts of India are, in their essentials, imperishable. Whether the Indian people hold to them or not, they will be taken up and added to the cultural wealth of the greater amongst the white Âryas (*Shukla varna pinggala kesha*) of the West from whose Eastern branch in ages past, the coloured peoples of ancient India, in part at least, received them. These essential ideas will then in any case remain because, as humanizing man for the spiritual end which they place before him, they are those of a great and true Civilization.

APPENDIX

SIR JOHN WOODROFFE ON INDIAN CULTURE[1]

By A. K. JAMESON, I.C.S.

UNDER the somewhat startling title of "Is India Civilized?" Sir John Woodroffe, late a Judge of the Calcutta High Court, published in November, 1918, a series of essays dealing with the main features of Indian culture (the word has acquired unfortunate associations but there is no exact equivalent). Sir John being an authority respected more particularly amongst the educated Indians, the first edition of the little book was quickly exhausted and a second called for as early as May, 1919. It may therefore be not unprofitable to consider the nature of the exposition which has evidently commended itself so favourably

[1] Reprinted with permission from the "Calcutta Review" April. 1920.

to Indian opinion. In form the book is a reply to criticisms brought against Indian Civilization by Mr. William Archer in "India and the Future," but it contains much more than a mere refutation of other peoples' views; it is a constructive effort to set out what the author believes to be the essence of all that is distinctively Indian. Before dealing with it, however, it may be as well to state definitely that we hold no brief for Mr. Archer, whose pronouncements, whatever amount of truth they may contain, suffer from that confident dogmatism and violence of statement which so often afflict those who write about matters Indian—whether favourably or the reverse—on the strength of a very superficial acquaintance.

The chief object of the book, then, is in the author's own words, "to state summarily and correctly the main principles of Indian civilization". Emphasis is laid strongly on the correctness, for it is asserted that Mr. Archer's criticisms are based on a distorted conception of what those principles really are, and that they lose their force when confronted with a true statement. There is, however, a subsidiary object in the mind of the author, namely, "to explain the general cause of the

attacks which have so constantly been made
upon " Indian Civilization, and a large part of
the book is taken up with analysing this cause.
He divides it into three branches, racial,
religious, and political, and carries it back
right to the very constitution of the universe,
exhibiting it as a secular example of the
struggle of Spirit, the sole ultimate reality, to
organize the matter in which it has involved
itself into finer and finer forms, until at last it
releases itself from the trammels altogether.
In the lower stages of this process, conflict is
not only inevitable but beneficial, for it tends
to the evolution of ever more complete modes
of expression of Spirit, the better thrusting out
the inferior, until a point is reached where
competition may be replaced by co-operation.
The fact that the proximate motive of the
individual persons or races engaged in the
struggle is in the main self-regarding, and
that they are for the most part unaware of the
rôle they are playing as vehicles of the evolving Spirit, does not alter the beneficial character of the process, because Spirit can work
through unconscious or even rebellious agents
to accomplish its great purpose. But when
man in the course of his development has

attained to a stage where he is conscious of the process but is not yet sufficiently advanced to adopt the ultimate ideal of co-operation, he begins to clothe his naked political selfishness with apparent altruisms, and pretends that when powerful nations strive to crush alien cultures they are impelled by the solemn duty of raising the ruled to the cultural level of the rulers. This the author brands as objectionable hypocrisy, and it is of this that he accuses Mr. Archer and all who make similar attacks on Indian Culture, a hypocrisy which leads them to traduce and belittle it in order to justify an attempt at eliminating it altogether by pretending that it is so hopelessly and fundamentally bad as to be intolerable in a world which aims at progress. The real motive, however, according to the author, is simply the fear that if an alien culture should be acknowledged to have worth and be allowed to strengthen and propagate itself, the culture of the critic's own country might be in danger of being swamped or altered out of recognition. This is asserted in respect not only to the intellectual, artistic, and political elements in culture, but also to the religious. As we said above we are not concerned to defend

Mr. Archer, but the allegations which the author makes against European missionaries in this connection cannot be altogether passed over in silence. He asserts that they have identified Christianity absolutely with the institutional form which it has developed in Europe, that they are simply units in the army which aims at the total destruction of Indian culture from purely selfish motives, and equally concerned with the others to impose European culture in its totality on India regardless of the real meaning of their religion. The reason he gives is that they are afraid that, if simply the principles of Christianity are presented to Indians and they are allowed to interpret them and to build up an organization in accordance with the inherited traditions and bent of mind of India, the resultant form may cease to be a useful instrument in the maintenance of European supremacy. In so asserting he is surely guilty of the very sin of misrepresentation of which he accuses Mr. Archer ; but we shall return later on to his attitude towards Christianity in general.

It has been said that Mr. Archer's attack is of the most comprehensive nature, directed against every branch of Indian culture, and a considerable section of it is devoted to Indian Art in its widest sense, including architecture, sculpture, painting, and music. The reply, however, dismisses all this in a couple of sentences. "These comparisons in matters of taste seem to serve no useful purpose. Let each mind feed upon what it likes best, and do not let ourselves intrude on the peace of its enjoyment." This is simply to abandon all attempt at finding a standard of value, and in any case it hardly does justice to Mr. Archer's position. For he grounds his criticism on an examination of the philosophical basis on which the admirers of these elements in Indian culture rest their support of them. In fact here, more than in most other parts of his book, Mr. Archer satisfies Sir John Woodroffe's constant plea for going back to first principles, a course which he alleges to be unfamiliar to western critics. The line which Mr. Archer takes is that the approbation of Indian art so freely lavished by critics of the school of Mr. Havell and Dr. A. K. Coomaraswamy depends on certain presuppositions which properly speaking do not belong to the artistic sphere at all but to what he calls the " theologico-philosophical," and that it forms part of the claim to spirituality as the sole basis of Indian culture as against the material, or at best mixed spiritual-material, basis of European culture. He denies the validity of the claim, and as a strong supporter of it Sir John Woodroffe might have been expected to join issue with Mr. Archer on the point; had he done so it would have been interesting to see his method of dealing with it.

In fact, however, Sir John Woodroffe confines himself to the religious and philosophical branch of the attack, recognizing, in our opinion rightly, that "Religion is the most important element in culture". In estimating the worth of a culture one cannot go far wrong in devoting the largest share of attention to its religious aspects, including therein not merely the metaphysical or theological grounds but also the results of these in actual practice—an important addition as we shall see later on. For in the ultimate analysis all other branches of culture depend on the view which man takes of his place and purpose in the universe; for according to that view all his other activities are moulded. We may be grateful to Sir John Woodroffe for his resolute insistence on this fundamental principle, too often over-looked in an age when more superficial aspects of human existence attract greater attention than at any previous stage of history, and this whether we accept or reject his application of it to the facts he seeks to elucidate. But first, in order to answer the question propounded in his book " Is India Civilized ? " it is necessary to define what is meant by Civilization. The definition which is given is strictly in accordance with the point of view indicated above and is worth quoting in full. " The vital progressive impulse of which we are conscious is the impulse of Life to so organize itself that it may become a more and more perfect vehicle of Spirit. This impulse it is which organizes matter into gradually ascending forms, and which, when man is reached, works in him to effect his spiritual development. True Civilization is a process which has the same end. It may and does produce some material comfort but this is not an end in itself, but when rightly employed a means whereby man's mental and spiritual nature is given greater play on its increasing release from the animal cares of life. That then is true Civilization which, recognizing God as

364

its beginning and its end, organizes men in society through their material and mental vehicles with the view to the manifestation of Spirit in its forms as true morality and true religion." This is well put and affords an adequate basis for the discussion. But obviously much, in fact everything, turns on the interpretation to be put on the words " true religion ". That is to say, a true religion being alone capable of manifesting Spirit, an organization which purports to manifest Spirit through a religion which is not true, cannot be a true Civilization.

Turning then to the author's exposition of religion, we find that, true to his pursuit of first principles, he begins with a definition of religion. " In its most fundamental sense Religion is the recognition that the world is an Order or Cosmos of which each man is a part and to which he stands in a definitely established relation ; together with action based on and consistent with such recognition and in harmony with the whole cosmic activity." It may be objected that in his endeavour to make it as comprehensive as possible he has leaned unduly to the side of vagueness. Such a definition would, for instance, not exclude the attitude of mind of the scientist of the school of Herbert Spencer, and though it may be conceded that such an attitude is in a sense religious, there is little to be gained by expanding a term which has a definite connotation in its application to the vast majority of mankind in order not to exclude a small group who would be perfectly content to have their tenets described as philosophy instead of religion. For to all except the unqualified nondualists of the school of Sankara religion has reference to a personal being, and even in India there are other authoritative teachers besides Sankara. Applying, however, this conception to the religion of India, he finds that it consists of certain fundamental ideas the chief of which is Dharma or Cosmic Order conceived as inherent and manifested by all beings, that, in fact, which constitutes them what they are. The root of all activities is desire which seeks for itself the fruit of its actions and thus manifests itself in action or Karma, which may be either in accordance with Dharma or opposed to it, the former leading to happiness and the latter to suffering either in this birth or in subsequent births the conditions of which are determined solely by the nature of the previous Karma. Both forms of action bind the soul to the world of forms, but escape from that world to the eternal bliss of the unchanging formless world of pure Spirit may be attained by the practice of morality, by spiritual discipline, and by direct knowledge of the Real as opposed to the unreal and transitory of which alone the senses give cognizance.

The phrase "Religion of India" has been used because the author himself uses it throughout. He is, of course, not unaware that many have held it to be a misnomer on account of the almost infinite diversity of both belief and practice which appears to characterise the religious life of India. And indeed while justifying it on the ground that the outline given above embraces the fundamental conceptions of every apparent variety and that there is thus a spiritual unity at the back of them all, he is still compelled to admit that even in relation to these basic concepts there are real differences of opinion, as for example the identity or otherwise of the individual and the supreme Spirit. He, however, minimises these in asserting that they do not affect the question of the worth of Indian civilization because, whichever of the opinions may be held, all alike possess great value. He himself writes from the standpoint of the Shakta school whose tenets are to be found in the Tantras, and he is satisfied that its principles afford the most wonderful synthesis of the rival claims of the World and the Spirit. It may be doubted whether the followers of the better known and what are generally considered more orthodox systems of the Vedanta would be quite so willing as he is to admit the equal value of the two interpretations. One had an idea gathered from the works not only of European but also of Indian expositors of Indian religion that the Tantrik systems were looked at askance, and that their pretensions to affiliation with the Vedas were at least somewhat doubtful. And this idea is certainly not lessened by a perusal of the reviews of Sir John Woodroffe's own work " Principles of Tantra " (written under the pen name of Arthur Avalon) copious extracts from which are appended to it. The general impression left is that the Tantras have been systematically neglected and misunderstood by all the best known and most competent interpreters of Hindu religion of whatever school, until

Sir John Woodroffe rescued them from oblivion and established their claim to legitimacy as exponents of the true Vedanta. His answer to this probably would be that the disrepute into which they had fallen—a fact which admits of no doubt—was due to attention being rivetted on certain objectionable practices which had sprung up among the followers of the school due to an incorrect interpretation of its principles, and that when the latter are studied impartially and only such practices are observed as are really sanctioned by them, this prejudice will disappear. Of the practical aspect we shall have something to say presently; but even granting his contention it may be considered somewhat doubtful whether a system which is so open to misconstruction as to have in fact been habitually misconstrued for centuries by all the leaders of Indian thought has any just claim to pose as an authoritative exposition of that thought.

The system in brief may be expressed thus. The Universe is a manifestation of the Power (Shakti) of the Supreme Consciousness or Self which is theologically called Shiva, and in His aspect of manifestation is known as the

Great Devi or Divine Mother. The two are twin aspects of the One, being respectively, in the language of western theology, the Transcendent and the Immanent. Spirit involves Itself in matter and then gradually evolves Itself therefrom, and thus, though of Its own nature blissful, yet as and through man It suffers and enjoys. Man, who is spirit, mind, and body, is divine, and that not only as spirit but also as mind and body ; for these are manifestations of the Divine Power (Shakti) there being no other. "There is no need to throw one's eyes into the heavens to find God or Shiva. Man as spirit is God. Man as mind and body is the Power (Shakti) of God. Man is thus God and His Power . . . To those who have this outlook on life every physical function and thought is a religious rite . . . There is no need to renounce anything except ill-thinking and ill-doing which brings ill-fruit. For what can man renounce when all things and beings are seen to be the Mother ?" It would indeed be difficult to reconcile this, especially the tenet of the divinity of mind and body, with the true Vedantic doctrine of the illusory nature of everything phenomenal, but we are not concerned here to adjust the differences between various schools of thought. What we set out to consider was the nature of this particular defence offered against the attacks made on Indian religion as the essential element in Indian civilization, and for this purpose it is immaterial whether the statement of that religion is strictly on orthodox lines or not ; for the defence is one which, right or wrong, has been accepted as valid by many of the educated classes. The danger, however, is obvious in such teaching that the qualification in the way of renunciation of ill-thinking and ill-doing may be forgotten or ignored, especially when the necessity for it is based not on a moral imperative nor on the nature of the power that is worshipped but simply on the ground that its neglect may result in misfortune. Probably the shadow under which the system lies is due to such neglect having been frequent in practice.

All that has been said hitherto deals with the philosophic bases of Indian religion and so far no mention has been made of its actual practices. The author indeed in his Foreword acknowledges that India is no exception to the general experience of the difference between

ideals and facts, and he lays it down as essen--
tial that the facts should first be accurately
known, then the true principles studied and
the extent to which they have failed of realisation, when finally a decision can be arrived'
at as to the nature and extent of the changes
that may be necessary. In the body of the
book. however, there is remarkably little
attempt to carry out this programme. From
beginning to end there is not a word to
indicate the nature of the organization which
exists for carrying the tenets of religion into
practice, nor how far it succeeds in translating
ideals into facts. Yet surely this is a most
vitally important subject for consideration.
According to his own definition of Civilization
already quoted an *organization* for the manifestation of Spirit in its form as true religion
is an essential part of it, and indeed it is
obvious that, in judging of the worth of any
civilization as an instrument for human
progress and not merely as an idea, its power
of realising itself through its fallible human
vehicles is a matter of the greatest moment.
The most perfect system of belief which
it is possible for man to conceive, while it may
be fit for eulogy as a product of abstract

thought, has value for progress only in so far
as it is effective in securing the manifestation
of Spirit in the lives and conduct of the human
beings who accept it. If this view is correct
it was surely incumbent on the author to
indicate, even if briefly, how far the organization for practical religion of the Tantrik school
of which he is an adherent is adequate for the
realization of its ideal, or, if that would have
unduly swelled the contents of his essays, he
might have referred the student to other
works where the practical aspects of Tantra
are to be found. He himself has written several
of these, under the pen name of Arthur Avalon,
from which the curious may learn whether
the description given of the system by Daya-
nand Saraswati, founder of the Arya Samaj--a
name not unhonoured among the modern
champions of Hindu civilization--is or is not
justified. It appears from these other works
of the author that the system is one which
cannot be properly estimated without a very
profound investigation on account of the great
difference between the apparent and the real
meaning of its rites, one in fact in which
without esoteric knowledge the follower would
be apt to go far astray. As such its value as

an instrument in raising to a high spiritual level the ordinary man who has neither the time nor the capacity to acquire such knowledge is perhaps questionable. Such a restriction of the benefits of the system to an elite would, however, perhaps not be considered a drawback by an author who offers for our consolation the thought that, "Men are not yet Man. Some have been and are so. The rest are still candidates for Humanity".

But even where the author does profess to estimate the practical results of Indian beliefs he does not always come into real contact with actualities. This is strikingly illustrated by his treatment of the doctrine of Karma. After a brief exposition of what he considers to be its main features he sums it up in the words, "So far then from Karma being fatalistic it is the doctrine according to which man is the master of his destiny". Whatever may be said for this as the meaning of the doctrine for philosophy, it is gravely misleading as an indication of the results it produces in Indian conduct. There can be no doubt that to the vast majority of Indians it does in fact produce a fatalistic attitude towards life, a view which is held not only by Mr. Archer but by almost the entire assemblage of European observers, who surely cannot all be accused of blindness and prejudice, and it is amply confirmed by the every-day experience of those who have to deal with the average Indian in daily life.

The same tendency is noticeable in his treatment of caste. There is a certain disingenuousness in his statement that there are to-day practically only two main castes, the Brahman, and the Sudra, and that sub-castes have arisen in the latter according to occupation, as though the facts were in any way altered by calling them sub-castes and endeavouring to minimise the degree of exclusiveness of these; nor is it in the least degree correct to attribute, as the author does, the untouchableness of the Pariah to the fact that he is physically unclean. His whole treatment of this subject is vitiated by his theory that the modern developments of caste can all be traced back ultimately to an origin in difference of colour and the desire to keep the Aryan blood from free contamination. This is, of course, the orthodox Brahman theory, but one had thought that the labours of a host of investigators, Indian as well as European, had finally proved the inadequacy of this facile explanation for an enormously complicated system. One observes, however, in several places a curious lack of appreciation of the results of such labours, which appear to rank for the author as not much superior in validity to the onslaughts of Mr. Archer. It is, for example, somewhat late in the day to maintain that a purely Aryan culture existed uncontaminated by any aboriginal elements until Buddhism broke down the rigid exclusiveness of caste. If modern historical research has proved one thing more clearly than another it is that caste in a rigid form did not begin to exist until long after Buddhism had reached its zenith and that it was in fact the Brahmanical revival in the early centuries of our era that saw the hardening of caste rules. But indeed it is hardly possible to expect any very exact recital of fact from an author who avers that in dealing with India he has in mind "not any soiled or hybrid developments of the time but the principles of the civilization of old India—India of the Hindus". For in spite of modern investigation into pre-Muhammadan India it cannot be said that we possess as yet anything approaching a detailed and accurate picture of the actualities of those times, which at a conservative estimate extended over two thousand years. We are still dependent in the main on a literature whose purpose was not that of historical record but rather the presentation of what its authors considered the State ought to aim at, which, even when not written with a partisan purpose to exalt a particular class, is didactic rather than descriptive. Until we are able to check its statements by reference to contemporary records of a different sort it is much as though we derived our knowledge of Greek life solely from works like Aristotle's Politics. Where such check is capable of application, as for instance from the early literature of Buddhism, it is frequently found that ideas hitherto accepted as correct have to undergo considerable modification; instances may be found in Rhys Davids' "Buddhist India," to name only one example. Such being the case it is obviously not difficult to present a picture of India beneath the sway of uncontaminated Hindu ideals which may for all we can say bear remarkably little resemblance to fact.

While one may question the value of a defence of Indian civilization framed on the lines indicated, one would not need to cavil at it so long as the method were consistently applied throughout. But this is not the case in Sir John Woodroffe's book. The author disclaims any intention of estimating the relative value from an abstract point of view of Indian and European cultures, or more particularly of the two vital elements in them, Hindu and Christian religion. The book, however, being in form at least a reply to an assertion of the absolute superiority of the one culture over the other, it was almost inevitable that, in so far as the form was adhered to, comparisons should emerge even if incidentally; and in fact they do emerge constantly. But the disclaimer of making any formal comparison has led to a result which can scarcely be regarded as fair to the European side of the question. On the one hand the author's intention of stating " summarily and correctly the main principles of Indian civilization " enables him to present it as an ordered system dependent on certain fundamental ideas which he analyses at some length, whereas on the other hand he is precluded by the restrictions he has imposed on his work from doing the same for European civilization. In consequence when reference is made to that civilization it is in the form of isolated facts, taken for the most part from modern developments of European conditions, which are stated without any attempt to consider whether they are truly representative of the underlying philosophical basis of the system or are abuses not sanctioned by it. Set over against the completed picture of Indian civilization both theoretical and practical, with all the high lights on the theoretical aspect, they naturally appear at a disadvantage. In all fairness it might be demanded that if Indian civilization is to be considered as an expression of the " Racial Soul," " which is not to be confounded with any of its products," the same criterion should have been applied to European civilization in so far as it comes under reference.

There are many instances throughout the book of this presentation of isolated facts, not indeed with the definite statement that they are typical of the Christian attitude to life, but in such a context as to lead those who are not well acquainted with Christian thought and practice to infer that they are typical. What justification, for example, is there for selecting an incident from an American paper in which a clergyman is said to have exhorted his hearers to " hammer the face off the Germans," and to have expressed a desire to be able to tell his God, " I gave the Germans at least one good wallop before I shuffled off ? " Would Sir John Woodroffe approve of a critic of Hinduism who cited as typical of its tenets " the ears of a Sudra who hears the Vedas are to be filled with molten lead and lac," an injunction which occurs in Manu, a much more authoritative exponent of the Hindu spirit than the anonymous American clergyman is of the Christian. Or again the sneer at missionaries because of their alleged fondness for converting Mukhyopadyaya into Muggins on baptism is surely somewhat cheap, even if the alleged fact is true, which one takes leave to doubt. It may, unfortunately, be true that on certain occasions missionary effort has been used as a cloak for commercial gain, though one would have liked the author to give specific instances of it which he does not do ; but to deduce from this the sweeping proposition that in modern days the Christian religion has been turned into a means of money-making and Empire-building is to assert what is simply not true. The author would have done well in these instances to remember his own dictum which he freely applies in dealing with things Indian. " We must distinguish between ideals and the human channels by which they are given expression," and to have given Europe the benefit of it as well.

But even admitting that these crudities are not characteristic of the argument as a whole, the defects of the method are equally serious though not so glaring in other connections. Take, for example, the oft repeated assertion that India's special contribution to the progress of the race lies in the essential spirituality of her civilization. To begin with it would have been well if the author had applied his demand for first principles to the definition of the term " spirituality ". In itself the term is colourless and the value of the conception depends absolutely on the nature of the spirit which is posited. It is not inconsistent with an extremely low level of culture, for all savages are intensely spiritual in the sense that they have ʋan ever-present consciousness of existence of non-material powers affecting their life for good or ill and guiding all things. The difference between such savages and those higher in the scale consists entirely in the quality of those powers. It has been asserted in derogation of India's claim to occupy a high place that her conception of them is for the mass of her population low and inadequate. We do not say that this view is correct; all we desire to point out is that the mere assertion of the spirituality of India's culture is not conclusive as to its place in the scale without further definition. But granting that her spirituality is of the highest quality conceivable, the question still remains, is it in fact the leading characteristic of her culture? to such an extent, that is to say, as to justify the broad distinction drawn between the spiritual east and the material west. It is not implied, of course, by this phrase that every individual in India is engrossed in the contemplation of the spiritual world to the exclusion of material interests, nor that the reverse applies to Europe; one speaks merely of the " leading motive and determining power " governing the general attitude of the two races. Even accepting this restricted application of the phrase it would still not be difficult to point to facts which render the justification doubtful. One may suppose that the spirit of a nation finds its most adequate

expression in the leaders of its thought and that
their writings and speeches afford a criterion by
which that spirit may be judged. On this
supposition the insistence of practically all
the prominent men of the present day in
India on the vital necessity of the development
of industry, of the spread of an education
whose main object is to foster the practical
capabilities of the race, of allowing—nay
compelling—the people to busy themselves
with the secular government of their country
and to pay attention to problems of sanitation
and medicine, becomes hard to reconcile with
the theory of spirituality. It is not contended
that the leaders entirely neglect the other
aspect of things, but in the form which the
author has chosen to give to the question it
is one of " leading motives," and it can hardly
be said with truth that the development of
spirituality is the " leading motive " of the
modern Indian public man. Sir John Woodroffe would have an answer ready for this
objection at once. " This emphasis on the
material," he would say, " is a modern development due largely to the evil influence of the
west ; it is not the legitimate expression of
the true Indian spirit, but an ephemeral

383

morbid growth which will be sloughed off
when India returns to its ancient faith, and
the due proportion between material and
spiritual will once more be exhibited." We
have no intention of deciding which point of
view is the more correct ; let us take it that
India's claims to spirituality are established
in full. Our point is that if Christianity and
the civilization founded on it are examined in
the same spirit of getting down to essentials
which has been applied to Hinduism and
Indian civilization, the sharpness of the contrast between the two in this respect would
be largely blunted. The mode of presentation
of the facts cited about European civilization,
and such phrases as " India alone up to now
has refused to surrender the worshipped Godhead and to bow the knee to the reigning idols
of rationalism and commercialism " cannot
but produce the inference either that Christianity is of such a nature as to lead to and
justify the coarsest materialism, or that it is
so devoid of power as to be unable to influence
the actions of those who accept its tenets. In
either case the result would be its condemnation as a spiritual force. No impartial
critic can possibly hold the former alternative

as true ; the point needs no labouring for the
high spiritual nature of Christ's teaching is
as freely admitted by Indians who have
studied it as by Europeans, and Sir John
Woodroffe himself elsewhere makes passing
reference to the fact, though he fails to bring
it out clearly. He apparently accepts the
second alternative in asserting that the
worship of purely material progress is the
leading motive in Europe at the present day,
which worship, he grants, is not in accordance
with the precepts of Christ. But do the facts
really support this view? Surely the events
of the last six years are the best answer.
Nothing in the war was more remarkable than
the spontaneity with which the entire population of the allied nations rose to defend the
spiritual principles of right and justice and
mercy to the weak against the challenge of a
power which had rejected Christianity as an
outworn creed and proclaimed a return to the
ideals of the old Teutonic gods of brute force.
It is not that Christianity failed in Germany,
but her rulers deliberately turned away from
it in the belief that the ends they proposed for
her would be better served by a different creed.
The victory of the allies, a victory admittedly

25

due largely to moral forces, shows that Germany was wrong, that Christianity is still more potent as an inspiration to self-sacrifice than a stark materialism however powerful; and the peace which has followed, whatever its faults may be, has at least been marked by an earnest endeavour to carry into practice a high idealism. Perhaps Sir John Woodroffe in bringing his indictment against European materialism was thinking of the period immediately preceding the war when worldly comfort did seem to be the ideal of the majority. To a superficial observer it might have seemed justified, yet for those who held that even then a higher ideal had not been altogether lost, the war has come as a vindication. The Racial Soul of Christian Europe may have been clouded over by forces alien to it, but it has repelled them and has proved its claim to be based ultimately on something higher than mere materialism.

A final example of Sir John Woodroffe's method of argument may be given; it is one which is not peculiar to himself, but occurs frequently in the writings of those who uphold the claims of eastern as against western civilization. Throughout the book numerous statements are made of fundamental dogmas of Hindu religion. These may be accepted as correct, but they are open to this criticism that they appear in such a context as to lead one to believe that they are the exclusive property of that religion and find no place in Christianity. Yet on examination many of these will be found to be every whit as strongly emphasised in Christian teaching as in Hindu. The Gita, for instance, has surely no monopoly in teaching that we are all parts of a great Divine order making for the fuller realisation of Spirit and that it behoves us to take up our position therein and fulfil our part in the Divine purpose without vulgar animal hatred, without "desire for personal gain, but selfless-ly as soldiers in the human hosts of the Lord," or that self-sacrifice is the supreme law which should govern our relations with our fellow men. "To do good to others is the highest religion," is a sentiment with which a Christ-ian may well agree, and to present it as the peculiar glory of Indian thought is not to do justice to a religion which declares "Thou shalt love thy neighbour as thyself" to be one of its chief commandments. Nor can one say that Hinduism stands alone in holding that, "as between the soul and its material environment the former is of primary importance". In one of his concluding pages Sir John Woodroffe sums up the essentials of Indian religion as follows : "India has taught that the Universe is in its ultimate ground, Spirit ; that what is material is the expression of the Eternal Spirit in time and space ; that Man is essentially either that self-same Spirit, or a part of, or akin to, it ; that the Universe is governed by a just Law which is the very nature of its true expression ; that all Life is sacred ; that Morality is the law of humanity which is the master of its destiny and reaps only what it has sown ; that the Universe has a moral purpose and that the Social Structure must be so ordered as to subserve it." As an exposition of part at least, though not the most important part, of Christian thought this might be accepted with few changes and it is simply grotesque to put it forward as though it were an achievement of Indian thought alone. Sir John Woodroffe has probably been too busy editing and translating the Tantras to pay much attention to modern works of Christian theology ; had he done so, however, it might have saved him from stating that according to Christian ideas God is something "merely extra-cosmic," who has "arbitrarily produced and governed the Cosmos," and he might also have learned that the conception of God as at once Transcendent and Immanent is not to be found only in the Tantras.

We must emphasise that the author cannot plead that he is not guilty of misrepresenting Christianity on the ground that he does not represent it at all. When an author gives as a portrayal of Hindu religion a full and careful examination of all that is best in its theory with only slight reference to its practice and, while refraining from any similar ordered view of Christianity, allows himself to make frequent citations of isolated facts all of which tend to produce an unfavourable impression of the conduct of professedly Christian people, it is idle to pretend that such a procedure does not result in a distorted view of Christianity. Sir John Woodroffe as a former Judge of the High Court has no doubt often applied the doctrine that a man is liable for the reasonable consequences of his acts whether he deliberately intends precisely those consequences or not, and he can hardly object to being judged by the maxims he applies to others. Our contention is that in fact his method must and does result in producing a totally wrong idea of the essential qualities and value of western civilization in the minds of those who are not in a position to supply the necessary corrective to the one-sided arguments employed from their own knowledge. It is not so much his facts to which we object—though we are far from accepting all his statements as accurate—as to the mode of presentation of them, which is such as to create an atmosphere of prejudice against the system of which they are taken as examples, although in many cases they are not in the least typical of it. We have no desire to assert that Sir John Woodroffe intended any such result, but we regard it as most unfortunate that one whose words carry so much weight among Indians should, while maintaining a powerful plea for justice to India, have so written as in effect to deny that justice to Europe. Much of what is written at the present time in defence of India's culture is to a western mind somewhat alien in form and expression, and it loses effect by a tendency to indiscriminate eulogy. The value of a work such

390

as the one under consideration is that it presents clearly and without extravagance the outline of the arguments on which such a defence must be based if it is to convince one who comes to the subject without any presuppositions in its favour. The value would, however, have been much increased had the author confined himself more rigidly to the point he set out to prove, namely the intrinsic worth of Indian culture. For this purpose references to European culture were not absolutely necessary and they should either have been omitted altogether, or if they were thought desirable they should have been to essential principles and not to superficial aspects. Dealt with in such a manner the studies in this book would have afforded surer ground on which to build up that synthesis of all that is best in the two cultures which is Sir John Woodroffe's ideal as it must be that of every right-thinking man.

Malda   A. K. JAMESON

INDEX

26

Printed in the United Kingdom
by Lightning Source UK Ltd.
131406UK00001B/120/A